HEALING THE TERRORIST WITHIN!
Self- and Other-Esteem

Florence Pittman Matusky, Ph.D.

with

Jeanne Elodie Matusky, B.F.A.

Healing The Terrorist Within!
Self- and Other-Esteem

Published by

6137 East Mescal Street
Scottsdale, Arizona 85254-5418

www.CloudbankCreations.com

ISBN: 0-9651835-1-3

Library of Congress Control Number: 2003108986

Printed by Lightning Source
La Vergne, TN

Acknowledgments

Special thanks to International Business Machines and United Technologies for their teachable-moment
ads in *The Wall Street Journal*, 1980 and 1984; Stephen C. Lundin, Ph.D., Harry Paul, and John
Christensen for their book's — *Fish!* — business sense; Matthew Fox and Caroline Myss for their East-
West teachings on spirituality and healing; Daniel Goleman for his many Science articles on the brain in
The New York Times and his book, *Emotional Intelligence*; Nathaniel Branden in whose 1970's NYC Self-
Esteem Intensives we learned the language of self-esteem which led us to other-esteem; Thomas L.
Friedman for his N.Y. Times' Op-Ed columns in which his voice of freedom rises above the military-
political-religious din and admonishes all people in our interconnected world to live with restraint, with
civilized internal boundaries for our mutual survival; and the many writers whose quoted words helped us
to illustrate our story of esteem.

＊

2
0
0
3

Healing
The
Terrorist
Within!

Children learn what they live
And live what they learn.
— Dorothy Law Nolte

CONTENTS

Foreword I

OUR STORY OF SELF-ESTEEM began years ago in a New Jersey shopping center parking lot, the day before Jeanne's fourth birthday. She was run over by a car driven by a seventeen-year-old. She had a deep cut over her right eye; the femur of her left leg was crushed. She was bleeding and crying, "Mommy!" "Mommy!" "Mommy!"

Three horrified women inside me vied for attention and control. I was the distraught woman who wanted to let go of reality, to faint, to go back in time to undo what had happened. I was the mother who was scared to death that Jeanne was going to die, and my inner voice repeated, over and over, "It's my fault!" "It's my fault!" And, I was the scared-sensible woman who knew she had to take charge of what she could. So, I did. A police car arrived; I asked the police to take us to our town's hospital, where Jeanne went into shock. After providing her medical history, calling our pediatrician, and requesting specific specialists, I called my husband at his NYC office. "If Jeanne dies, I'll never forgive you." His words echoed in my head as I hung up the phone, but my question prevailed, "Would I ever forgive myself?"

Jeanne spent three weeks in traction in the hospital before she was partially encased in plaster. As the cast dried, it constricted her chest; it was a fearsome time for her. Once at home, we fed her healthy food and vitamins to hasten her healing. We encouraged her to draw, paint, and look at books, and we read to her to keep her mind active while her body was inactive. After three months in the cast, it had become her protector, so she felt vulnerable when it was removed, and she had to learn to walk again. When healed, physically, she had minor scars on her forehead and legs, but, psychologically and emotionally, our whole family was affected.

That Fall, I could barely drive my car any farther than the grocery store or church; I could not look at myself in the mirror for months. Her five-year-old brother needed extra attention because his sister received extra attention from us and our friends and relatives. "Why didn't I break my leg?" he lamented. I talked with no one about my inner turmoil; I kept busy being a suburban housewife and mother; I lived Boxer's maxim, "I will work harder!" Boxer was the horse in George Orwell's *Animal Farm*, which I had taught in 7th grade English. For all Boxer's efforts, he was carted off to the glue factory anyway. In attempting to make up for my not measuring up to all of my own and others' standards for being a good mother, I ended up not liking myself. I didn't know at the time, but it was a recurrence of an old issue of negative self-esteem.

When Jeanne entered the first grade, I chose a Human Development master's program from a university's catalogue for more personal than professional reasons. It was the required twelve credits in journal-keeping, known as the Direct Study of Human Beings, that appealed to me the most. I wanted to get back in touch with the person I could be to counter who I was becoming. I had already decided, from my experiences teaching seventh grade, I needed to study more psychology in order to better respond to the students who revealed their innermost feelings and problems through their writings.

Much writing and reflection led to my acknowledging that I had evolved from a spunky little girl who grew too tall too quickly, with no affirmation for the tomboy she was, and plenty of encouragement to be obedient: to be "seen and not heard" — an old British tradition for childrearing. My mother wanted me to be just like her, a housewife. I had other ideas: my father said I could be anything I wanted to be. I adored mother's sister Aunt Nellie, a teacher. I sought out her company when she came to my grandfather's house for the summers and holidays. She taught me to sail and to paint. At age three, I attended Uncle Lin's one-room schoolhouse where he taught grades I-XI. Cousins Annie and Max were my playmates, but their mother was very strict and blamed me, rightfully so most times, for whatever they did, and I suffered her scornful laughs, though she sent birthday cards to me every year until she died at age 96! Annie loves to tell the story about my giving her a ride on my sled down Gin Cove Head. Daisy, the cow, ran out in front of us; Daisy kicked Annie and gave her a black eye. Aunt Louie wanted to kill me. My father interceded; he was my hero. He used to say, and practiced, "If you can't say anything nice about somebody, don't say anything!"

From my father, I learned to keep my own counsel, especially about not liking my physical looks: I had heard too many times, "You look just like your Aunt Peg!" At that young age, I associated looking like with being like. Aunt Peg was the Queen Bee of my mother's family, also a teacher, also strict, and I was scared of her. It took me a long time to understand and to appreciate both aunts who had haunted my childhood. It took me a longer time to be willing to be seen and heard; I blushed whenever attention was drawn to me personally. I felt comfortable, though, hiding behind my academic, athletic, and professional selves. I now know that we make better life choices when we have positive self-esteem because we go after what we want and let go of what we do not want or of what others want us to want.

During graduate school, I knew I was improving when I spoke out against the dismissal of the headmistress of our children's private elementary school in favor of "a more educated" man. Martha Johnson was wonderful. She knew her two hundred students by name and by idiosyncrasy! She brought her

Golden Retriever to school; the students loved to pet him, as he napped on the rug in front of her desk. At the public Board meeting, the president congratulated the Board on not having tenure for its teachers; then he proceeded to impress us with the number of years each Board member had served the school: "Mr. So and So has been on the Board for twelve years and Mr. So and So has been on for fifteen...". Having heard enough, I stood up and questioned the "tenure" of the Board and its double standard for teachers. The audience laughed in support. It did not make a difference to the Board's decision, but I had made my point and had found my voice. Several of us mothers helped Mrs. Johnson compile her speeches and memoirs into her book, *Very sincerely*. Then she became a college professor!

For years, with my earned credentials and diverse working, teaching, learning, and living experiences, I have looked for the positive messages in negative life experiences. Still, knowing the difference does not necessarily lead to changed thinking or attitudinal changes. Emotions have their own embedded knowledge, instincts, motivations, responses, and behavior, which supersede, override, or undermine the best of rational and good intentions.

Jeanne's accident is etched in my brain forever. I have found that forgiving myself is not something that is over and done with. The "I'm not good enough" and "I don't deserve anything" feelings bubble up when I least expect them, especially when I feel "down" about something or receive too much negative feedback from an important-to-me other. Those personal judgments are signals that it's time for me to refocus on my positive self in the here-and-now. I believe there are no accidents, that all of life's negative and positive experiences and the many people who touch our lives are opportunities to discover who we are, what we want to know, and why we are here on Earth. We are where we are and with whom we need to be until we learn life's lessons: our biography is destiny until we dare to intervene, love, and heal ourselves. Jeanne's accident was the impetus for undertaking the study of esteem: what it is, how to facilitate it, and to better live what we learned. It was also an opportunity for mother and daughter to work together as peers to research a topic that interested both of us.

Much of the book's research was done before September 11, 2001. The transnational terrorists' attack refocused our attention. We consider our book to be a chart, rather than a map. We learned that esteem does not exist in isolation: everyone and everything in the world are connected in some way to everyone and everything else. We have chosen to present the big picture of esteem with a multifaceted approach, in one book, rather than a fragmented approach, in two or more volumes. Since our esteem presentation moves from one aspect of life to another — human, cultural, moral and ethical, personal and professional, and spiritual — as you read, keep in your mind's eye the book's main focus: self- and other-esteem.

We are indebted to and we thank the many authors, journalists, and writers whose books and articles are cited in *Healing The Terrorist Within!* Each of them, as well as our many students, friends, relatives, acquaintances, and living and learning experiences, helped us to illustrate our story of esteem.

Sincerely,
Florence
Scottsdale, Arizona

Foreword II

"It was twenty years ago today since you were run over by a car," announced my mother on the eve of my twenty-fourth birthday. I didn't know she'd been counting. It has been a lifetime for me since that hot day in August when I insisted it was more important to stay in the car to play with my coffee can full of leaves than it was to accompany my mother and brother into the hardware store. It was the impetuous determination of a four-year-old that resulted in the event that altered my life course.

To this day, I'm convinced I've become an artist because of "the accident." I might have been a lawyer or an actress. Somehow, the accident altered my perspective on the world. Becoming aware of the consequences and the fragility of human life at age four allowed me to become more reflective than some children — perhaps more observant, cautious, or different. I am pleased with having chosen to be an artist. It fits me, but it has not been easy...

I am still working on carving out my niche in society without succumbing to the stereotype of the "starving artist." As an overprotected young girl, my challenge has been to be an artist in a society that is not particularly artist-friendly. I decided to teach art in an inner-city charter school after September 11th. It is mentally, physically, emotionally, and creatively challenging. My resistance, fears, abilities, beliefs, and self-imposed limits are magnified by the teenagers' own defenses, fears, and limiting beliefs in every interaction I have with them. I never lost sight of my intention to leave this world a better place than when I found it. Now I have the opportunity to teach inner city kids to express themselves — kids who have been "run over" by their families and the society in which they live. I make a difference in their lives while I enrich my own.

Completing this project unleashed my creative energy to take off on my own. I learned, through this book and years as a freelance artist, that we create our lives from the inside out. "Not every man is an artist, but there is an artist in every man," said the ancient religious philosopher Meister Eckart. We can look at our lives as a sculptor views his stone: full of possibility. It's as if the stone has a soul that must be set free - and to free it is a labor of love. A passerby may see only a hunk of stone, a lot of work, and a long journey. Woe to be a passerby of one's own life!

As Goethe writes, "Whatever we think we can do or dream we can do, begin it. Boldness has genius, power, and magic in it."

Bless your heart!
Jeanne Elodie
Lambertville, New Jersey

One

Do you know what you are?
You are a marvel. You are unique.
In all the years that have passed,
there has never been another... like you.
— Excerpt from Pablo Casals' poem

Human Beings' Polarities and Possibilities

PLANET EARTH IS INHABITED by nearly seven billion human beings who live in at least two hundred and fifty countries with more than five thousand living languages. The U.S. population is less than three hundred million! "For every person in the world to reach present U.S. levels of consumption with existing technology would require four more planet Earths."[1] The present U.S. consumption level is not available to all Americans: over thirty percent live below the poverty level, are unemployed, homeless, on welfare, or in the prison system. Other Americans are subsidized by their families to help them get established, and many middle-class Americans live from paycheck-to-paycheck with considerable credit card debt, while others are sixty days away from bankruptcy. The U.S. is rapidly becoming like most countries, where there are huge gaps between rich and poor people and few middle-class. People migrating from war-torn, disaster-plagued, and impoverished nations to other nations increase international, cultural, and economic tensions as they vie for a share of resources in a non-solidarity world. Billions of human beings yet no two on Earth are alike! Individuals' genetic inheritances, the plasticity of the human brain, and ongoing responses from and to environmental conditioning, nurturance, and other influences account for the diversity and possibilities of human beings' nature and potential.

Focused individuals in all countries — the Americas, Africa, Europe, Asia, and the Pacific — become leaders of other human beings for better or for worse through popular vote, fraud, brute force, or inheritance: family or established institutions. To improve the primarily negative human condition on Earth to a more humane and positive one begins with one or more thoughtful and committed human beings. It requires human beings in each country whose hearts, minds, and spirits are more focused on the greater good than on self-serving power, money, things, and status that are usually gained from other human beings' labor and at their countries' expense.

It is a matter of simple addition: together, two or more human beings can lift up more of the downtrodden and influence more people than they can as individuals. Both positive and negative actions are not only additive, they are exponential: they unite, attract followers, and gather momentum. When respect or esteem is missing, human beings may emerge as terrorists. Negative actions appear to have more power and energy than positive ones, just as bad news attracts more attention than good news. What needs to happen for human beings to choose to be humane?

For human beings to choose an inner and outer world of peace, health, happiness, and integrity over war, power, money, greed, and terrorism requires an awareness of and a willingness to act on alternative possibilities. Alternatives are not readily available to human beings who have been trained since birth not to think for themselves and to unquestioningly obey orders, as in totalitarian families or societies, or to those people who believe or behave as if they are superior or inferior to other human beings. It is a matter of freedom, which is not simple.

America's red, white, and blue star-spangled banner is a symbol of Americans' personal freedom. Freedom is the foundation of our values, from individualism, self-reliance, love, and trust to opportunity, generosity, and courage. The human mind, though, is divided: one side may like peace while the other may prefer turbulence; one side may be cognitively literate while the other side may be emotionally illiterate. Integrated or dynamically balanced minds include love and esteem. Love and esteem are complex human qualities, which are dependent upon the quality of an individual's humane development and life experiences. It is easier to be a loving adult when we have had a loving childhood. Freedom does not guarantee we will love ourselves; we cannot love other human beings if we hate ourselves. To feel love, we must experience it and acknowledge its existence. To love ourselves, we accept our past and our

2

human condition. Loving ourselves does not mean that loving others is an automatic process. The inability to love self and others leads to many human tragedies, from narcissism, abuse, and terrorism to the lack of intimacy, empathy, and compassion. Freedom without responsibility for ourselves and to others is a threat to society, democracy, and all humanity.

There is freedom in loving, reciprocal relationships when there is no need to use others and when we are not used by others to compensate for ego deficits, real or imagined, or to provide material wants. Parents who are not free of their own negative childhood experiences pass them on to their children: "No social injustice is felt more deeply than that suffered within one's own family."[2] Children and adults will have problems with the fine lines that exist between love and narcissism, freedom to and freedom from, and inner and outer power and control when (a) they are deprived of basic physical needs; (b) they do not have caring, respect, acceptance, understanding, empathy, consistent rules, and judicious discipline, or (c) they are overindulged and believe they are the center of the universe with entitlement privileges. Even in a free society, we lose touch with our inherently possible selves when we experience external demands or assaults that diminish our spirit. People who live in a free society, though, may take advantage of opportunities to learn and earn a keen sense of self, to esteem themselves and others, despite all drawbacks.

Self-esteem is the difference between a human being's *raw ego* and a *nurtured ego*. *Raw egos* react actively to negative stimuli with the fight or flight syndrome (mostly male). The mostly female response is passive: freeze (feel powerless, a victim: do or say nothing) or feign (excuse, deny, rationalize, or compensate: overwork, overeat, overshop). Repressed emotions surface later as psychological or physical diseases. *Nurtured egos* dynamically balance emotional, cognitive, and experiential data. Self-esteem crosses all boundaries; it crosses all disciplines. The body, mind, emotions, and spirit are interconnected, not separate as the 15th and 16th century philosophers and mathematicians taught; their impact, however, continues. The lack of esteem for self and other people leads to a wide range of problems and to terrorism. Group-esteem unites like-minded individuals in a common or religious cause against different others when it is not combined with self-esteem and other-esteem. Awareness of our individual freedom; knowing, accepting, and being oneself; and completing the process of becoming whole persons with esteem forestall our becoming blind followers, abusers, cultists, or terrorists.

Freedom is the enemy in the minds of those who demand obedience; their followers choose dogma and security over freedom. "Whether scientist or religious, the dogmatic person is one who fears secretly...that his truth will disappear unless he puts a firm stockade around it."[3] People who represent freedom are a threat to leaders and clerics who fear the loss of their power; they rule by controlling the minds of men, women, and children or by imprisoning dissenters. Respect, rights, esteem, tolerance, responsibility, and acceptance are the currencies of freedom. Genocide, repression, suppression, intolerance, hatred, and violence are the currencies of dictators, religious extremists, and terrorists. Freedom's adversaries believe their destiny is to destroy those unlike themselves, individual freedom, and the governments and icons that represent different forms of truth, both Eastern and Western.

September 11, 2001, left us — Americans, America's guest workers, visitors, and friends around the world — shocked, outraged, saddened, stressed, fearful, but not cowed by the terrorists' acts of violence, bloodshed, and intimidation. Nineteen terrorists commandeered four commercial jets — loaded with fuel, passengers, and crew — and flew them into New York City's World Trade Center's Twin Towers, the Pentagon in Washington, DC, and a field in Pennsylvania. Thousands of innocent people were killed. Millions mourn. The media informed us of the terrorists' identities in the air and of their cohorts on the ground.

The power of a lone individual's (Osama bin Laden) passion, resources, and ideas to unite with the Taliban and Al Qaeda forces, to ignite the passion of many others, and to wage a war as individuals, not as a nation, is an example of human ingenuity at its worst. Those transnational terrorists executed their 9/11 plan in a devilishly simple, sadistically masterminded way, with an in-your-face attitude. They selected our national emergency number 911 as the month and day to strike and targeted "American" and "United" airlines to fuel our adversaries' glee.

We now know the Islamic-extremist terrorists' long-term goals are to demoralize us as individuals and as a nation, to undermine our human rights and freedom, to destroy us personally, economically, politically, and psychologically, and to make us retreat from the world. They believe that we

4

— *their* infidels — are the problem. Why? Those "educated" terrorists were predisposed and chose to be brainwashed to hate us by those who have the will, charisma, resources, but not the courage, to solve their own personal, religious, and political or power problems. They confronted our personal, cultural, national, and corporate "sins," not their own nor their culpability.

The Islamic-extremist terrorists believe our religious roots and multi-culture are inferior to theirs, and they desire to punish us for *their perceptions of our sins*: we are descendants of The Crusaders of the 11th, 12th, and 13th centuries; we help our allies (specifically, their enemy, Israel); we rescued Arab nations (Kuwait, for example) from other Arab nations while supporting unpopular regimes; we granted American women equal rights; we are a pleasure-oriented, science-driven, rich, and powerful country; and our "big businesses" wield power at home and abroad. Those suicide-terrorists believed they were doing their extreme version of Islam a favor by exterminating us, as if we were germs or vermin. By becoming martyrs, they believed they were securing their own salvation. In some Muslim circles, those who commit suicide-terrorism, in the name of their political or ideological interests, are considered martyrs. The waves of terrorism against Israel by young Palestinian suicide bombers appear to be due less to religion than to feelings of hopelessness, cultural humiliation, and intergenerational issues. "There is no teenager capable of making the political decision to commit suicide. You can bet it was older men who encouraged her to do this and who wrapped her in dynamite. This is not martyrdom, that is ritual sacrifice."[4] Although some young women are avenging family and friends' killings, Islamic-extremists' closed minds use others as adversaries to give meaning and purpose to their lives. Americans ignored their negative impact upon the Muslim world until 9/11.

The 9/11 suicide hijackers-terrorists appear to fit a cultic profile: middle-class, bright, well-educated, and idealistic. Instructional letters were delivered to them the day before 9/11, pointing to the existence of mind control tactics to ensure the success of their plan. It appears that cults under the guise of religion are created to satisfy individuals' ego and power wants and needs, both in the East and in the West. We have been experiencing the proliferation of cults: the exercise of mind control over individuals by charismatic leaders who consider themselves God's "chosen people" with the power to promise their followers divine permanence and ultimate truth. Many Americans do not fully appreciate the psychology and power of cults, the vulnerability of ordinary and extraordinary people to manipulation, emotionally, intellectually, physically, and spiritually. Whether cultism or terrorism, the ideology is similar to the German Nazi's practice of dehumanizing its targets to rationalize and justify exterminating them. The war of ideas and for human minds has begun.

Again, we are confronted with the age-old battle for human beings' minds, emotions, bodies, and spirit: totalitarianism where people are subservient to the voice of authority versus the democratic ideal where people are free to participate in developing their own behavior and destiny. Compromised freedom continues to reign in the USA and in many countries around the world; however, as our nation confronts terrorism, and not its sources, many Americans are exploring and examining the diverse webs of relationships and consciousness that divide human beings and affect world peace.

When we disperse the seeds of terrorism by plowing/bombing the ground in which they flourish, it will produce more terrorists and more hate with nothing left to lose but to strike again. When we do not create environments for human beings to esteem themselves and others unlike themselves, we help perpetuate the "we versus they" mentality so prevalent today. Peace may not be the answer, but it must be the goal, since no terrorists, whatever their origin, will fade away. We have homework to do to uncover and heal our historical, economic, political, cultural, moral, spiritual, and personal assumptions.

What do we mean by healing? Healing and curing are not synonymous, for healing may occur when curing may not be possible. Essentially, to heal means to make whole. Most of us would choose happiness over suffering; it is the human mind, though, that exerts the greatest influence on our mental and physical selves. Disturbing emotions undermine our ability to be happy and healthy. Healing brings a sense of peace, joy, well-being, and inner self-worth. A sense of healing occurs when we take responsibility for and resolve any physiological, psychological, emotional, spiritual, or interpersonal issues, and adversarial communication patterns that are obstacles to loving and living with oneself "as is" and with other people who are unlike us. When we are whole, that is, our body, mind, emotions, and spirit are synchronized, we do not need to impress other people with our importance or try to make ourselves look good at another's expense. A transformation occurs when we are willing to share our real, vulnerable selves to become a separate but interdependent person, that is, not dependent on, co-dependent with, or independent of other human beings. Having a well-developed sense of self means we embrace love, intimacy, commitment, and grace. The sharing process may be with a confidant, a trusted person or a journal.

To heal ourselves, we go beyond the symptoms and seek the cause of problems within ourselves first, then outside ourselves, and take responsibility for them. When we uncover the invisible bases of irrational or biased opinions, prejudice, and assumptions, we recognize that our perceptions of what is going on are our interpretation of an event or situation. A story illustrates the point that our perceptions are clouded by our assumptions: a young man loved to drive his sports car on mountain roads and "screech" around blind curves. One day, he encountered an oncoming car, seemingly out-of-control; they missed each other by inches. As they passed, the young woman driver screamed, "Pig!" Infuriated, he yelled back, "Sow!" Proud of his retort, he accelerated around the curve and ran into the pig! Esteem for others begins with esteem for self; both are required to heal our inner terrorist. We live in the present when our self-knowledge frees us from hooking into others' unresolved issues, for we can distinguish between what is our problem and what is theirs.

Terrorism has many forms and terrorists wear many hats. What do we mean by the term *terrorist*? The word was coined during the 18th century when French Revolutionists overthrew King Louis XVI. "Liberté, Egalité, and Fraternité" ignited a Reign of Terror on July 14, 1789. In 1795, Edmund Burke, a British conservative, labeled the revolutionists as "terrorists." In our Western society, *terrorists* are those who threaten or use violence to intimidate civilians or governments. Terrorists' actions usually involve killing innocent people, instilling fear in others, and causing infrastructure damage. We utilize the term *terrorist* to also describe those individuals, groups, corporations, or nations who use money, fear, force, or threats, including verbal or psycho-logical abuse, to intentionally demoralize, intimidate, kill, kidnap, rape, or subjugate any human being for any reason or for self-serving purposes.

Are terrorists born? No, they are man-made, and they are self-made. How? The roots of terrorism, violence, and hate are stored in the human brain, in

7

the amygdala (ah-MIG-dah-la), as feelings and emotions that guide behavior, known as schemas[5] or mental images. As children we learn what we live and live what we learn. Without a keen sense of self, we can be brainwashed to believe people unlike us are the enemy and the group's needs and wants are more important than an individual's. The natural dynamic of living beings is to grow and learn to be a unique self. However, every unmet need, abusive act, or unfulfilled desire is a negative emotional experience waiting in the wings to be magnified or resolved by ensuing negative or positive life experiences, belief and value systems. Schemas inform and drive our behavior; they become active when confronted with negative stimuli from the environment. Children who are raised to obey, think, and do what authority figures say, ignore their own wants or needs and have a subjugation schema. Put-downs by important adults become an unlovability schema. Maltreatment becomes a mistrust schema. There are at least ten negative schemas, similar to scripts or tapes, that put us into an automatic emotional-brain-response mode seconds before our cognitive brain tones down the message. With awareness of our schemas, emotional control can be learned to bring reason to emotions and healing to others and ourselves.

All of us know people who are proud of their information of how the world works, their technical skills or special talent, or of their material things, status, money, and power. Some of those people are fully focused on the outer world, and they are illiterate when it comes to the workings of their inner world. They rationalize their emotions, and they cannot form mutually rewarding intimate relationships. They thwart the natural development of those whose lives they touch. The self-esteem pioneer, Nathaniel Branden, wrote, "I am not living consciously if my consciousness is used for everything but self-understanding."[6] Without self-understanding, we have little compassion or empathy for others.

Universally, many human beings have a dislike of the unlike and fix the blame, not the problem, by projecting their problems onto others to deflect attention away from the self or their group. Negative self-esteem is evident when individuals perceive other individuals or groups as inferior and themselves as superior. Negative self-esteem also ensues when people choose not to develop their whole selves, despite positive environmental influences, or to have intimate relationships. They overlook a universal truth: we do not grow and develop in a vacuum; therefore, "The I needs the Thou in order to become a Self."[7] As adults, we are responsible for modifying our negative experiences and reactions, managing our image and responses, and ousting the terrorist within to create a world of peace, love, respect, and an acceptance of or a tolerance for differences.

The Russian dramatist, Anton Chekhov, noted the nature-nurture difference between human beings and other animals: "In nature a repulsive caterpillar turns into a lovely butterfly. But with human beings, it is the other way around: a lovely butterfly turns into a repulsive caterpillar."[8]

Forms of Terrorism

There are *(A) International* and (B) *Domestic* terrorists. The Islamic-extremist terrorists come from different nations; they are the *Transnational* terrorists who attack Americans because they hate our country and what we stand for. They use their interpretation of religion and brute force to destroy, control, or contain us. In our own country, we have *Domestic* terrorists. They are the people who, through deceit, secrecy, power, control, and financial greed, seek to rule human lives for their own or group's selfish purposes. There are at least ten forms of *Domestic* terrorism:

(1) The *Corporate* terrorists: Their executive elitism leads them to act as if they embody "the divine right of kings" to circumvent laws by enriching themselves at the expense of companies, employees, investors, other countries, and taxpayers who pay for governmental bailouts and losses. They equate self-worth with net-worth; they opt to cover-up not own-up to wrongdoings; they lack integrity, trust, and stewardship.

(2) The *Eco-terrorists* endanger the sustainability of the Earth, its inhabitants, resources, and democratic structures. Eco-terrorists are those whose decisions and self-interests are best served by ignoring, exploiting, capitalizing on, colluding in, or demonstrating their perceived entitlement to more of the Earth's resources. Other Eco-terrorists take the law in their own hands or seek fame for their "causes" without attention to their negative impact, even if for the greater good in the long-run.

(3) The *Intimate*[9] terrorists are fear- vs. love-oriented; they "attack" human beings personally, from self-abuse to other-abuse. They live within our midst and appear normal. They quietly intimidate, coerce, bully, or ruin character or reputations. In addition, they abuse people financially, physically, mentally, emotionally, verbally, or sexually, sometimes even to the point of murder. Intimate terrorists are psychologically, emotionally, and spiritually illiterate; their victims are unsuspecting intimate family members, friends, or even themselves when addictions, from food and drugs to habits, overpower them and/or when they tyrannize the self with "should," "ought," "can't," "won't," or "didn't."

(4) The *Invisible* terrorists are those who use their financial resources and powerful connections — through design, inheritance, marriage, governments, corporations, or membership in international organizations — to manipulate and dominate cultural, educational, and political systems and the world's economy,[10] from behind-the-scenes, and to control people: the masses. For profit and more power, they create crises, discredit both national and professional authorities, provoke and fund wars, control human beings' and nations' destinies through their secretive machinations. "The terrorist attack on New York City in September 2001 came only a year after candidates in America's millennial presidential election had described how money and wealth in the United States were crippling democracy. Politics, they said, was being corrupted as the role of wealth grew."[11] Since the election and 9/11, government in the interest of the rich continues under the guise of "stimulating" the economy. Enormous wealth and power in the hands of capitalists, a diminishing middle-class, and a growing minimum wage and unemployed group mean our freedom, labor, and democracy are For Sale.

(5) The *Protection* terrorists — including gangsters, goons, drug lords, and others — "protect" their own legal and illegal businesses, thus "kill" the competition; run "protection rackets" by exacting payoffs or bribes; blackmail legitimate businesses as the "cost of doing business" to "protect" them from strikes or damage at job sites/factories; ensure delivery services, "protect" reputations, jobs, or people; and/or kidnap for ransom, kill-for-hire, and extort "protection" money from their victims.

(6) *Racists, Sexists, Rapists, Homophobes, and Extremist Religionists, Isolationists, and "Patriots"* are underdeveloped, insensitive, or undereducated human beings: they fear — thus, hate — those people they deem to be vulnerable, enslavable, unlike, or

10

perceived to be inferior to themselves. They project their fears onto others as they use all forms of terrorism to assert their self-righteousness.

(7) The *Random* terrorists: From Columbine High School in Colorado and the Son of Sam terror in New York City to the Muhammad-Malvo killing spree in the Washington, D.C. area, snipers snuff out innocent lives randomly and impersonally. Our culture embraces violence, glamorizes killers, forgets victims, and tolerates the relentless dehumanization of thousands of people by rage-filled, drunken, or drugged others who are "accidents waiting to happen" or are ego-deficit-opportunists, so they murder, rape, assault, destroy others' lives, livelihoods, or reputations instead of working on their own problems.

(8) The *Savior* terrorists. Their individual ideology is opposed to big government, taxes, programs for the poor, immigrants, diversity, gun control, or open minds. They spread rumors, put pipe bombs in mailboxes or send letter bombs or anthrax through the U.S. mail. Other *Savior* terrorists have fundamentalist beliefs; they bomb homes and clinics to kill to "save" a life, or they directly or indirectly engage in ethnic cleansing.

(9) The *Technology* terrorists: They create viruses or tamper with computer systems throughout the world to destroy data or to prove how "smart" they are. Other *Technology* terrorists steal individuals' and nations' patents, inventions, or creative work; or they create or design "foods," drugs, or products for human consumption to sell and enrich themselves, while endangering people's health. The use of technology by administrators who lack a discerning morality or who fail to listen and assure safeguards for human life has proven to be disastrous, such as the Challenger and Columbia shuttle tragedies.

(10) The *Workforce* terrorists abuse personal and system power. Many are in the bowels of bureaucracies and corporations, or they run small companies. Their negative-esteem, narcissism, cutthroat competitiveness, or incompetence undermines other employees' motivation, productivity, well-being, and careers. Employee-terrorists offend, ignore, or terrorize customers since the way they think, feel, and behave affects the customers' reactions. Other Workforce terrorists live unexamined lives and do unto others what was done unto them, diminishing the lives of those they touch.

11

The Terrorist Within Ourselves

Terrorists operate within ourselves and within our world. The terrorist within operates in the inner world whenever we choose negative or victim attitudes about ourselves, others, our work, learning, play, and life. Children who are told "You're stupid!" "You're not good enough!" "You're a slob!" or "You don't deserve anything!" often perceive themselves as such and act accordingly, even as adults. Others' prophecies become self-fulfilling prophecies! Feeling unlovable has at its core a feeling of being flawed or defective, so they overeat, overdrink, overreact, or overcompensate. Feelings of deprivation stem from lack of nurturance and affection; the result is loneliness or sadness. Learning that "Rules don't apply to me" leads to feelings of entitlement and conceit. For whatever reason, many of us believe our terrorist within is a friend when we say, "That's the way I am!" or "You can't beat the system!" or "I'm looking out for Number One!" "I'll like myself when I lose fifty pounds!" or "I don't care!" Self-centered people are toxic consumers of energy, material things, and other people. Acceptance of one's past, which drives today's behaviors, requires awareness of one's past and the insight to change. Until we resolve the unsolved mystery of self, we will harbor and perpetuate the terrorist within and be vulnerable to terrorists outside ourselves.

The silenced feelings of abused children may emerge later, driven by an unconscious desire for revenge. They take their hate, repression, depression, or boredom out on others and/or themselves by bullying, killing classmates or their own families, or committing suicide. Forms of violence and corporal punishment stifle empathy and compassion for oneself and others. Punishment stems from society's need to deter violent behavior for the common good or safety. However, it also stems from an individual's or a group's need to control behavior perceived to be a threat to egos or power bases. One of the few freedoms available to children in our society is rebellion. Many silenced and abused children grow up to be terrorists. Many manipulative children fail to strive and thrive; their negative esteem may be expressed as blaming, victimizing, terrorizing self or the world. An ideology of male toughness is reinforced through gangs' bonding rituals and gang rivalry. They also terrorize neighborhoods and nongang members by forfeiting their individual humanity.

12

The violence in our society stems from ignorance of and indifference to what diminishes and thwarts human growth, causes emotional pain, and interferes with cognitive learning. While avoiding mistakes is not the purpose of human life, rising to meet challenges and preserving freedom are worthy goals. Taking responsibility for ourselves and for our world is the first step to overcome all forms of terrorism. It also means we have to be vigilant observers, even if it reminds us of Big Brother in George Orwell's *1984*. If we take care of ourselves only, and ignore a neighborhood child, a cry for help, or a terrorist in our midst, our freedom will not lessen the universality of terrorism or its ongoing threat to all in the free world.

The Terrorists Within Our World

The terrorist in others operates in the real world whenever we are perceived as passive, weak, powerless, vulnerable, different, nonhuman, or belong to a disvalued or hated group or organization. Dependent women attract the terrorist in emotionally illiterate men. Some women collude in their unimportance, accept insignificance, and believe that they deserve the ill treatment they get. Dependent people are apt to be followers; their locus of control, or center, is outside themselves. Followers are the fodder for an ego-driven leader whose power and strength are based on followers' weaknesses and helplessness. Employees who have unresolved life issues are fair game for power-and-control-narcissists in the workforce. Many children are conditioned psychologically to obey a father or mother as all-powerful symbols of authority. When they become adults, they may blindly follow and have no respect for themselves until they mature to do their own thinking and to pursue a life of their own making. Underdeveloped people are vulnerable to charismatic leaders and cults and are prone to brainwashing.

Whoever is successful in this world, individuals and nations, is at risk of becoming a target. People in the limelight attract not only media attention but those people who want their fifteen minutes of fame as well. Ordinary people with extraordinary talent, looks, or skills are also terrorists' victims: "The commonly seen hatred or resentment or jealousy of goodness, truth, beauty, health or intelligence is largely determined by threat of loss of self-esteem, as the liar is threatened by the honest man, the homely girl by the beautiful girl, or the coward by the hero. Every superior person confronts us with our own shortcomings."[12] If we are perceived as superior as individuals or as a superior nation by terrorists, then there is always the possibility that we will be targets of their resentment, jealousy, or hate.

Peace is dynamic, not passive. Peace is not attained by avoiding a battle but by asking ourselves the meaning of a possible battle: What values are involved? What values are we considering fighting for? Turning the other cheek is not a response to those who are the products of centuries of intergenerational, negative imprinting. Their experiences remain encoded in the brain and in the body for life, creating fear, anxiety, and hate; all of which displace love. "Love is natural; hate is created."[13] The purpose of psycho-therapy is to help people become more aware of what they are doing, what they are up against, and what will help them out of the victim role, the better to manage their negative feelings, thoughts, and impulses so they may become functioning human beings. Terrorists, inner and outer, need our help to get to the stage where they are free to accept responsibility for their situation and to choose a new way of life, of being, within what is realistically possible.

The Isms and Esteem

Healing the terrorist within is possible when we recognize, acknowledge, and learn how to deal with or heal the various forms of terrorism and other internal and external dangerous positions and situations that we are bound to encounter in our lifetime. Some of us are not terrorists but passivists; we want freedom from tension or change through the status quo, nonparticipation, or sulking. When we wish dangerous facts away, repress our awareness of danger, or take refuge in withdrawal, we are using passivity as our defense. We prefer the safe mainland to the waves of the sea. Until we confront our emotional or cognitive rationale, defenses, fears, and/or our apathy leading to passivism, we will be a magnet for or will condone others' negative behavior.

Most people want to be users of life, not passive bystanders. Pacifism is in opposition to the use of force under any circumstances. Pacifists, though, take a stand against negative behavior and practices. Mahatma Gandhi (1869-1948)

14

achieved his goals for India against the British through pacifism; he went on a hunger strike; he was assassinated later. Martin Luther King, Jr. (1929-1968) led nonviolent sit-ins, parades, and hymns, and gave inspiring speeches; he was assassinated. King's nonviolent conduct, Rosa Parks' refusal to sit in the back of the bus, and many other Black and White human acts of courage and nonviolence were initially met with violent responses but, eventually, brought new laws and positive social changes in racist practices in the U.S. Pacifism and nonviolence practiced by Gandhi and King were successful in dealing with countries with humane value systems, such as Britain and the U.S., but they would not have achieved the same results with totalitarian, communist, or fascist regimes where human beings are expendable. During World War II, the French Underground and the brave souls who hid Jews from the Nazis are examples of the personal risks and inner rewards involved in behaving courageously and humanely. Sometimes, even lovers of peace have to stand up for freedom to protect it from ideological narcissists and terrorists.

Good and evil, fear and trust, love and hate, power issues, terrorism, passivism, and pacifism coexist within each of us, and our choice or ability to act depends upon our level of human and humane development. It takes nine months of incubation to become a human being and eighteen years (until puberty, in some cases) of loving nurturance to become a humane human being. If we are subjected to inhuman, inhumane, cultic, or terrorist treatment from the people who touched our lives, we are at risk for becoming a future terrorist in our personal and/or professional lives. There is also a cultural-political-psychological-economic chasm between the U.S. and most of the Muslim world, which has been neglected for so long that it will take years of good intentions, on both sides, to heal the open wounds. Demonstrating unconditional positive regard for different others, all living beings and things, and the Earth is the best way to prevent terrorism; however, that is an impossible task for those who are invested in perpetuating, "I am right and you are wrong!" Fear, though, is the bottom-line for those who resist change.

In essence, "All pathology is merely physiology struggling under stressful ordeal...Hate is hurt (hindered) love, deviltry is hurt (hindered) divinity, doubt is hurt (hindered) belief, fear is hurt (hindered) safety."[14] The refusal or the inability to affirm oneself as an individual may be a way to escape the painful burden of selfhood, which often manifests itself through obsessive-compulsive

15

behavior: addiction to drugs, alcohol, shopping, overeating, or work. It is never too late for us, human beings everywhere, to develop or enhance self-esteem, to reparent ourselves.

Most people do not know who they are. They identify with their job, roles, reputations, ethnic background, talents, possessions, or company and with the way they are used to feeling, thinking, doing, and being. When threatened, or in unfamiliar situations, their automatic response is to resist or rebel, and to take it personally, as if they were protecting their real selves. When we are protecting who we think we are, or someone else, we do it more forcibly and angrily. The more we know who we are, the less need we have to prove ourselves to anyone. What is more, we are less likely to wait for someone else to intervene in a life-threatening situation and are clear about what needs to be done, so we are perceived as a leader.

A child's basic needs for loving care, nutrition, security, belonging, and respect are best met during the first seven years or so of growth and development. Those childhood experiences set the stage for later life: for positive esteem and behavior through positive reinforcement or for negative esteem and behavior through negative reinforcement. Even those children who had adequate caretaking are at risk during exposure to negative conditioning, such as, assaults on their dignity or core culture and to cognitive teachings promoting hatred through biased history and ethnic, religious, racial or moral supremacy. Intergenerational traumas and conflicts are also absorbed and perpetuated, which impair independent, logical thinking, emotional literacy, and normal growth and development.

Learned behavioral patterns, schemas or mental images, are stored in the human brain and predispose human beings to act unconsciously, impulsively, or deliberately upon real or imagined environmental stimuli. Re-education programs take time to undo years of negative programming, or brainwashing, incurred by default or design. With a high degree of self-awareness, individuals choose to let go of past programming and to live in the present. In times of crises, the innate fight, flight, freeze, or feign syndrome is activated. Passengers on United Airlines' Flight 93 learned what they were up against via cell-phones. Some of them took responsibility for knowing they were in a worse-than-hijacking-situation: they thwarted the transnational terrorists' plans to use the plane as a bomb to destroy more American icons and to kill even more

16

human beings. The plane crashed into a field in a Pennsylvania farm area. There were no survivors. Other lives were saved by their act of courage. Terrorists outside and inside the self depend upon our fear, silence, or passivity to collude in their goals.

Our individual and national survival and humanity depend upon our state of physical, psychological, emotional, spiritual, and international health. Americans united on September 11, 2001 and rallied around the flag. Now we may be able to let go of decades of me-ism or self-centeredness to concentrate on our collective well-being. We can choose good over evil, trust over fear, love over hate, and disown arrogance. We can also choose to understand the core of Muslim rage, treat them with esteem, and channel their rage into rebuilding their economy, society, and schools that teach more than religion. Their individual survival and humanity depend upon changing the conditions under which most Muslims live today: lack of esteem by the West; once-proud now-humiliated by poverty, war, and repression; perceptions that Islam is the best of all religions; and no investment in upgrading to the 21st century. With esteem and trade relations beyond oil, there is hope for peace and humanity. The future need not be a repeat of the past, for there are more people today who desire peace and seek truth than there are people who wield power and seek profit from war, deceit, and secrecy.

Self-Esteem: A Process

A pediatrician and a child psychologist (Drs. Swihart and Cotter) composed a useful definition of the self-esteeming process to keep in mind as we explore self-esteem in the various states of being human:

> Self-esteem is a dynamic, ever-changing set of beliefs about oneself. It is manifest in a sense of personal competence, self-confidence, and worthiness. It varies from time to time and situation to situation. It is self-generated and requires effort to maintain or expand. It is not a possession that, once acquired, is permanent; rather, it is a set of feelings about oneself that require constant renewal. Self-esteem cannot be given to someone, but the skills to build it can be taught. It is not egotistical; it does not thrive on the defeats and failures of others or even comparison with others.[15]

17

Another way of defining self-esteem is cautioning what it is not. Branden defines self-esteem as a "consequence" of what we experience, internally or externally. He writes, "Self-esteem is not an all-purpose panacea...it does not guarantee fulfillment, but its lack guarantees some measure of anxiety, frustration, or despair...[it] is not a substitute for a roof over one's head or food in one's stomach, but it increases the likelihood that one will find a way to meet such needs...[it] is not a substitute for the knowledge and skills one needs to operate effectively in the world, but it increases the likelihood that one will acquire them."[16]

Self-esteem is based on love (a state of being from the heart: caring, nurturing, forgiving, purity of motive) and may be perceived as our inner compass to guide our personal, professional, and universal relationships, and our own life course. The valuing or esteeming process begins with the small self's experiences of family or human development processes. The quality of the connection between an individual and his society's inherited, created, and diverse ways of being depends upon the quality of the relationship with self, and whether or not one can transcend the personal needs and deficits of the small self to develop a healthy, relational, larger Self.

The relational, larger Self is often neglected in a large capitalistic republic where some people are valued more than others, based upon "old money" or new money, who-you-know, looks, age, status, money, power, gender, race, or ethnic origin, and a lot of intolerance for any differences. Hence, the need for all people to develop self- and other-esteem with a unifying vision of respect for due process, individual rights, cultural differences, intellectual, emotional and skill development, and spirituality for healing. The terrorists' self- and other-esteem were absent on September 11th but group-esteem (positive for them, negative for us) and hate for America prevailed as they fulfilled their mission. They shattered the illusion that our shores, skies, and we are safe. We are isolated and insulated no more. Conspiracies exist, and we have been woefully ignorant of many of them until 9/11. We have become aware, though, of the powerful and greedy corporate types or elites who rule America behind-the-scenes with disastrous economic effects for the majority.

International, national, and interpersonal conflicts and terrorists' tactics are perpetuated by insecure people whose egos are driven by money and power or by the fear of their own extinction. Those who think in terms of power only do not have a humane, compassionate, or empathic view of humankind, nor do they want their followers or their opponents to have esteem for self and others beyond family ties for blackmail or for hostage purposes. Leaders who think in terms of peace must be able to transform raw aggression from within, and from without, into creative negotiations for peace, as Mahatma Gandhi and Martin Luther King did. Leaders must be willing to fight for peace, as a last resort. We have learned from first-hand experience and from history that some people do not cherish life and are willing to sacrifice innocent civilians for their cause. Haile Selassie (the former Emperor of Ethiopia) was no angel; he was a ruthless leader, but he knew the difference between good and evil. He said, "'throughout history it has been the inaction of those who could have acted, the indifference of those who should have known better, the silence of the voice of justice when it mattered most, that has made it possible for evil to triumph.'"[17]

America's State of Esteem

America may be one of the best countries in the world in which to live. After the Mayflower immigrants from England, other immigrants came here from all over the world for a better life than they had in their homeland. Many had to confront other immigrant groups to integrate themselves into our society, work hard, and, after a generation, their offspring spoke English only. Today, though, many immigrants are asylum seekers or are educated; they cherish their roots, so we are becoming a nation of entrenched, diverse identities: multilanguages, multicultures, and multipreferences. To avoid the internal strife encountered by monocultural nations divided by diversity, we need to learn the lessons from our 9/11 and ensuing experiences. America remains the land of opportunity and the home of the free and the brave. However, America is not perfect.

While the primary American values of individualism and self-reliance conflict with those of most non-western cultures, individualism in earlier days included honoring community values.[18] Today, though, it is evident that individualism focuses more upon "What's in it for me?" Individualism has become greedy self-interest or narcissism. Individualism as raw self-interest is

19

an example of being "stuck" in adolescence, at the small self level. The statelessness of esteem — our ignorance about it, our fear of it, or our lack of love for others and ourselves — is a global social problem and a fundamental human problem until we learn how to heal ourselves and seek ways to contribute to making the world a better and safer place for all.

Democracy proceeds from the will of an empowered people; it is a natural process for those who esteem themselves and others. Our democracy is threatened by terrorists and other external forces and by the vested self-interests of its citizens, residents, and visitors who override the interests of the common good and take advantage of our open democratic system. Consumerism promotes "Get rich now!" Corporate leaders get golden parachutes for downsizing and saving money for the short-run. Missing in our political, educational, and corporate leaders today is commitment to and faith in humanity and in the democratic process for the long-run.

The arrogance of people in powerful positions, from government to corporations, and even in the family, who believe they can do what they please because they have the power to do so, must be addressed publicly. History is chock-full of the blindness of self-indulgence: the Renaissance popes whose actions led to the Reformation and the English kings whose policies led to the Declaration of Independence by the American colonists. The U.S. government's history of favoring big business has led us to the oil wars, to stock market manipulations, and to corporate CEOs who downsize and seek cheap offshore labor to make themselves look good on paper for the short-run. Corporate executives pay themselves huge salaries and receive "perks" out of proportion to corporate earnings while front-line workers' wages and lives are marginalized. Those corporate and governmental actions are destroying America's middle-class and are demoralizing our nation's workforce. Many "brilliant" business titans are graduates of our Ivy League business schools. Apparently, morals and ethics and human relations are secondary to bottom-line economics, creative accounting, and profit. Enron's MBA executives were so competitive and hell-bent on success in "free markets" that they brooked no dissent, created cutthroat corporate cultures, faked profits, hid debt, and bankrupted companies in their wake, while they personally pocketed millions of dollars.

Democracy is not one-view-fits-all. The U.S. has struggled with the wish to promote diversity and the desire to Americanize its immigrants and to respect individual rights. Each individual's value is a prerequisite for a democracy to work well for all, just as a democratic environment is a prerequisite for capitalism to work for the majority of people. Our democracy and freedom are jeopardized (1) when people fear different others, family commitments, relationships, learning something new or taking action to right wrongs by revenge or retribution; (2) when people are obsessed with work, money, sex, or success at others' expense; (3) when educational systems ignore multiple intelligences, emotional development, and do not foster learning with respect for individual differences; (4) when capitalistic practices create huge economic and psychological gaps between investors, owners, managers, and workers; and (5) when mass unemployment ensues from American industries' preoccupation with short-term decisions without long-term visions. Think globally, but act locally needs to change to "act 'Glocally,'" that is, with due regard to balancing both global and local needs and conditions."[19]

Our democracy is continually compromised by demagoguery in elections. Those who do not trust people to think or to evaluate issues for themselves arouse human emotions and biases. Demagogues prefer to persuade and manipulate through propaganda rather than to educate through positive, substantive messages. Stand-up comics, late night TV hosts, and their writers have a distorted sense of free speech, sometimes, when they say and do whatever it takes, even "sell our nation's soul," for laughs. Some "jokes" are beyond satire and reveal more about them than those they malign when they demonstrate no respect for any office, profession, or human beings. Negative self- and other-esteem become visible to all when our democratic principles are undermined by those who attempt to impose their dogma, beliefs, attitudes, and values or to deny individuals' rights, freedom, health, and independence.

Changes are needed in parenting, education, working, and relating to develop whole people and to preserve the biosphere that sustains us all. Our public schools are an investment in America's future; we need a holistic approach to education. Our media programmers satisfy the basest instincts: the bad news, not the good, is newsworthy. The media is letting America down when owners of the media, reporters, and commentators do not seem to understand or realize the role they play in helping citizens understand their democracy. Entertainment has a higher priority than news. Our films' themes run the gamut of the best to the worst, which glorify violence, undermining our values and international image. Despite the increasing gap between the haves and the have-nots in the U.S., we are the world's best advertisers, largest consumers, and worst polluters. For the world to match the U.S. consumption level, with today's technology, may require four more planet Earths.

Many nations and people perceive us as "pushers" of our culture and of our military and financial might. They would like to see us fall. We have had a wake-up call. People learn more by example and hands-on experience than they do by talking, preaching, or punishing, or by having money thrown at them. A nation that really values human dignity, human relationships, meaning, and community as much as productivity and profits does not resist creative solutions to our current quantitative approach to life, work, and international relations.

Warning signs to a free society are the widening of the gap between the haves and the have-nots and the battle for open or closed human minds. Both are seeding the roots of resentment, jealousy, and hate that the have-nots have already unleashed upon themselves — dropping out of school, addictions, crime, violence — and that the closed minds have unleashed upon us all: the status quo. We have been experiencing terrorism in our homes, schools, workplaces, and on our streets since World War II. Chairman Prescott's[20] 1938 warning about educating the whole person to counter future destructive anarchy has become a reality. Another danger to our society is we are not prevention-oriented: there are no tax incentives for healthy, but costly, lifestyles. Unhealthy lifestyles, with attendant dis-eases, are enriching the fast-food, medical, and drug industries. The gap is also widening between people who want to take charge of their wellness with food supplements, exercise, and alternative medicine and those who do not or cannot; the latter are bankrupting the system. U.S. laws grant a near-monopoly on "health" to the traditional medical field and pharmaceutical companies. Few Americans or visitors can afford to get sick in this country. Esteem is undermined by illness, by the inability to afford wellness, and by laws that limit choices.

Crisis: Danger or Opportunity?

We are at a crossroad. "Nature is big, man is small; the quality and level of human life has always depended on man's relation to nature."[21] Today, though, human nature and science have created heaven and hell here on Earth. "All religions are based on the idea that there are forces greater than our own, that we are not the masters but the fruits of creation…If there is a creator, the greatest homage we can pay to him is the study, understanding and appreciation of his creation."[22] Instead, many human beings are devouring the fruit and each other.

Dollars, statistics, and youth seduce the U.S. public, primarily; there is no provision for a dynamic balance to maintain or restore harmony, beauty, and well-being. Many arts activities and emotional development research are neglected or devalued even though they contribute to growing whole human beings and to a more harmonious society. The arts are considered "frills" even though they offer a means of increasing cognition and enhancing self- and other-respect and esteem. Expressing emotions and feelings is generally considered unmanly and is relegated to women, and art and music programs are the first budgets to be cut or criticized. Artists exist "on the fringe" of society, supporting themselves as waiters, bartenders, or at minimum wage jobs until a few of them get a "break" or media or public recognition. Parents have become patrons of the arts while the government and corporations adhere to "appreciation of the arts" and ignore the benefits of the practical application of the arts to life, in school, and at work. Resistance to change exists at all levels of society, from individuals to bureaucracies. Creativity is stifled.

The pollution of the Earth through man-made and man-caused waste, abuse, negligence, and disrespect coincides with the number of broken spirits, meaningless lives, and rage-filled, power-driven, or greedy human beings. "Mother Nature" is being destroyed by human nature. Human nature is suspect when some human minds are focused on "nothing succeeds like excess" or on eternal martyrdom. The transnational terrorists believe, "There is no better way to show God you love him than to sacrifice human lives to kill as many of the enemy as possible." Bottom-line economics and an obsession with material things appear to pale in comparison to man's inhumanity to man, but they are related. The pollution of the human mind that leads to killing people or to "making a killing" (money!) in the stock market prompts formulating questions and hypotheses that are soul searching (How can we live together on this Earth? When will we humanize and democratize institutions and organizations?) or by becoming ecology-oriented, instead of settling for soul shriveling answers: War, Revenge, Ethnic Cleansing, Disease, Pollution. Most of us who live on this still beautiful but endangered Earth believe it is ours. It is not ours. "The living Earth is not our mother, not our resource, and not ours. Our habit of naming things creates in us the illusion that we have power and control over whatever we give names to."[23] Earth's relationship with stars and other planets in the cosmos is more important to its existence than its relationship with its inhabitants. But we — the creatures of the Earth — have benefited from its gifts. To continue our relationship, it is in our best interest not only to receive but also to give something back. Our relational Self needs to respond.

On our highways today, we use "one out of every seven barrels of oil produced in the world...to make our country stronger, safer and a better global citizen in the world...[begins] with how we use energy."[24] One way we could give something back to our Earth and our country is to dry up terrorists' dollars via less dependence on OPEC (oil cartel) or Arabian oil. We could use existing technology to manufacture more vehicles that run on our own renewable energy resources [The State of Arizona's alternative fuel-vehicle-rebate fiasco, in 2001, is not the way!]. Our own per gallon oil resources may cost more in the short-run but less, in the long-run, than the cost of more wars and lost lives and a U.S. trade imbalance. It is time to pay more respect for the Earth's unrenewable resources and its inhabitants, many of whom are endangered. Through mutual respect and esteem, we may improve the substance and the quality of human lives everywhere and relearn "that all life is interconnected and that all the parts form a whole web of existence."[25]

Silent Spring was Rachel Carson's[26] wake-up call, in the 1960s, informing us that man's use of chemicals poison the insects as well as the birds and pollute the rivers, the fish and, inevitably, man himself. We heeded her call and billions of dollars have been spent to clean up our rivers, toxic waste sites, and oil spills. We even drove 55 miles per hour for a while to save fuel. As soon as Arab oil prices dropped, and we discovered that supplies were plentiful all along, Americans wanted the gas guzzling cars again. Now we have global warming, cities engulfed by pollution again, and American dollars and American lives invested in preserving the world's oil sources.

The Closing of the American Mind was Bloom's[27] 1980's controversial discourse in which he predicted the decline of Western civilization: closed minds lead to impoverished souls. Twenty-three years later, we do have people with closed minds, big mouths, and impoverished souls throughout the world. We also have open minds who are soul searching. However, there is widespread disrespect in our society for traditions, values, legitimate authority, teachers, older people, the wisdom of the ages, and other cultures. There is a huge emphasis upon youth, looks, material things, and image. Even when authority was challenged in the 1960s, and collective freedom was flaunted as narcissism, the me-generation's underlying, but unrecognized, issue was negative self-esteem. Then and now, a common public perception of self-esteem is that it is all about ego, selfishness, and narcissism. Self-esteem is about inner and outer freedom, human rights, equality, emotional literacy, choices, sharing, empowerment, and interdependence.

Betrayal of Trust: The Collapse of Global Public Health is Laurie Garrett's millennium response to the politicization of public health at a time when global travel makes it impossible to keep "third world diseases" out of our country. In her chapter on biowarfare, she explored the danger to our society of historic hatreds. She reports:

> The new globalization pushed communities against one another, opening old wounds and historic hatreds, often with genocidal results. It would be up to public health to find ways to bridge the hatreds, bringing the world toward a sense of singular community in which the health of each one member rises or falls with the health of all others. [28]

Health is the basis for individual and national survival: physical, psychological, emotional, and spiritual. One nation's health, including financial, affects all others. Terrorists' ancient wounds evoke ancient images of the wicked cities of Sodom and Gomorrah in tortured minds. Anthrax attacks on government and media people and anyone who comes in contact with the spores represent the pestilence visited and wished upon us all. Health is more than the absence of symptoms and disease. Health begins in a human mind at peace with itself and its world.

The danger is each of us and our nation may not learn from our transnational and domestic terrorist experiences. Research on people's inhibited behavior led to finding that cities, countries, and even civilizations inhibit disclosure, fostering a conspiracy of silence. For example, "Within each culture, citizens are loath to openly discuss their deepest feelings about their nations' humiliations...Americans live with Vietnam, Germans with Hitler, Russians with Stalin."[29] When people feel unfree to discuss important or traumatic life experiences, they may incur stress-related illnesses, from physical to psychological problems. The 9/11 terrorists brought about nearly three thousand deaths including the severely burned and the injured. There is much grieving, needed healing, and there are so many stories of heroism and escape. In the mind are vivid television images of the jets ramming the towers, the flowers and candles at firehouses, and the donations and prayers. All will live on in memory. Humiliation? No! Americans are communicating at a deep level and many are saying, "I'm going to live my life differently from now on." After what happened on September 11, 2001, few of us can ignore and not be changed for better or for worse, especially those directly affected by the loss of loved ones.

Ignorance usually means lack of knowledge. "But to ignore is not just to be without knowledge, it is to choose not to look, not to see, not to hear, not to feel"[30] and not to benefit from mistakes or tests. We liberate ourselves from evil, disease, ignorance, and our past when we take the time to work on ourselves to become more people- than material-oriented. Our government will become responsive to citizen's needs at home when it begins rebuilding our nation with innovative economies that employ people at livable wages and affordable national health care. Many Americans have no health insurance. Currently, we have a huge wage disparity between the tops and bottoms in the workforce. All ignored inequities promote the have and have-not syndrome, undermining our democracy.

Freedom and Responsibility

Our Founding Fathers' Bill of Rights did not include a Bill of Responsibilities. The fulfillment of individuals' responsibilities was taken for granted in their decentralized society where people were neighborly and helped each other, knowing they needed each other to survive. The omission of individual responsibility was noticed later by the British Historian Macaulay who wrote President Madison (1809-1817) to the effect that the American Constitution is "all sail and no rudder."[31] Without a rudder, a ship is a victim of the winds and the waves, not under a captain's direction. Without responsibility to others and for themselves, individuals' rights are disconnected from society's reasonable needs to be free from antisocial and antihuman acts of irresponsible and incorrigible individuals as well as from transnational and domestic terrorists.

A Harvard Law School professor's study of "rights talk" led to observations and comments that current lawyers perceive constitutional rights as "absolute, individual, and independent of any necessary relation to responsibilities."[32] It was estimated that the ratio of lawyers to engineers graduating from our universities was about 4 to 1. More lawyers reflect a litigious, consumption-oriented society — which has become overly focused on making others responsible for individuals' irresponsible actions and personal choices, whether deliberate or by default — and not on making things or products. Japan, on the other hand, produces more engineers than lawyers.

Our Declaration of Independence granted us the "self-evident" and "inalienable" right of individual freedom; the Supreme Court, though, is charged with providing the necessary limits. What we have arrived at is a grave misunderstanding of freedom: freedom is confused with license and irresponsibility. True freedom has been replaced by materialism, hedonism, and terrorism. Thus, we are experiencing in our society that "Freedom without responsibility leads to destructive anarchy."[33]

The American selfhood concept of self-reliance, popularized by Ralph Waldo Emerson in the 19th century, has eroded in practice but not necessarily in value. "Political freedom is to be cherished indeed. But there is no political freedom that is not indissolubly bound to the inner personal freedom of the individuals who make up that nation, no liberty of a nation of conformists, no free nation made up of robots."[34] Thomas Jefferson knew that liberty is a fragile thing; therefore, he repeatedly warned Americans to be vigilant and to get educated because nobody's liberty is secure in a democracy if a large group becomes incompetent or negligent of its civic responsibilities. Freedom is and has been a deeply entrenched American value. For many Americans, freedom means freedom from others' values, ideas, lifestyles, and authority. However, many more Americans practice the values that undergird our freedom to protect us from terrorists, biowarfare, and diseases once thought to be history but now a reality to be overcome again.

Reality Check

The opportunity presented by the 9/11 terrorists' attacks is to develop and foster esteem in everyone at all institutional and organizational levels. Esteem is a grassroots solution to complex personal, business, social, international, and ecological problems. It is a necessary healing process. To accomplish healing, changes need to be made at all levels of society, beginning with parenting, the public schools, and government agencies. The antecedents of people's ego problems, resentments, and discontent are not directly due to external causes but indirectly to our Western intellectual tradition and its institutions, including the family, for most do not nurture children and adults' inner lives: the whole self. With a lot of help from others' input and hindrance, individuals construct their own reality and often spend the rest of their lives projecting and defending their underdeveloped egos. More than an attitude adjustment is needed!

Children who do not have the foundations for positive self-esteem (love and respect) live with perpetual stress; they may feel worthless, so they act-out against self, others, or society. Without self-respect or self-esteem, they are not prepared emotionally or cognitively to learn. "America's literacy [reading] gap is a disgrace...with such high-income nations as Canada, Germany, Great Britain, and Sweden, the U.S. ranks 12th out of 20."[35] Children who are difficult to get along with, disruptive in the classroom, or are loners are asking, in their own way, for special attention. In effect, they are crying for help: "If you really accepted and respected me, you would see through my façade or armor and know that I am scared, fearful, or hurting and you would help me learn or cope with my family or get along with my peers." Our friend and colleague, Dr. Alice Castner, says that none of the teacher training courses she had to take to be an elementary school teacher, before she became a university professor, was as important to her as her German-born mother's advice, "Get the worst kid in class on your side."

Despite our multicultural diversity, our dominant culture is white male-oriented. Our society emphasizes the Western intellectual tradition — ideally, logical or analytical reasoning; in reality, it is more about rote learning — without acknowledging or attending to the role that emotional intelligence plays in learning, loving, relating, morals and ethics, and working. Our educational systems are educating one-half of human brains, leaving the other half to be preyed upon by cults, radicals, zealots, fundamentalists, and terrorists, including the intimate terrorist. We ignore the role that spiritual intelligence plays in our beliefs, values, and integrity; in our quest for meaning; and in our ability to have compassion and to learn from differences. Even our citizenship tests are more about history, dates, and laws than about values.

It is no accident that America is awash in therapeutic techniques, self-help literature, and diet books to purge us of the mental blocks and blindspots that prevent us from having the esteem we desire or the money to "buy" esteem with material things. Many flag-waving Americans settle for treating others as inferior beings in order to feel superior. That is a misuse of freedom and responsibility for ourselves and to others, resulting in some Americans and foreign students being exposed to other Americans' prejudice or arrogance. We have the expertise to open closed minds, deprogram brainwashing, and build self- and other-esteem. We do not legitimize or practice it.

Many of the transnational suicide terrorists were "educated" in American and European schools where they personally encountered culture shock: loss of pride and dignity to their group-esteem and culture due to their being treated as having lower status by underdeveloped Americans or other unassimilated immigrants. Their living experiences in America or Europe contributed to their festering emotional brains and hardened hearts. The transnational terrorists-to-be gravitated to militant Islamic preachers to reclaim their dignity and to channel their rage. Islamic-extremist religion became their panacea to exact their revenge by rubbing our noses in freedom.

America is not alone in having underdeveloped human beings who feed their egos by physically or verbally abusing others. America is the bearer of the torch of democracy for the world. All Americans have the responsibility to be the best representative and upholder of freedom at all society levels, from the ghettos and barrios to the bowels of bureaucracies, boardrooms, and the Oval Office. Xenophobia (*fear and hatred of foreigners or strangers or of anything strange or foreign*) is alive and well throughout the world. Wherever there are Muslims — in the U.S., Canada, England, or other westernized countries — they experience identity crises or the futility of assimilation, especially when many cannot find employment or are not accepted by their neighbors or the larger society. In Tipton, England, for example, four Muslim young men, outraged by the U.S. bombing of Afghanistan in response to the 9/11 terrorist attacks, joined forces with the Taliban. Three of them were captured in Afghanistan. In England and in other Western countries, despite asylum seekers' education, language skills and Western dress, a Sheik said, "They want to keep calling us Pakis, bloody Arabs, brown Kaffirs."[36]

Each year, hundreds of thousands of people from Africa, Eastern Europe, the Middle East, Central Asia, China, and South America enter not only the U.S. and Canada, but other wealthy nations, such as, Austria, Belgium, Denmark, Finland, France, Germany, Greece, Ireland, the Netherlands, Spain, Portugal, Sweden, Italy, and Britain. Those asylum seekers are a drain on each nation's resources; some find menial jobs; a few fit in; others are in limbo. In monocultural nations, some natives perceive outsiders as intruders. Interestingly, all nations willingly spend money on arms for war, but few are willing to invest in arming individuals' minds with esteem and education for peace. Whenever we denigrate people, we reap what we sow. By our negative, irresponsible actions, we collude in feeding our chosen victims' anger, desire for revenge, and violence. Paradise was lost again on September 11, 2001. It may be regained by reuniting hearts, minds, spirits, and resolve, but not in the same old business-as-usual or abusive ways that are far too common in our history. Do we have the resolve to become change-agents for peace? Are we willing to upgrade from our small self to our larger Self?

30

Consilience:[37] Multiple Intelligences and Multiple Approaches

The future is in us now. Understanding now teaches us how to plan for a terror-free future. To do so requires a consilience of interdisciplinary knowledge, experience, and approaches to confront the fact that wrongs done unto individuals or groups live into successive ones. Peace requires justice. Healing wounds and psyches begins with identifying, punishing, reconciling, or forgiving the perpetrators. Psychic wounds heal when there is a commitment to making the world a better place for all human beings and working on it.

History and the classics are excellent texts for teaching children and adults that men's inhumanity to men, women, and children is learned. Aggressiveness and violence are not inherent human traits but survival instincts to perceived threats to the human ego or learned ways to feed fragile egos. Unfortunately, we have replaced the mindless fist with a facsimile of the human mind congealed in computers. We have relied upon technology for our protection, not upon people's knowledge, wisdom, and experience of what makes human beings love, hate, greedy, or generous and/or upon the people-skills necessary to relate to those still in the mindless fist age or guided by baser instincts. Unless we learn from the past and present mistakes, we are doomed to repeat them in our future.

Terrorism accelerates identity crises. Esteem is in crisis and our democracy is in crisis. The perquisites (perks) of freedom, power, and politics are becoming the sole domain of those people at the top who have the money, contacts, or the raw ego to override the democratic process. Terrorists and narcissistic people do whatever it takes to win. At the bottom, behavior translates into negative esteem, helplessness, and hopelessness. The American Dream is already a nightmare for many. For most Americans, a job is their life, not a better life anymore. Many citizens are just a paycheck away from homelessness. Before 9/11 our economy was in trouble. Since 9/11, businesses have closed and unemployment rates have risen, which are usually double the national average for Blacks and Hispanics. A job is a buffer against losing one's self-esteem, health, family, and home. The currency of the prevailing definition of self-esteem in America includes money, status, TV visibility, and power. If you have a top job, academic or athletic status, or are a movie/video or TV star — America's royalty — then you are a Somebody by those external criteria.

One of the first psychologists to recommend an attitude of openness to reach and to work with problem children or adults was Sidney Jourard[38] in *Disclosing Man to Himself.* The self-esteeming process involves whole persons working with whole persons (physical, mental, emotional, spiritual), understanding their personal meanings constructed from family and culture, and utilizing principles and practices that integrate head, heart, and spirit with academia where people and their feet are. When we redefine what it means to be an educated person by acknowledging that there are multiple intelligences, along with the "3 Rs" (reading, 'riting, 'rithmetic), and the other "3 Rs" (reasoning, responsibility, resilience), we will stop growing losers and start rebuilding human lives: people will learn to perceive themselves from a wider perspective and to enlarge self-imposed boundaries. "The body will not grow if it is not fed; the mind will not flourish unless it is stimulated and guided. And the spirit of the child will suffer if it is not nurtured."[39] When we become inner activists, instead of inner terrorists, we stand up for our basic human rights — our natural self — and rekindle the excitement of exercising our talents, unfolding our wholeness, and healing and enhancing our connection to all. When we esteem ourselves, we have the resilience to confront all forms of terrorism: we refuse to be puppets controlled by puppeteers, and we untangle the web that would deceive or enslave us to find our truth. Living our truth will keep us free.

It is not enough to work on ourselves; we must help others regain their human rights for respect, esteem, and worth. On a visit to Romania in the 1980s, the number of parents who were dispirited, unmotivated, suicidal, and overly protective of their children dismayed us. Most had a dream: to be free, to talk freely without fear of arrest, or to leave their country. A Romanian living in America informed us that his people have experienced centuries of despots and that it would take years for their mentality to change. He escaped, and he changed!

What has yet to be acknowledged in our society is, "every human being's central need to express himself — to show himself to the world as he really is — in word, in gesture, in behavior, in every genuine utterance from the baby's cry to the artist's creation."[40] Many artists see and know what is important; they cross internal and international boundaries to awaken stone hearts by using metaphoric language — visual, musical, poetical — which is more accessible across cultures. What has yet to be put into practice in America is a whole person approach to teaching, learning, relating, working, playing, the arts, and healing. Then each human being may discover, within self, the capacity for personal development, a sense of relationship and connectedness to all, and a realization of wholeness or healing.

The basic skills that build character and foster healthy child and adult development are not included in the Western intellectual tradition of judging students by IQ and achievement tests. The basic skills that build character and foster child and adult development are intellectual, emotional, and spiritual development in addition to the wisdom learned cognitively and experientially. Self-discipline is learned through self-understanding, learning from and managing one's emotions, and by experiencing satisfaction in being inner-directed. The ability to learn is hindered by emotional illiteracy. Spirituality includes loving self and others and empathy, which is the basis for altruism, caring, and compassion. It is evident from the violence in our society and in our schools that a bold new vision — a consilience of knowledge from diverse disciplines and the wisdom of experience — for rearing and teaching children and re-educating adults is needed to save us all from man's inhumanity to man and to find a raison d'être beyond self.

After 9/11/01, not only in America but in all nations, most people finally comprehend the full meaning of the term "globalization." Trading and transportation between nations have connected and divided nations for eons, but today's technology has extended individuals' reach and allows most of us to penetrate each others' lives. Globalization occurs when technology, trade, and transportation are integrated: shrinking the globe, knocking down physical walls between nations and individuals, increasing mobility, creating market and financial dependencies, and sharing instant communications through the media and the Internet. Technology has flourished in the past fifty years; however, human beings' basic needs remain the same for love, food, sex, a home, a sense of belonging, and meaning. Underdeveloped human beings have learned more and more about building psychological walls around ideologies, religions, and interethnic issues while learning and caring less and less about the world, other people, and themselves. When angry or power hungry individuals unleash their fury on other individuals, they are unaware of the unconscious programs, recurring patterns, and fear that rule their lives. Individual esteem and global-esteem are missing from technology and from educational and religious systems. Individual self- and other-esteem are prerequisites for living, working, and relating in a globalization paradigm. The greatest gift members of the human race can give to each other is the willingness to stand in each others' footsteps every now and then to free themselves from the unconscious grip of negative esteem and culture.

Each human being is unique and each is a work of art so it is important for each to develop to capacity and to show himself to the world as he really is; otherwise, he will be bereft of the knowledge and connectedness needed to live a fully human life. Pablo Casals (1876-1973), a Spanish cellist, conductor, and composer, survived World War II in France; then emigrated to Puerto Rico. Casals wrote about a newborn baby:

You are a marvel,
Each second we live is a new and unique moment of the universe,
a moment that will never be again. . .
And what do we teach our children?
We teach them two and two make four, and that Paris is the capital of France.
When will we teach them what they are?
We should say to each of them:

Do you know what you are? You are a marvel.
You are unique. In all the years that have passed,
there has never been another child like you.
Your legs, your arms, your clever fingers, the way you move.
You may become a Shakespeare, a Michelangelo, a Beethoven.
You have the capacity for anything.

Yes, you are a marvel. And when you grow up,
can you then harm another who is, like you, a marvel?
You must work—we must all work—to make the world worthy of its children.

34

There is hope for all humanity when we acknowledge and practice that we are all interconnected here on planet Earth by the air we breathe, the water we share, and the thoughts, feelings, and behavior we choose. Water is more than a liquid for survival or for our various uses, and some of us have more access to drinking water than others. Dr. Masaru Emoto[41] of Japan has researched and photographed (using a magnetic resonance analyzer) frozen vials of pure, sterile, and polluted water "as is" and after exposure to humans' positive and negative emotions, written or spoken statements, and classical or heavy metal music. The results of his photographed frozen water crystals — like snowflakes (positive impact: beautiful, unique crystals; negative impact: few or deformed crystals or ugly structures) — have compelling messages for human beings, since we are composed of over two-thirds water — as is the Earth — that the state of our world, people, esteem, and diseases are reflections of what we individually and collectively think, feel, say, do, and create. Knowing this, can we then intentionally or unintentionally harm another?

There is also hope for the world in Margaret Mead's words: *Never doubt that a small group of thoughtful, committed citizens can change the world: indeed, it's the only thing that ever has.*

Two

Who do you think I am? A Nobody?
I'll have you know, I'm A Somebody!
—Florence at age seven

Human Beings' Esteem: A Work in Progress

WITHIN CASALS' QUESTION, "when you grow up can you then harm another who is, like you, a marvel?" is the ultimate answer to the difference between terrorism and humaneism: negative esteem versus positive esteem. The seminal questions, "Who are we humans? Where did we come from? What is our purpose here? Where are we headed?" remain unanswered. We do know that we are all a work in progress. Yet, most of us do not do in our lives what we believe in our hearts. To do so is to live authentically. We do know that it is not natural for human beings to harm each other; it is learned for survival and from experience. Terrorists become terrorists through default or design: their own or someone else's. Esteem is an antidote for terrorism.

Throughout history, as societies grew larger, more complex, and industrialized, differences in abilities, occupations, and motivation automatically separated some people and nations from others. The Western term *individualism* and the emphasis upon self can be traced to the Industrial Revolution's division and specialization of labor in the 1600s and to the Protestant Reformation. The word *self* entered *The Oxford English Dictionary* in 1674 with the meaning: *a permanent subject of successive and varying states of consciousness*. Self-framing words, such as *self-made, selfish, self-conscious, self-worth, and self-esteem,* have become part of our Western language since that era. *Self, individualism*, and *identity* are democratic terms. *Image* — that is, an unreal or false self — is becoming more acceptable to "sell" oneself or one's company's product or service in our institutions and organizations.

In collectivist Eastern and Asian societies, identity identifies one's place or status in the group. Group-esteem is more concerned with maintaining traditions, preserving group identity, and savings one's face rather than one's skin, that is, not "losing face" or shaming the group's pride. Collectivist cultures comprise more than half the world's population; their loyalties are to family, tribe, group, religion, or employer. They are more prone to distrust differences and to fight with other ethnic groups. When human beings' thinking is enslaved by "distorted symbolic meanings, illogical reasoning, and erroneous interpretations [the tactics of extreme religious fanatics!], we become in effect deaf and blind"[1] to our own shortcomings and keenly aware of others' criticism, real or imagined, and of others' "faults." Thus, "criticism is a dangerous spark—a spark that is liable to cause an explosion in the powder magazine of pride."[2] A group's perceived loss of pride or dignity ignites individual passions (for example, resentment over America's prosperity, business practices, anger at Americans for ignoring their group, religion, or nation, and hatred of infidels' behavioral and cultural impact). A group's loss of pride or dignity, real or imagined, releases the terrorist within those whose identity is based in the group, not self.

Individualism emphasizes individual ability and achievement; whereas, collectivism emphasizes individual effort. Ability and achievement lead to competitiveness and success or failure. Effort and hard work lead to success and self- and group-esteem. In our culture, effort is seldom rewarded. Individual raw egos without self-esteem are accidents waiting to happen; they welcome charismatic leaders to fill their felt inner emptiness. In collectivist cultures, individual effort contributes to the success of the group, company, or tribe, if their charismatic leaders have the present and future welfare of their people and nations as primary goals. The welfare of their people or of moderate Islam was not part of the 9/11 conspiracy by Osama bin Laden, the Taliban, and Al Qaeda forces.

Self-esteem, with its many interchangeable names and similar definitions, remains surrounded by confusion and mystery, still mired in semantics and controversy. Most people agree we must have self-esteem, but there is little agreement about what it is or how to get it. There is agreement about one thing: Nobody wants to be a Nobody. Everybody wants to be a Somebody. Human beings become a Somebody through self-esteem; some become a Somebody via narcissism, money, status, or power. Others become a Somebody via the many forms of terrorism, from the transnational suicide terrorists whose ideology and hatred sustain them to the domestic terrorists

37

who live among us. In *The Anatomy of Terrorism*, David Long[3] found that suicide bombers and hijackers have feelings of worthlessness; their violent acts are desperate attempts to be an admired Somebody in the here-and-now and in the hereafter. The 9/11 transnational terrorists' suicides earned them esteem and fame in the eyes of their fellow terrorists and others in the Middle East and around the world. Terrorism is not a solution to world economic, poverty, or esteem problems. Neither is war. The complacency and incompetence of America's security agencies toward Americans' safety reflect individuals' ego problems and our politicians' economic biases in favor of business, which allow the rich to become richer and to pay less taxes, decreasing workers' job security, increasing economic inequality instead of equality, and tarnishing the nation's image abroad. Thinking "outside the box" requires making people's esteem, health, education, and safety a priority.

Two months before 9/11, a military analyst and two U.S. Marine officers wrote, "Arguably the most serious direct and immediate threat to U.S. National security today is not another state, rogue or otherwise, but the transnational terrorist organization Al Qai'da."[4] They had also warned that the terrorists' targets would be our cities and economic base, not military bases, and that our next war would not be with nations but against groups, including the Taliban, and individuals from various Muslim countries. On a trip to the Middle East in the early 1980s, it was visibly apparent that the economy of some Arab nations was light years behind Israel. Israeli lands were irrigated and colorful with citrus and sunflowers. Across the highway, Arab land was barren and rocky, but the seeds of resentment were already sown in the people who did not have the outer resources to compete or the inner resources to initiate change. The general perception we encountered was that the United States government had underwritten Israel's economic boom.

In researching and attempting to illuminate the term *self-esteem*, we became aware of the baggage that the term carries and with it the limitations of language to transfer the meaning of something that is lived, not just read or reasoned and communicated verbally and nonverbally, through action or passivity. A seventh grade English student's voice of frustration comes to mind: "Why do I have to study English? I've been talking it all my life!" His response may be similar to yours, "Why should I study myself? I've been living with me all my life!" What we single out, name, learn about, pay attention to, and give importance to will, inevitably, shape our selves, our lives, our relationships, and our responses to terrorists and to the world.

Old and New Definitions

In a 1940's textbook, self-esteem was reported to be synonymous with conceit and egotism. An acquaintance, self-professed to be "spiritually enlightened," believes self-esteem is the same as SPS, or Self-Praise Stinks! In the 1960s, a *Random House Dictionary*'s definitions of self-esteem ranged from *an objective respect for or favorable impression of oneself* to *an inordinately or exaggerated favorable impression of oneself.* In the 1990s, a Webster's dictionary definitions of self-esteem are *a realistic respect for or favorable impression of oneself; self-respect and an inordinately or exaggeratedly favorable impression of oneself.* The Final Report of the California Task Force to Promote Self-esteem and Personal and Social Responsibility verified that "the common public perception of 'self-esteem' as a condition of highly individualistic narcissism has resulted in confusion and misunderstanding."[5]

Bad press has contributed to the emergence of and the preference for terms other than self-esteem, from self-concept, self-respect, self-regard, and self-worth to identity. Self-esteem encompasses all the terms. Other substitutes for self-esteem have been suggested by psychologists, from self-efficacy, self-discipline, self-responsibility, and self-control to self-appraisal, but the term *self-esteem* keeps emerging with all its past history and present stories of controversy. Esteem's linguistic roots are French — *estimer* — and Latin — *aestimare: to value, appraise, estimate.* Hence, rather than a static process, esteem is dynamic and ever-changing.

Business pamphlets in the 1980s labeled people who think they're always right, are quick to blame others for their problems, and lash out when frustrated as having super-high self-esteem. It was predicted that super-high self-esteem was more difficult to correct than low self-esteem. Super-high self-esteem masks super-high ego deficits, not an overdose of self-esteem; it demonstrates not high but negative self-esteem. Self-esteem is a dynamic balance of intellectual literacy, experiential learnings, and integrated emotions and feelings. Most negative-esteem people are emotionally illiterate. Self-esteem will be misunderstood, mired in semantics, and a problem for all until emotional literacy is taught and considered to be as important as intellectual literacy. Terrorism will be a problem until we focus on the complexity of or the many roads that lead to esteem.

Self-Esteem: Simple or Complex?

The official definition of self-esteem, as promulgated by the California Task Force to Promote Self-Esteem and Personal and Social Responsibility, is:

> *Appreciating my own worth and importance*
> *and having the character to be accountable for myself*
> *and to act responsibly toward others.*[6a]

The Task Force's "Key Principles" outlined a further definition, of its first sentence, which involves "accepting ourselves, setting realistic expectations, forgiving ourselves and others, taking risks, trusting, and expressing feelings. It also rests on appreciating our creativity, our minds, our bodies, and our spiritual being." While the words "and others" were not inserted between "my own" and "worth," the "Key Principles" include: "'Appreciating the Worth and Importance of Others' means affirming each person's unique worth, giving personal attention, and demonstrating respect, acceptance, and support. This principle also means setting realistic expectations, providing a sensible structure, forgiving others, taking risks, appreciating the benefits of a multicultural society, accepting emotional expressions, and negotiating rather than being abusive."[6b] The "Key Principles" also enlarged upon the meaning of accountability for ourselves and responsibility toward others.

Thirteen years later, despite the linking of self-esteem to other-esteem by the California Task Force, its definition of self-esteem and its lofty aims have not impacted the populace, including those of us who profess to be literate in the mental health or teaching professions. The controversy over the legitimacy of self-esteem goes on and on. The Task Force's *Conclusion*, a poem by T.S. Eliot, was prophetic:

Little Gidding
We shall not cease from exploration
and the end of all our exploring
will be to arrive where we started.[7]

An old but widely used self-esteem assessment, Sociologist Morris Rosenberg's[8] ten questions, consists of five positive and five negative questions, which explore one's feelings about self. It was presumed, from the assessment, that a high opinion of oneself meant high self-esteem and that a low opinion of oneself meant low self-esteem. Today's researchers attempt to measure self-esteem by asking a series of standardized questions, such as "Are you generally successful in your work or studies?" and "How well do you get along with other people?" On standardized self-esteem tests, Nicholas Emler[9] found no correlation between high or low self-esteem and academic performance; he did find that low self-esteem people might try harder so they succeed. Roy Baumeister[10] found that people with a low self-esteem condition to be more socialized; whereas, people with high self-esteem were more likely to maim or kill and are less socialized or considerate of others.

Intrigued, Baumeister conducted extensive research on self-esteem and found that high self-esteem people who feel great about themselves may be more of a threat to those around them than low self-esteem people who feel bad about themselves; therefore, he said, the assumption that low self-esteem leads to violence or aggressiveness is wrong. *Narcissism* is defined by clinical psychologists as "an inflated or grandiose view of self, the quest for excessive admiration, an unreasonable or exaggerated sense of entitlement, a lack of empathy (that is, being unable to identify with the feelings of others), an exploitative attitude toward others, a proneness to envy or wish to be envied, frequent fantasies of greatness, and arrogance."[11] Baumeister formulated hypotheses around threatened egotism, designed a study of aggressives, using a combination of standard self-esteem and narcissism scales, and the study's results "supported the threatened-egotism theory rather than the low self-esteem theory."[12] In addition, his study of violent inmates indicated that they scored in the middle on standard self-esteem tests; whereas, on the narcissism test they "had a higher mean score than any other published sample."[13]

From our more complex self-esteem perspective, which includes other-esteem, it appears that the standardized tests do not correlate with reality or assess subjects' behavior toward others. It is what people do, not only what they say they do, think, or feel, that betrays their self-esteem status. The problem with most self-esteem tests: self-esteem is not being tested. The tests purporting to test self-esteem are being tested and found inadequate for those who are antisocial or into self-deception. Also, testing to label people only is not helpful to individuals or society; test results that may be utilized to make interventions would help people learn and grow, if they choose to change, and would be helpful to all. Medical tests indicate where problems lie and how to help solve them. Mental tests need to have the same goal. To avoid the confusion of hierarchical terms (high, low, and moderate), we think esteem is viewed best in terms of positive or negative to understand the thought and feeling processes that currently create these two opposing states of being and behavior. High- and low-esteem terms are not as informative as positive esteem, which works for us; and negative-esteem, which works against us in all aspects of life and work. Negative or low self-esteem people may be passive not aggressive, but the body responds to ego threats anyway and pays its chemical toll to either the fight, flight, freeze, or feign syndrome. "The capacity for violence is part of our early instinct for self-preservation. It enables us to fight for our very life."[14] Positive esteem people respond assertively (aggression modified by cognitive input). Researchers found no soft underbelly, or a hidden core of self-doubt, in bullies and murderers. In ego-threatening environments, their brain's limbic system's "fight syndrome" is locked in the "ON" position.

Many youngsters, who were into drugs during their adolescence, bypassed the emotional tolerance stage, so they remain emotionally illiterate and obsessed with power over others, for they have no felt sense of inner power and control. Also, the root cause of human violence may be traced to the lack of affirmation or caring by an adult, leading to aggressively affirming oneself at the expense of others' lives or esteem while inserting oneself into the larger society beyond family. Aggressives' ego constructs are by default or by design. Fetal Alcohol Syndrome (FAS) babies do not have the brains of normal babies, nor do babies who are born to drug addicts. Babies of mothers who smoked cigarettes or pot, or had inadequate diets before and during pregnancy, do not

42

have the same ability to develop and learn as babies who are born to mothers who did not abuse themselves. Early trauma, including in utero, derails normal and humane development as well as compassion. Deficient nurturance, all forms of abuse or neglect, and emotional conflicts are the fodder for developing humans to construct a false self to counteract the assaults on the original self. Therefore, they do whatever it takes to survive and thrive.

It appears that, "Psychology is not yet adept at measuring hidden aspects of personality, especially ones that a person may not be willing to admit even to himself or herself."[15] Most self-esteem assessments depend upon self-reports and are not geared to cover all aspects of a human being's life that influence self-esteem. Hence, self-esteem continues to be perceived in simplistic terms and has been the subject of intense scrutiny and criticism since the 1990's California Task Force's serious study of self-esteem. That Task Force had no impact on the "feel-good" Self-Esteem Movement that undermines self-esteem rather than building or enhancing it. In 1992, *Newsweek*'s article, "The Curse of Self-Esteem: What's Wrong with the Feel-Good Movement,"[16] illuminated narcissistic, self-absorbed, enlarged, and endangered egos, which included "When you're as great as I am, it's hard to be humble" and other quotes from well-known personalities. The article accentuated the negative and eliminated the positive aspects of self-esteem. Less newsworthy are people who are narcissists' opposites: those who value others more than themselves, so they become sycophants, abuse victims, ardent fans of those in the limelight, or dependent upon others or things for their sense of self. Self-esteem has been vaguely defined with similar words and has been ignored as a basic human need. Evidently, something that cannot be defined properly can be safely ignored. However, like the sign in our dentist's office, "Ignore your teeth and they'll go away," self-esteem keeps troubling us.

A decade later, *The New York Times Magazine* article, "The Trouble With Self-Esteem," documented the findings of researchers using standardized self-esteem and narcissism tests with violent populations: pride is dangerous and few know how to be humble. The author postulated that the demise of self-esteem would be an economic blow to the mental health profession since its treatment modalities are based upon *the self*. The old joke about neurotics build castles in the air, psychotics live in them, and psychiatrists collect the rent is akin to the assertion: "I am by no means saying mental health

43

professionals have any conscious desire to perpetuate a perhaps simplistic view of self-esteem, but they are, we are…the 'cultural retailers' of the self-esteem concept, and were the concept to falter, so would our pocketbooks."[17]

People and esteem are not concepts; they are real. The tests are geared to simplistic views of esteem. While many self-esteem researchers prefer the term *self-concept* to *self-esteem,* "it's possible to have a self-concept containing mostly positive beliefs — a positive self-concept — and still lack self-esteem."[18] A simplistic view of self-esteem is one that undermines, in practice, the esteeming process: counselors and therapists who do their best to artificially boost antisocial young men's opinion of themselves and parents and teachers who "have students make lists of reasons why they are wonderful people or sing songs of self-celebration. With a simplistic view of self-esteem, parents and teachers are afraid to criticize kids, lest it cause serious psychological damage and turn some promising youngster into a dangerous thug or pathetic loser. In some sports leagues, everyone gets a trophy."[19] Feel-good exercises may make counselors, therapists, teachers, and parents feel good about doing something to feel competent, although they do not bring about the desired outcome. Many follow mandated guidelines that look good on paper but do not work in real life. Common sense is missing in both approaches. Adults who have positive esteem model it naturally when working with children. Adults who lack positive esteem latch onto fads and try them out on children rather than on themselves first. Children know when they are being "conned;" they have no respect for those who hide behind a mask of exercises, methods, and state licenses. They respect those adults who treat them with respect and honesty that is backed up by knowledge, wisdom, and the courage to be a real person, which means the adults have done their own selfwork. The old and prevailing view is, "The lack of love is…at the bottom of the lack of self-esteem."[20] The lack of love for self means our emotions need attention.

The complexity of self-esteem illuminates another problem with self-esteem assessments, studies, and research. Self-esteem cannot be reduced to ten statements, it cannot be improved or enhanced just by repetitions of self-affirmations, and its status cannot be ascertained by reporting on emotional literacy not taught in any curriculum; although, some people learn emotional tolerance at home or through positive and negative life experiences. Self-esteem tests and assessments of an individual's feelings about his qualities or condition are not testing self-esteem; they are testing fluctuating emotional states and encouraging self-deception. Self-deception is the currency of psychological preservation, just as the fight, flight, freeze, or feign syndrome is the currency of physical survival. The problem, then, is not that people have too high or too low self-esteem with attendant behaviors. The problem is most people are emotionally illiterate, and self-esteem development requires emotional literacy as well as experiential, cognitive or intellectual, physical, and spiritual development. A divided self is not an integrated, congruent, or dynamically balanced self:

> People who are highly competent sometimes feel deeply inadequate; people who are inferior feel superior; people with an ordinary appearance feel beautiful; and people who are attractive feel ugly. More impressive yet, some people who have lived exemplary lives are torn with severe guilt to the point they no longer wish to live, while others who have committed horrendous crimes suffer not a twinge of conscience.[21]

The above quotation shows that affect (feelings and emotions) biases one's perception of self; therefore, one's affect is not representative of a whole person's self-esteem. Feelings have two basic aspects: pleasure or pain. Feelings are experienced through the senses and are stored in the amygdala. Emotions, such as love, fear, anger, are names given to diverse feelings. Hence, self-esteem is not a valid indicator of individuals' successes or failures unless they are emotionally literate. Emotional literacy requires self-knowledge, self-understanding, physical and mental health, and self-work. Taking constructive versus destructive action in one's life is a way to dynamically balance the whole self and to earn self-esteem; then self-esteem may be equated with self-worth, when it includes the whole Self.

While we are enmeshed in a controversy over whether or not self-esteem is a cultural retailer's commodity or a basic human need, the assaults on the self and self-esteem continue. Our society overuses academic IQ and other achievement tests to label kids' academic abilities and possibilities; then the fall-outs, drop-outs, and the antisocial are often shunted to another social agency where they are subjected to finding their dis-ease in the DSMIV

(Diagnostic and Statistical Manual, 4th edition), published by the American Psychiatric Association. Mental health professionals with heavy caseloads overuse the DSMIV to diagnose, label, and have drugs prescribed for those who do not conform to societal or psychological norms. However, we shun from applying new technologies (magnetic resonance imaging, cat scans, etc.) to work with aggressives' possible brain defects to determine if behavioral problems are functional or organic. True, the communists had their "yellow houses" in Siberia where dissidents who did not toe-the-party-line were incarcerated, brainwashed, and drugged into submission. Some of the resistance to using technologies that pinpoint brain abnormalities is the cost; however, most of the resistance comes from the moral minority's paranoia. Thus, we expect those who are violent and hostile — whose underlying motive is to dominate or harm us in our homes, workplaces, schools, and on the streets—to have the same human values and to be assessed by the same unhelpful tests as the rest of us. "To appear civilized — to become a kinder, more concerned human being — demands of most people that they come to terms with their inner nagging drive for power. The more a person knows about himself, the more he matures, the less there is a need for a cover-up façade behavior."[22]

Our civilized, democratic response to self-esteem is to engage in controversy revolving around the words to substitute for *esteem* because our self-esteem tests, assessments, and scales do not work for narcissists, bullies, murderers, and other deviants. They are terrorists! They make life, school, learning, and work more difficult for the rest of us. Life is the only test, and without love, respect, trust, accountability, and responsibility, individuals' violence informs us that democracy is under siege: destructive anarchy. Society pays and so do the taxpayers. Both transnational and domestic terrorists are successful in our democracy because we trust and expect everyone to abide by our democratic values or "rules." They betray our trust and endanger our lives when they abide by their own rules in our country. No terrorist is going to change, including an intimate terrorist, unless there is an incentive. When people are emotionally and spiritually illiterate or brain-damaged, sometimes they don't know how to live or relate. In fact, they don't even know they don't know!

With personal and professional experience working with pathological liars and murderers in prison, Florence has learned that self-deception and "whitewashing" one's dastardly deeds are such finely tuned arts that current tests cannot penetrate the surface of their armor. Where there is raw ego or uncivilized egotism, there is no esteem for anyone and no conscience or compassion. Yes, we must "beware of people who regard themselves as superior to others, especially when those beliefs are inflated, weakly grounded in reality or heavily dependent on having others confirm them frequently."[23] They are beyond the realm of so-called high self-esteem; they have negative esteem for all; they cannot be tested as regular law-abiding human beings, even when they go through the academic motions of working on a Ph.D. and attain it. They learned to "con" themselves first, and then they "con" anyone willing to collude in enabling them to be who they think and say they are. Human beings' lives may be reconstructed by learning emotional tolerance and through psychological and spiritual interventions, but criminals/terrorists must be invested in changing and in doing the necessary rehabilitation work; otherwise, they just learn new ways to use others and the system.

The popular "cure" for low self-esteem relies upon a misuse of the French psychologist Emile Coue's[24] autosuggestion, "Every day and in every way, I am becoming better and better," thus leading to today's narcissistic self-affirmations, which cloud deeper problems that, when faced, might make people more accountable, responsible, or esteemable. It appears that today's self-esteem movement, as practiced, is more about outer dependence — false praise, unearned "stars," and kid-glove treatment — than it is about capital-izing on one's inner and diverse resources to earn a self. Those practices are making self- and other-esteem into a laughing stock. Coué's reality-based affirmations keep us on an even keel where we feel equal to others; it is the opposite of saying affirmations that convince us that we are something we are not.

Snobs think they are superior to others. Snobs are rarely accused of having too high self-esteem. In America, only people who physically harm or kill others are studied and reined in. Those who psychologically or socially harm others are left to flourish unchecked and are rarely chastised. The barnyard pecking order appears to be inherited animal traits; snobs, though, are made, not born. It starts early. Young girls ostracize other girls and make lives miserable in schools. Boys also label each other: Jocks look down upon Nerds. Designating people as "in" and "out" are ways snobs control others' status and behavior; they set the fashion brands and the fads. Adult snobs have "in" dogs, cars, writers, designers, and vacation spots. The word *snob* entered the English language around the 1800s when the newly rich, commercial middle-class people within England's caste system could not rise above their birth status and were snubbed by royalty. Those middles that had achieved wealth, and felt more equal than others, affected lofty "airs" to demonstrate their felt sense of importance. America has more than its share of snobs with their arrogance, haughtiness, condescension, and rudeness; they disdain those they consider "below" them. Some of those snobs are corporate elite terrorists. From our self-esteem perspective, snobs are people with negative esteem for self and others; otherwise, they would not have to engage in affected behavior, wear masks, and seek others' approval by impressing everyone with their so-called specialness. In fact, they fail to impress themselves. Health is not the absence of disease. Mental health is the presence of esteem for all.

No human being is perfect, and there will be transition times when positive esteem may fluctuate until allostasis is achieved through conscious effort and with spiritual literacy, which is necessary to develop other-esteem. Pagan religions taught the sacredness of all life: the sacred is in everyone, everything, and everywhere. Western civilization's institutions and organizations excluded paganism and divided our lives into two separate categories: the sacred and the profane, that is, spirit from matter. We have lost sight of the fact that the same processes that give the Earth abundant life are the same ones that give each of us a sense of self, the ability to contemplate our navel or the world, the capacity to make choices, to feel horror when tragedy strikes (9/11), to experience love when we make connections to others, and joy when we believe "God's in his heaven; All's right with the world."[25] With positive self-esteem we have the power and control over who we are today and who we will become tomorrow, as Marvin Minsky's parody points out to us:

What controls the Brain? The Mind.
What controls the Mind? The Self.
What controls the Self? Itself. [26]

48

Self-Esteem's Sources: External and Internal

While most researchers agree that human beings' *personae* are fifty percent inherited genes (nature) and fifty percent environment (nurture), the predisposition for self-esteem is inherited, but it is learned and earned since "there are no genes to carry the feelings of worth."[27] Early experiences become the basis of our regard for others, ourselves, and our view of the world. The whole self is developed by the exposure to many domains. The family system is the first domain to impact our esteem. Our own culture (with people like us) and subcultures (with people unlike us) and their institutions and organizations are major influences that affect the development of whole selves and the course of lives. So each of us has a story, a history of being raised in a "good enough" or dysfunctional family or caretaking system within a particular culture, of attending schools and community or religious functions, and of following our own passion or others' interests in pursuing our career.

Each of us has a particular inheritance — physiology, psychology, and emotionality — which was further influenced, positively or negatively, by individual responses from and to significant others, peers, and adults. The history of each individual's experience is different when we consider class, race, gender, or status. The experience is also different for those who lived in small towns, cities, one country or several countries. Self-esteem in individualistic countries, such as the United States and Canada, for example, is a different process from that in collectivist countries, such as Japan and China, where the emphasis is upon the group, not the individual, or in Middle East countries where the emphasis is upon the group and religion. Islamic-extremists interpreted the Koran to suit their religious views; they inculcated the young to hate the West and to disown their autonomy and selfhood. People are not cognitively, emotionally, or spiritually literate when they use other human beings as adversaries to ignite their zeal.

The source of internal self-esteem, according to Branden, are the "six pillars of self-esteem:"[28] 1. Living consciously; 2. Self-acceptance; 3. Self-responsibility; 4. Self-assertiveness; 5. Living purposefully; 6. Personal integrity. Five of those six traits require a self that is not dependent upon a group or an ideology for an identity; whereas, living purposefully could mean adopting the group's purpose as one's own. To live consciously requires awareness of the consequences of actions, behaviors, and goals. The transnational terrorists were willing to martyr themselves to make a bold statement, to live "ever-after" in Islam heaven, and to kill as many adversaries as possible, without assessing the consequences of their actions upon the world, their families, allies, or their religion. Love is the foundation, says Branden, for achieving the six pillars of self-esteem. Love, though, must be experienced externally, through parenting or from significant others; then it must be felt internally, before it can be expressed authentically.

Parenting

Raising children is the most difficult job anyone will ever undertake. There are no licenses or existing degrees, but books may be read or courses taken; however, the experts' advice changes with the times. Most parents, though, parent as they were parented by emotionally unavailable parents. Statistics on juvenile crime, the divorce rates, and the number of births to unmarried women in recent decades[29] are indicators that children and adults are not getting the kind of love and respect they need to love and respect themselves and others. Parents who have inner environments of peace, security, and love (despite their outer world) and have bonded with their children, born without medical intervention, are more likely to have rewarding child rearing experiences.

In his 1950's research, Daniel Prescott found that love was missing from the human development literature. He wanted to find out if "love is a genuine human reality or a romantic construct within our culture."[30] He discovered that "Love is not rooted primarily in sexual dynamics or hormonal drives. It is rooted in the individual's value dynamics...The good effects of love are not limited to the beloved...to love is not altruistic but self-realizing."[31] He concluded that love is a genuine human reality and became convinced that "it plays a most important role in human development."[32] "Being loved can afford any human being a much-needed and basic psychological security."[33] Love, though, needs to be dynamically balanced with consistent rules and judicious discipline that are in the child's, the parents', and society's best interests.

Literature on how to rear children to fulfill their potentialities has been available for years in the libraries and in the bookstores. Studies have correlated parents' character with their children's behavior; a child's personality is reflective of the emotional atmosphere of his home. "Any list of undesirable attitudes and characteristics will include those of parents who are overemotional, overprotective, childish, alcoholic, seductive, overconscientious, or divorced."[34] Parents who are unemotional, cruel, narcissistic, underprotective, or zealously attached to a cause, from religion to health, spend more time on defending their egos or absorbing dogma than they do on building self-esteem. In turn, their children may become like the parents, through default by becoming like the hated parent (negativity attracts negativity) or through habit by leading unexamined lives: we learn what we live and live what we learn.

There are many steps for parents to guide their children along a humane development path. An infant's basic needs for food, water, warmth, etc. are accompanied by safety and security needs, the need to be loved and to love, and to belong to a family or group. When an infant's needs are met, higher growth is possible. Higher growth is blocked when needs are not adequately met, and the frustration experienced stunts an infant's growth potential. Foremost are the needs to respect ourselves, to be strong, and to have positive self-esteem. Unconditional positive regard validates the essence of *being* in children and adults. Parents' unconditional positive regard promotes children's faith in their resources, helps them function freely and with maximum effectiveness, and teaches them they are valuable in all respects. Unconditional positive regard is the basis for optimum development.[35]

In essence, three conditions must be present for positive self-esteem before other-esteem is possible; they are:

(1) Acceptance—expressed by warmth, interest, and concern for
    the individual's well-being by persons significant to him;
(2) Clearly defined limits, goals, and relatively high demands
    and expectations for performance; and
(3) Respectful treatment and latitude of individuals for persons
    who abide by the established limits.[36]

People with positive self-esteem carry within them the experience of having a parent or significant other who loved them whether or not they were handsome, did well in school, or took out the garbage. They probably had someone who was proud of their successes and was accepting of their failures, while maintaining realistic expectations for effort and achievement. These empowering relationships instill a sense of uniqueness, which is not dependent upon educational, social, or economic "norms" set by others.

From mythology comes the story of Narcissus who could not love another, just himself. He fell in love with his own reflection in the water (instead of seeing himself reflected in his mother's or a significant other's eyes); hence, narcissism is the term applied to people who are obsessed with themselves and are self-centered. Narcissism is healthy and necessary to get our needs met as infants when we cry for food, changing, and attention, so it is not surprising that self-esteem is equated with narcissism. However, narcissism in adults results when the natural impulse to grow and learn is thwarted but not destroyed.

Boyhood experiences with potatoes stored in the cellar became Carl Rogers' life theme. The potatoes developed pale white spindly sprouts — unlike healthy green ones when planted in the soil — while reaching toward the distant sunlight. "They would never become a plant, never mature, never fulfill their real potentiality...Life would not give up even if it could not flourish."[37] Similarly, people who have had a deficit upbringing, or had inadequate bonding with a caregiver, are striving to grow in their own way, even if it takes the form of addictions, narcissism, violence, or hate.

On the way to a personal-powered or to an overindulged, negative, or violent self, human beings experience five power levels.[38] If an infant gets positive responses to his crying and movements and his narcissistic needs are met, he feels loved and affirmed. When needs are met, and a child feels loved, the stage is set for loving and affirming self which prepares him to successfully enter the world beyond narcissism and family in a day care center or kindergarten. When a child is overindulged, or "smothered," he may remain narcissistic and expect to be treated by everyone as if the universe revolves around his needs and wants. If, however, a child's needs were not met, and he does not feel loved or affirmed, then his entrance into the world beyond family may be aggressive- or passive-oriented. Caretakers and teachers love passive children, not realizing the future danger of what is lurking within them. It is the narcissistic child, however, who gets the most attention, just as the squeaky wheel gets the most grease. Most abused children respond aggressively to all provocative social situations; they are penalized for their behavior, and violence becomes the ultimate power level where the violence may be directed at themselves or others.

Human attachment or bonding is about love. Attachment or bonding processes usually occur within three months of birth between an infant and the caregiver. Whether attachment or bonding begins early or much later, it is a necessary and important process for the development of functional, empathic human beings. During the years 1784 to 1838, 146,920 out of 183,055 newborn "foundlings" died at the University of Vienna, Germany, Children's Hospital. They wasted away from the lack of loving care.[39] Research on infant monkeys of the attachment process by Harry Harlow[40] found that they clung to the cloth "mother" as a source of warmth or comfort, rather than as a source of food. Human babies are deprived of regular face-to-face and skin-to-skin experiences when mothers do not nurse them, use bottle props, or hold the infant at arm's length.[41] Such feeding practices negatively affect the mother-child bond and the baby's developmental processes.

Historically, parents have not responded to their infants' distress when put down for the night. They believe that their children will just "go off to sleep." And there are still parents who "do unto others what was done unto them" by letting their infant "cry itself to sleep."[42] Holding and hugging children when they misbehave, even against their will until they calm down, "does not break a child's spirit; rather it frees his spirit from the burden of anger and other negative feelings which interfere with his self-expression and fulfillment."[43] Premature babies in incubators thrive when they are regularly touched, if only by one finger. Parents who provide opportunities for their children to acquire life skills and allow them to accept responsibility and learn from failure are demonstrating their belief that their children have what it takes to survive and to achieve. Many American parents, though, feel guilty when they say, "No!" to their children, so they finally give in to their whining.

Generally, positive self-esteem has three foundations: first, respect and approval from other people; second, actual capacity, achievement, and success; and third, the acceptance of and willingness to put effort into acting upon our own inner nature. Further, we also have cognitive and aesthetic needs, which must be satisfied to be humanely developed. Human development, therefore, is a never-ending process; so is self-esteem. Each of us who has experienced being shaped by others and our environment also has the capacity to shape and re-shape ourselves. So, the good news is, children of deficient parenting or caretaking can rebuild positive self-esteem, despite their family history and environment. Some find significant others (real people or a distant role model) to learn how to parent themselves. Others earn esteem by finding meaningful work, fulfilling relationships, belonging to an esteemed group, or having a life mission. Our locus of control must be inside, not outside self, for esteem fluctuates with changing situations.

Positive Self-Esteem

Misperceptions of self-esteem are common. Most self-esteem gurus and writers about psychology are most concerned with the egocentric, emotional dimension of self-esteem or the small self. Defining self-esteem as how warm and loving one feels toward oneself self is not enough. Why do we feel warm and loving toward ourselves? Is it because we own a lot of status things? Is it because we have a powerful job? Is it because we feel good about ourselves when we outwit, take advantage of, or compare ourselves to others, so then we feel we are better or superior to others? Or is it that we are warm and loving toward ourselves because we are self-reliant and accept self *as is*, and are also responsible, virtuous, competent, and a relational Self?

Self-esteem is not a preoccupation with a self that is detached from other human beings. A self is subject to familial, educational, cultural, and a myriad of other interdisciplinary and experiential influences; therefore, self-esteem is not only what I think of me but what others think of me too. Just as the body and mind are not separate and act as one, even if incongruently, we are affected or influenced by others since we are all interconnected and interdependent.

Positive self-esteem people have many positive qualities that are visible through their behavior and personae. Some of those are: they feel equal to others; they do not have to criticize or put anyone down to feel good about themselves; they do not put someone on a pedestal or "name drop" to feel important by association. They have examined values they live by but are

54

willing to modify them, if necessary; they have integrity, honesty, and are able to live with differences. They do not spend time worrying about the future or obsessing over past mistakes; their work is satisfying and rewarding. They are not easily led or dominated by others; they trust themselves to solve their own problems. They are sensitive to others' needs and situations, and they do not take advantage of others in business or in their personal lives; they do not use sex to feed their egos; they do not need extramarital affairs, drugs, alcohol, food, or approval to compensate for any felt emptiness, and they do not fear commitment. They look for the best in others, do not carry grudges, and are responsible for themselves and their families while being responsible to others and the Earth.

Positive self-esteem is similar to the automatic pilot on a small plane. An automatic pilot does not adhere strictly to the course but strays to the left and right, constantly changing altitude and attitude in response to changing environmental conditions. However, it always returns to its intended setting and stays on course. We can develop a positive core of self-esteem that is not negotiable by difficult or different people, cultures, or situations. We may stray off our course while learning new things or experiencing new people or situations, but we are able to rescue ourselves when we become aware that our self-esteem is faltering. We are more able to put ourselves back together again after facing periods of self-doubt, if we learn from our stressful life experiences instead of avoiding them so we do not have to repeat them later.

When we have positive self-esteem, we are less encumbered by the "Don'ts, Can'ts, Shoulds, and Oughts" embedded in us when we were growing up and by today's regrets over yesterday's "Didn'ts." It is our choice and assessment of a situation that ultimately is the deciding factor in our esteem, even if our first reaction is to succumb to the internalized cautions and fears. With positive self-esteem, we show our feelings, laugh at ourselves, and feel at ease or comfortable in most situations, all of which enables others to feel comfortable around us and to like themselves better in our presence.

Negative Esteem

In the late 1980s, it was reported that many young people were subject to about 15,000 negative statements and about 5,000 positive statements during the twelve years it takes to get out of high school. It was also estimated that about twenty percent of students entering school had negative self-esteem; whereas, eighty percent had negative self-esteem by the fifth grade, and ninety-five percent of the seniors in high school had negative self-esteem. Something happened to their positive esteem while in school! Schools are places where the emotional brain and emotions and feelings are not admissible; yet, they are places where students are vulnerable to teachers' and peers' emotional slights and judgments. Today, those 1980's students with the ninety-five percent negative self-esteem are the backbone of America's institutions and organizations. Let us hope they have already healed the terrorist within so that all may now focus on the terrorists in our midst.

Man without a keen sense of self can be persuaded and brainwashed by charismatic leaders to perceive dangers where none exist and to protect his perceived vital interests as well as his group's. "If others threaten him with ideas that question his own frame of orientation, he will react to these ideas as to a vital threat."[44] Man also needs "objects of devotion, which become a vital necessity for his emotional equilibrium...values, ideas, ancestors, father, mother, the soil, country, class, religion, and hundreds of other phenomenon — they are perceived as sacred...Even customs"[45] and his narcissism. In adults, narcissism is an example of negative esteem.

He who gains a sense of security from his self-construct, his perceived superiority over others, his quality of work, or achievements must "hold on to his narcissistic self-image, since his sense of worth as well as his sense of identity are based on it."[46] When either is threatened or slighted:

> a narcissistic person usually reacts with intense anger or rage, whether
> or not he shows it or is even aware of it...such a person will never forget
> someone who has wounded his narcissism and often feels a desire for
> vengeance which would be less intense if his body or his property had
> been attacked.[47]

It is conceivable that terrorists have a narcissistic self-image that can be programmed to seek vengeance on the so-called infidels who are perceived to have slighted them or whose way of life is a threat to their own. In Afghanistan, under the Taliban, women used to hide behind their veils and not show any flesh but their eyes in public. In Pakistan, women prefer to hide their faces. Reportedly, the rationale for Middle Eastern women wearing veils was to prevent warring tribes from kidnapping the younger women. In Saudi Arabia, women are not allowed to drive cars. Two of the 9/11 terrorists occupied an apartment in Florida; they draped a towel over the picture of a nude woman on their wall. To men who look down upon women, a nation where women are equal under the law is another sign, to them, of America's weakness and vulnerability. Certainly, each of the terrorists was not man enough to move beyond the myths of overblown manhood and dogma handed down by generations of macho fathers and religious fundamentalists.

People's negative behavior advertises to all the state of their esteem for themselves and others. Self-esteem deficits may be cognitive, experiential, relational, or emotional. Negative-esteem people are not dynamically balanced — emotionally and intellectually — whole human beings; they may be religious but they are not spiritually literate. People with negative-esteem may possess many things and pursue varied leisure and professional activities but carry within them the feeling that material things have been substituted for parental or others' time, involvement, and love. Other people with negative-esteem carry the burden of psychological abuse from disapproving or dissatisfied parents or significant others. Too often, parents have experienced being seen through others' critical eyes or hearing harsh words about their own alleged lack of ability and unimportance, so they pass it on to their children instead of growing from their own negative experiences. Parents' repeated negative criticism of a child's ability or appearance and siblings' and peers' bullying and belittling all foster negative self-esteem. John was about six when his father, an engineer, decided that he should be better at arithmetic. He would keep him up after his bedtime, drilling him with the multiplication tables. Finally, one night, John had enough and blurted out, "You know, Dad, you're not Mr. America!" Children see very clearly, but the ability to see so clearly is clouded after years of hearing, "You're not smart enough!" or "You'll never amount to anything!" The energy spent defending one's ego from assaults leaves less energy to spend on learning and esteem.

"People who have a negative view of themselves are typically muddling through life, trying to avoid embarrassment, giving no sign of a desperate need to prove their superiority. Aggressive attack is risky; people with low self-esteem tend to avoid risks. When people with low self-esteem fail, they usually blame themselves, not others."[48] Negative-esteem people are prone to be oversensitive to failure and criticism, to feel or expect immediate rejection, to take a long time to recover from disappointments, and to have a pessimistic view of life, as is observed in children and adults who have not experienced the security of a mother's, father's, or a significant other's love. Young people who feel something is missing in their lives may not be equipped to help themselves, so they develop a social system of their own, which may be gang-, drug-, criminal-, or leisure-oriented; all engender negative-esteem.

Some young people try to "buy" self-esteem; instead, they end up with negative self-esteem. Unsolicited credit cards are sent to students when they enter college or get a job. Many young people respond to the "You deserve it!" advertising and buy things to make themselves feel or look good. Many young women are burdened with $7,000+ balances on their credit cards at high interest rates. Other young people "max out" their credit cards and are hounded by collection agencies. They ruin their credit rating and their reputations by taking short cuts to self-esteem. Student loans are an entirely different matter: an investment in a future career.

Various studies have pinpointed three potential sources of negative self-esteem: (1) heredity, (2) lack of social skills, and (3) socialization processes that undermine self-confidence. Negative esteem is not an inborn character flaw; it represents a learned pattern of responses to an early negative environment, which colors our future encounters. Few of us live out our lives with the kind of love we want or need or without conflict, adversaries, and struggles. If we avoid the struggle to learn from our lived experiences, we may cover it up with behavior that diminishes us and those lives we touch: our body may betray us by expressing physical back pain, migraines, or tantrums to prevent hidden emotions from surfacing, such as antisocial or inferiority feelings, anger, resentment, repressed unlovable behaviors, or assaults on young egos.

Continuous self-praise and boasting are symptoms of negative self-esteem; otherwise we would not have such a great need to impress others or ourselves. Much has been written about the importance of encouraging children by giving them substantial praise. Too often, though, praise has the opposite of the desired result, especially if the praise is not sincere or reality-based. To praise someone is to presume that we know something that the person we are praising does not, thereby assuming a position of authority, rather than one of a peer. Praise causes more harm than help 99 percent of the time.[49] Many children are both cynical about praise and dependent upon it; the worst possible mixture for esteem to flourish.

What children want and need is "thoughtful attention. They want us to notice them and pay some kind of attention to what they do, to take them seriously, to trust and respect them as human beings. They want courtesy and politeness, but they don't need much praise."[50] Feeling worthy of praise, through demonstrating our worthiness, is more important than receiving it. Children become hurt and angry when their basic needs for adequate love and attention are not met. When children feel free to express their negative feelings, they become free to express their positive feelings as well.

Children who are indulged too much, or who are insulated from the consequence of their actions by their parents, end up self-centered, thinking they are the center of the universe. "If you want a child to have integrity and character, you have to toughen them up a little bit."[51] Children who learn emotional tolerance early on have more positive childhood experiences than those who learn it the hard way do. Children who have experienced unconditional love have the basis for loving themselves; however, children who were overprotected may not be ready for independence. Overprotected children may take longer than others to learn how to handle life on their own.

The Afghan people have learned to endure. Philip Caputo reported he was with a platoon escorting refugees into Pakistan in 1980. A ten-year-old boy, separated from his family, hobbled along on slashed feet from five days of barefoot marching. Fearful that he would drown, Philip carried him across the rapids; the boy found his father. "The father slapped the boy in the face and poked me in the chest, shouting angrily...'Now,' he says [interpreter translating], 'his son will expect some stranger to help him whenever he runs into difficulties.'"[52] Fear and frustration expressed as anger is natural when people are placed in threatening situations or where they have no control over outcomes, as in the Afghan father's case. Similarly, a mother whose child runs into a busy street may slap and berate him to assuage her fear or frustration over what *might* have happened. Her underlying but unattended feelings are love for her child and real or imagined inadequacy as a parent. Love, hate, anger, and fear are intimately intertwined.

There is a difference between feelings of inadequacy and feelings of frustration. "Feelings of inadequacy seem to grow out of failure to meet successfully the expectations of others and the demands of institutional processes; whereas, feelings of frustration grow out of failure to achieve goals set by oneself and to feel the inner self-growth and development for which one has the potential."[53] A natural outcome of feelings of inadequacy are self-doubt, inferiority feelings, hopelessness in meeting life's demands; whereas, feelings of frustration may be demonstrated by hostility directed toward friends, authority figures, school, society, or even oneself.

If we believe that others can make us feel guilty, incompetent, unloved, or inferior, we have colluded in relinquishing our personal power to them. When we allow other people to judge us or to play god with us, we will be judged, and we will be punished. We are the authority on ourselves. Nevertheless, what an important-to-us person thinks of us does affect our self-esteem, positively and negatively, since we file away, consciously and unconsciously, every iota of sensory data. The saying, *Sticks and stones may hurt my bones, but words will never harm me*, is untrue. The harmful words are stored in the brain's amygdala for later retrieval, unless we make peace with them.

The lack of human beings' and society's wholeness led the former Roman Catholic priest Matthew Fox to assert, "Our society is sick with adultism. Adults set the economic, moral, education, worship, and work agendas. To the extent that adults are out of touch with the child in them, this agenda creates a false self and an unbalanced society. The wounded child in the adult screams out for attention, compassion, and healing."[54] Adults often deny their wounds and play out their wounded child on others for the rest of their lives. Many men prefer a macho, dominant stance with women or a distant one: they are so preoccupied with sex that they neglect their wives and girlfriends to view pornographic or sex films. Some all-male clubs exclude women from membership; their "bonding rituals" include having live girls — who may be prostitutes — entertain them: an Americanized version of the Japanese geishas — who are not prostitutes — for men with yen. Those men prefer to think they are oversexed, not overly vain or power-hungry; all are symptoms of negative self-esteem. It is said that all human beings are recovering from childhood. Many men do not acknowledge the importance of the limbic and frontal lobe areas of the human brain; therefore, they remain emotionally immature and miss out on intimacy. The lack of positive self-esteem is like having a virus we carry unknowingly in our bodies.

Developing Other-Esteem

Other-esteem is a deterrent to all forms of terrorism. To develop other-esteem, we start with ourselves; otherwise, we will be as guilty as indulgent parents who spend money, not their time, on their children. Taking the time to sit down, to listen to them, to talk with them, or to hug them fosters emotional literacy. Emotionally illiterate, money-indulged children acquire a sense of entitlement. To develop our esteem for others, we must have empathy for those unlike ourselves, then we can help others to develop theirs.

The forces that help develop a child into a caring adult have implicated fathers. Empathy — the ability to share another's feelings — has been intensely studied because it is a socially desirable personality trait. Research suggests that the strongest predictor of empathy in adulthood is the amount of time a father spent with his child. If the father's time spent with his child is to criticize him "for your own good," then he does not foster empathy or unconditional love. The child who is constantly criticized and reprimanded begins to feel bad and, sometimes, to act badly, and self-esteem suffers.

Self-esteem is situational; it is not a fortress; therefore, it is important to hear and acknowledge what others think of us to determine if what they think is an uncovered or disowned part of self or if it has more to do with them or what we evoke in them. When we disregard others' feedback, we miss an opportunity to learn more about our impact and ourselves. When we do not give feedback, our silence is assent, and we miss the opportunity to learn and grow through each other. When we collude in stereotypes of *The Ugly American*[55] at home, in restaurants, at work, or abroad, our narcissism is as evident as our disdain for others' feelings or welfare, and we incur resentment. Ralph Waldo Emerson mastered the art of writing between the lines:

> WHAT YOU ARE
> SPEAKS SO LOUDLY
> I CAN'T HEAR
> WHAT YOU SAY YOU ARE

Just as light travels faster than sound, our spoken words are second to our "first impression." It is our whole self that speaks. We see, hear, and feel nonverbal messages: what people are not saying is often more important than what they are saying. As the old saying goes, *Actions speak louder than words*. It is the hidden, unspoken message that captures our attention first. It is also what captures others' attention. The body does not lie. We send nonverbal messages with our eyes, how we move, carry ourselves, and breathe. If we do not appear assertive, physically and mentally alert, or self-caring, a prospective mugger perceives us as an "easy mark." Our level of esteem is visible to knowledgeable others. We can be more attuned and sensitive to other people when our own ego is not the center of our attention, and we may be more likely to understand and empathize with people who are unlike us.

People of different cultures have different systems of nonverbal communication and ways of doing things. Since our culture is deeply, and often unconsciously, embedded within us, we often insist that others conform to our ways and tend to become uncomfortable and anxious when they do not. "Language is not (as is commonly thought) a system for transferring thoughts or meaning from one brain to another, but a system for organizing information and for releasing thoughts and responses in other organisms."[56]

How frustrating it is when others' perceptions of us are the opposite of what we think we are all about! And, the harder we try to communicate who we are or to change another's perception, the more resistance we encounter. Understanding others and ourselves are related processes; therefore, the challenge is to reflect upon the resistance on both sides. Sometimes, though, the communication problem is, as Edward Hall[57] stated, "The trouble I have with him is me." The fewer value judgments and negative experiences or schemas we have, the more clearly we can perceive what we are up against. It takes a strong sense of self not to be dragged into a fray or to get out of someone's life as quickly as possible when we find we are dealing with a bigot, someone who has an investment in diminishing us, or one who fits us into some preconceived model from his unresolved past experiences.

Americans often annoy citizens of other nations. We are perceived to be aggressive, arrogant, ignorant, and affluent. At a workshop conducted for a group at a Canadian (Newfoundland) university, an Englishwoman reported that in England, in her training people for job interviews, she advises her students to "Walk in like an American! Act as if you own the place!" *The Foreigner*, a play by Larry Shue, is a wonderful example of Americans' perception that talking louder and enunciating better in our own language is the way to be understood by a foreigner who does not understand our language at all. This inflexibility and apparent ignorance of other cultures and languages are negatives that perpetuate the perception that Americans embody historical prejudice, cultural narrowness, and personal arrogance. Americans are also caring, generous, and peace loving, but our negatives get the best of us in unfamiliar situations. Some foreigners' negative perceptions are their bases for judging all Americans.

The myth is that open communication will heal the historical wounds between tribes, ethnic, racial, religious groups, and nations. Unfortunately, the more some people communicate and get to know one another, the more they may hate each other. Since understanding others and understanding ourselves are related processes, we can begin with us, or with others, and learn about ourselves through them by keeping a journal. Forms of nationalism or religiosity that despise others' ways of life are more difficult to overcome since embedded emotions in the amygdala are fused with real or imagined injustices.

The Islamic-extremist terrorists and their hosts who wrought such horror on our nation, killed nearly three thousand innocent people, left their families distraught, and injured others, shattered our illusion that we are insulated from the rest of the world. Prominent American voices implied that we got what we deserved for our alliances and actions or abortion practices. Such voices must be disregarded as morally obtuse; they sound similar to those who say a young woman gets what she deserves when she is gang-raped. We have spent billions of dollars and have lost American lives to rescue Arab nations from each other. Those rescued nations have allowed their press, schools, and mullahs to attack America with hateful propaganda. They support terrorist groups to deflect criticism away from themselves for accepting our aid or support and to bolster the Palestinian cause against Israel's occupation of the West Bank and Gaza.

Money we give or lend to other nations must be accompanied by mutual respect; otherwise, we are like indulgent parents who raise kids with entitlement attitudes. Generations of Arabs and Muslims have been raised on distorted views of America so they hate us and dance in the streets when

63

Americans are killed. Cold-blooded terrorists must not be ignored, though, for they will continue to play David and Goliath. The religious extremists need a lot of tough love, and we need to manage the perceptions of those leaders who bite the hands that feed them by reaching their people with more creative ways of communicating our values and intentions, from improving their future to overcoming corruption.

Tough love makes people responsible and accountable. Human lives and realities are about anger and fear. Fear comes in many forms and induces the fight, flight, freeze, or feign syndrome. The human brain is attracted to the negatives; the schemas in our amygdala are fear-based. It takes an awakened heart, and a reprocessed amygdala, to love those who have different values and ways of understanding and living. Empathy and altruism are not possible when our attention is fixed on ourselves, or when we cannot imagine our actions' impact upon another. It will take years to repair and heal Americans' and terrorists' hearts and souls.

The breakdown of wholes into disparate, manageable parts is the way our society of bureaucracies and corporations work, but it is not the way people work best. Without an awareness of the larger context — the big picture — we become fragmented and alienated from others, our work, the world, and ourselves. Then we burnout, get labeled, feel apathetic or unproductive, get depressed, or live for what is usually out of our reach.

When we heal ourselves and become the persons we were meant to be — A Real Somebody! — we learn to see and to celebrate life, from an ant crawling on a flower to the curiosity and wonder of a child. Wonder is akin to worship (*worship* is an historical construct from the word "work-ship"); wonder gives us the power to enjoy and to value life. Self-esteem is a basic human need and the underpinning of the life force within us all! Self-esteem is not only an inner quest to heal the terrorist within but an outward one, through other-esteem, to help heal the terrorist outside ourselves, to reconnect us with our whole selves, our human family, and our home: the Earth. Fluency in the language of esteem enables us to cross all human boundaries and to be the mirror that reflects terrorists' possible selves. In our individualistic society, we need to combine our mirrors to facilitate and accelerate the esteeming process.

64

Three

*I am as great to me as you are to you,
and you are as great to you as I am to me;
therefore, we are equal.* —Dee Hock[1]

The Language of Diplomacy, Terrorism, and Esteem

THE LANGUAGE OF DIPLOMACY, between officials of different nations, is usually organized around issues of power. The language of diplomacy is narrow, so it breaks down very easily; thus, war is more likely than peace in most diplomatic negotiations. However, the more diplomats, politicians, and leaders are at peace within themselves and with others, the less need there will be to play out their ego needs on other people or other nations. It is said, "A split within is illness, a split without is war...What we need to learn is to recognize and to solve our inner conflicts so we feel secure enough to move 'towards' another human being [and] towards humanity."[2] Anwar Sadat is quoted as saying, "My contemplation of life and human nature in that secluded place [Cell 54, Cairo's Central Prison, Egypt] has taught me that he who cannot change the very fabric of his thought will never be able to change reality, and will never, therefore, make any progress."[3]

Psychopolitics[4] is a term that encompasses an individual's psychodynamics. The dynamics of politics and psychology are rampant in national and international circles among politicians and world leaders. The word *politics* is derived from the word for *citizen*, but today's definition has more to do with power and control. Political and religious leaders who use their power to fuel their personal or group's ambitions have demonstrated throughout history that war is the inevitable result.

Power is essential for all beings. Power plays exist in infancy; it is the force — babies' cries, gurgles, and smiles — that gets caretakers' attention and care.

The term *power* originates from the Latin infinitive *posse*, or from the French infinitive *pouvoir*; both terms mean *to be able to*. Individuals have power, known as *personal power*, whose locus of control may be internal or external. Nations and their institutions and organizations have power, known as *system power*. Self-esteem — with love as its base — and power — with fear as its traditional base — are intimately intertwined. Power is allied more with fear than with love. Without love, the world is dangerous. Personal power derived from external sources only (power over others, possessions, money, and status, etc.) is negative-esteem-oriented. To change the fabric of one's thought requires a keen sense of self, emotional literacy, and a balance of external and internal personal power. However, power is perception, and Dee Hock's "MiniMaxim," quoted above, is a mantra to repeat whenever we find ourselves feeling unequal in the company of those with money, power, or status. The mantra also helps us to maintain our equanimity and resilience, especially when a terrorist attacks us or when we are in the presence of negative self- or other-esteem people. We maintain our power when we do not allow another's negativity to control our response, so we do not collude in their attempts to dehumanize or demean us.

Niccolo Machiavelli provided us, in the 15th century, with an analysis of statesmanship and power. In his chapter "Of Cruelty and Clemency, and Whether It Is Better to Be Loved or Feared," he contemplated, "whether it is better to be loved more than feared, or feared more than loved. The reply is, that one ought to be both feared and loved, but as it is difficult for the two to go together, it is much safer to be feared than loved."[5] That credo is still operative in leaders and clerics who are not dependent upon their followers' votes for their power positions. It is also the modus operandi of some heads of families, bureaucracies, and corporations.

In our democratic society, we elect our political leaders. The interrelationship between followers and leaders is one of the most significant of human relationships. A verse in the *Old Testament* (King James version of the Bible) reads, "All we like sheep have gone astray; we have turned every one to his own way, and the Lord hath laid on him the iniquity of us all" (*Isaiah* 53:6). In Margaret Rioch's article, "All We Like Sheep," about group processes, she proposed that "it is almost always possible for one of the sheep to play the role of shepherd of the flock...A. K. Rice thought of the ego as performing a leadership function for the individual, as a shepherd performs a leadership function for the flock, deciding which way it shall go, how it shall and shall not behave, and who shall be allowed to come in and go out."[6] When the simile about sheep is applied to human beings, the shepherd is also a sheep, just another human being. When we elect a politician, expecting a statesman to emerge, we are usually disappointed. It follows, then, that the quality of an elected leader or politician depends upon the quality of the voters. The language of positive self- and other-esteem crosses all personal, professional, and international boundaries.

Political and religious leaders' levels of self-esteem — an integration of intellectual and emotional intelligence, personal power, and experience — are the key to how they will react to their system power role: "a person with low self-esteem...will generally feel anxious about losing his power and will habitually use the power either for ego-protection or ego-building. A person with high self-esteem will generally use power more gracefully and will not let the trappings of the position seduce him into dependency upon them in order to feel significant and potent."[7] Positive self-esteem, with an internal locus of power, is preferable to dependence upon the trappings of power and things or to preoccupation with what other people think.

Psychopolitics is not limited to politicians and leaders; neither is the language of diplomacy their exclusive domain. Psychopolitics goes on in most interpersonal relationships, whether personal or professional. Our lives would be more peaceful, rewarding, and fulfilling if we were treated, and treated others, with more skill for dealing with people and nations and with more respect for differences that have evolved since Abraham: the ancient patriarch of Islam, Christianity, and Judaism.

The Language of Intimate and Other Domestic Terrorists

Our Western civilization was founded on Power Over[8] others. During the past fifty years, most human beings in our society have evolved to levels of higher human consciousness. Thus, our archaic system power structures and inherited beliefs about slavery, child labor, and physical, verbal, and sexual abuse have yielded to human rights and respect for human life and human dignity and to a more humane use of personal and system power. However, many individuals abuse their personal power. They perpetuate their control or dominance by physical force or psychological repression of other human beings who work for them or live with them, such as wives and children. Their personal power is based on controlling others since they feel out of control or powerless within themselves. The *workforce* and *intimate terrorists* usually maintain their power and control over others through verbal manipulation, covert coercion, or intimidation. Diplomacy, or skill in dealing with people, is *not* a verbal abuser's forte. Power Over others is manifested by verbal abuse by anyone of anyone, especially children or of people, employees, or service people in an unequal power position. A need for Power Over, a desire for revenge, and emotional immaturity lead to terrorism. *All terrorists* bypass their possible selves by protecting their ego constructs.

Through the maturation process, we learn to be emotionally literate in our family of origin and to express anger appropriately. If we do not learn from our parents how to express anger and other emotions appropriately, we miss a crucial learning curve. We learn what we live, so we become angry and abusive too. An individual's stored anger, from childhood or later experiences, motivates and perpetuates abusive behavior that has little or nothing to do with current events or relationships. Anger can be expressed in a healthy way. When it is not, it is hurtful and destructive to those who bear the brunt of unacknowledged abusive behavior and hostility that belongs to the abuser's past. Living with a verbally abusive husband and father undermines his wife's and his children's self-esteem. Some women are abusers, too. Working for abusers is equally destructive.

Personal Power's two sides — dark and light — are Power Over and Power With. The realities of people with Power Over and Power With orientations are diametrically opposed. Power Over is all about anger, hostility, dominance and subordination of another human being; therefore, one's power source is outside self, that is, stolen or bought. Power With is about love, collaboration, cooperation, participation, and mutuality; there is an expectation of kind words, accurate information, open communication, and caring interactions. Thus, Power Over others is a destructive form of personal power; it kills the spirits of both the abuser and the abused human being. Power With, or shared power, is a nourishing form of personal power. Power Over people's unresolved childhood experiences left them so insecure, vulnerable, and distrusting that they need to control others to avoid their feelings of powerlessness. Power With people promote the growth and well-being of self *and* others. There is a mutuality of interest, where each collaborates with and helps the other to live well and to enjoy life to the fullest.

A verbal abuser cannot accept a partner as an equal; her equality is perceived as his inferiority. He equates his worth with one-up-manship; therefore, her talents or achievements are a threat to his ego. Alternatively, he thinks so little of himself that there must be something wrong with her if she loves him. Thus, a verbal abuser misuses his power to discount, judge, criticize, undermine, trivialize, threaten, and withhold his thoughts and feelings from his partner and to treat her as an adversary, an enemy. An abusive relationship does not begin as such, but the signs are there, and the abuse escalates over time. Gradually, a partner is led to believe that there really is something wrong with her, that she is to blame for his anger and abusive behavior, that she is a "bad" person because she is not "perfect" in his eyes, and that *if only* she could communicate better he would understand her, *then* they would live happily ever-after, which is a *victim* stance. If she asks why he treats everyone but her more respectfully, he may retort, "They deserve it, and you don't!" "I paid for you!" "I own you!" "Any woman can do for me what you can do!" or "You always have to have the last word!" He behaves as if she is his lawful property and personal scapegoat. He blames her if/when he has an adulterous affair. To make matters worse for understanding what she is up against, everyone thinks her abuser is a "nice guy" for most of his abuse occurs in secret. Exorcising his terrorists or demons is his responsibility; however, he is not suffering; she is. He has little reason to change, unless she changes her response to his game, his rules, or leaves him.

When a partner is systematically conditioned by experiencing ongoing verbal abuse or unexpected verbal assaults, she learns not to trust her own worth, feelings, or perceptions. She may lose the ability to stand up for herself and her children, which she may later regret for not "protecting" them. If she objects to the verbal abuse, he labels her a complainer or a troublemaker. Her reality is not acknowledged; his is the only reality. Her negative situation compromises her immune system, and she may experience a crisis: a health problem, extreme sadness, or acute depression. A crisis is an opportunity. When we hurt enough, we will do something: seek outside help, keep a journal to record the words and actions that are breaking our hearts, realize that where there is control there is no love, and affirm self's worth, uniqueness, and right to be treated with respect and dignity. Self-esteem strengthens the body's immune system to withstand and counter verbal abuse or another's paranoia.

Most abusers — male and female — deny that they are abusers. To become conscious of their negative behavior and impact upon their family, or nation, would conflict with their self-image or ideal self. That is one reason why abusers do not apologize. Positive self-esteem people can acknowledge weaknesses and mistakes. Self- and other-esteem people do not abuse others. Abusive, negative-esteem people feel weak and inferior on the inside so they cannot admit to anything that makes them look bad in their own or others' eyes. An abuser's apology would help his victim to move past anger and toward self-esteem. If the abuser's apology is real and involves humility, it may act as a deterrent: not to repeat the abuse and to accept responsibility for his attitude and behavior. Instead, most abusers cling to their self-aggrandizement and Power Over behaviors to compensate for their felt impotence and to make themselves feel good momentarily; then they need the next "fix." There is no place in a loving relationship for terrorism. The Terrorist Game plays those who, once they recognize the game, allow the game to continue.

Patriarchy still exists in some segments of our society where women and children are dehumanized. The origin of abusive behavior is usually in an abuser's childhood. Children are especially vulnerable to physical and verbal abuse. When there is no outside-the-family witness to their abuse, children learn to suppress their feelings, to believe that the abuse is somehow justified, and to pass it down from generation-to-generation. Without caring parents or significant others, or by actively seeking to change oneself, it is difficult for human beings to refashion their lives so they have the last word about who they are and, in Winston Churchill's words, "up with which they will not put." When caring adults encourage versus discourage a child, they communicate confidence, choices, and limits. Self-esteem blooms. Instead, we are told, "Don't do this!" or "Don't do that!" Rarely are we told to "Do!" even by a caring adult.

Teacher, leader, shaman, and healer Thunder Strikes was instructed about his universal family by his Uncle John Two Crows, who told him that his life's identity and purpose would depend upon what he chose to accept as a measure of his self-worth:

> To make his point, he asked me, 'How much do you want for Smokey?' [beloved pony], and I quickly replied, 'I won't sell him to you. You couldn't give me enough money!' Then he raised an eyebrow and asked, 'Are you for sale? Do you feel that way about yourself? Throughout your life, there will be people who will try to buy you and tell you what to do and what you should be like. Will you be willing to sell yourself or, like Smokey, are you not for sale? That is your measure of self-worth.[9]

The Language of Transnational Terrorists

Self-esteem is influenced by culture, which also affects the psychopolitics of political and religious leaders and everyone else responsible for others' welfare. While many and varied societies are similar to the West's cultural pluralism, laissez-faire economics, and political democracy, the Middle East is not. Muslim societies do not separate religion and state nor do they promote women's equality. Moreover, most Middle East countries have had little interest in how the West thinks, writes, or creates works of art; they want little to do with Western cultures.

Since the 18th century, Ottoman, Arab, and Iranian scholars have called for reform and modernization due to global trends; however, there was a split into a Western-oriented movement and a conservative one that condemned those who had strayed from Mohammed's teachings, labeling them traitors who deserved more punishment than the infidels. With over thirty years of experience as a historian of the Islamic, Arabic, and Middle East worlds, Bernard Lewis[10] believes that the answer to our current Middle East terrorist problems rests with the Muslim world. He wrote, before September 11, 2001, that the Middle East's choice is between continuing their present course of hate, poverty, and insularism or healing their wounds, moving on, and joining their talents and resources for the greater good of all on planet Earth.

The Middle Easterners' psychopolitical choice, whatever it is, leaves Americans, and people of other free nations, the choice of revenge or diplomacy: to seek ways to soften our diplomatic language, so our positive intentions may be heard, and to examine the impact of our cultural imperialism and its perceived threat, real or imagined. Revenge is not a diplomatic response. The Islamic-extremists may not be aware of Machiavelli; however, they do concur with his tenet about keeping political control: "A prince, therefore, must not mind incurring the charge of cruelty for the purpose of keeping his subjects united and faithful; for, with a very few examples, he will be more merciful than those who, from excess of tenderness, allow disorders to arise, from whence spring bloodshed and rapine; for these as a rule injure the whole community, while the executions carried out by the prince injure only individuals."[11] The Muslim clerics overthrew the Shah of Iran in the 1970s; it was hailed by American left-wing groups as an improvement; instead, what followed was not democracy but clerical control.

We have history with the Middle East. Rollo May used a political example to question the morality of a decision by the United States Government regarding Iran. Years before, the U.S. is alleged to have been involved in the overthrow of the Iranian government in order to install the Shah "to protect the profits of the big oil companies"[12] and to provide cheaper oil for Americans and their industries. The Westernized Shah did not have the emotional support of his people; he was overthrown. Later, our country made decisions concerning the Shah's health and welfare, and Iran, ruled by the clerics, became our mortal enemy. In 1990, Iraq also became our enemy. Saddam Hussein, as president, became a hero to the Arab masses: "Proud bearers of an ancient heritage overwhelmed and humiliated by successive waves of conquerors and subjugators, today's Arabs yearn desperately for the dignity and vindication...[from] a deep seated sense of inferiority and persecution."[13] In 2003, our identified adversaries are: Osama bin Laden, Al Qaeda forces, Afghan's Taliban, and many governments in Middle Eastern nations. East-West conflicts have been going on for centuries. War is not a solution to history.

If the West has learned anything in recent years and from prior wars, it is about the power of the pen and of the human mind. Education is the best weapon for world peace. Traditional education is not good enough for today's world problems and conflicts. Traditional education does not integrate emotional and spiritual literacy with the basic 3Rs and technology. The fabric of human thoughts is the problem and the solution: intellectual and emotional intelligences are co-dependent languages of congruent human beings. Education of the whole man, woman, and child is the best weapon for world peace. To heal terrorism, we must be politically wise, learn from the past, and understand our deepest motives and truths that work for the common good of all: East and West. First, though, we must get along with our families and ourselves; then we may learn to get along with others. During that process, we may sense the meaning of our presence here on Earth.

The Language of Self- and Other-Esteem

All languages contain vocabulary, the words, and grammar: the body of rules for speaking and writing a language. The language of diplomacy revolves around the words, *power and politics*. The *process*, building a relationship, is ignored; therefore, communications and negotiations break down very easily. War is the usual outcome. The language of esteem revolves around many words: power, virtue, acceptance, competence, human development, love, culture, morals and ethics, personal and professional development, and spirituality. Since esteem for self and others crosses individual, cultural, political, national, and international boundaries, the *process* is primary; *loving relationships* are primary. Then a negotiated peace is a more likely outcome. Hawks advocate war, preying on emotions and small game.

Religious intolerance continues to separate human beings and nations from each other. Most of the world's religious beliefs are based on an exclusive truth and exclusive path to God. History, past and present, is rife with the costly engagements of diverse religions' vocabulary, grammar, and dogma. A grassroots organization is underway to initiate the process of building an acceptable spiritual relationship among the world's religious sects. For peace, the primary issues of power and politics between religious factions, nations, and individuals need to include love and mutually rewarding relationships. Peace or war? *To see or to perish is the very condition laid upon everything that makes up the universe.* — Teilhard de Chardin

Our Working Definitions of Esteem

Our research and experiences inform us that without other-esteem, there is no self-esteem, only narcissism or ego-deficits.

> **Positive self-esteem** is the result when a small self integrates developed physical, emotional, intellectual, and spiritual intelligence with lived experiences to become a larger Self: loving, accepting, virtuous, competent, and responsible human being by demonstrating those qualities in personal and professional relationships.
>
> **Other-esteem** is self-esteem plus the motivation to directly or vicariously learn about and respect different people, cultures and creeds, all life forms, and the Earth, and to act responsibly toward all. Other-plus self-esteem is global-esteem: a worldview vs. a selfview.
>
> **Negative self-esteem** is a result when human intelligences are underdeveloped or when people experience not being nurtured or blaming ego deficits on others. Negatives may be changed to positives by self-exploration and self-redevelopment through re-education and/or by journaling.

The Elements of Esteem:
Power, Virtue, Acceptance, and Competence

Despite our judgments of how or why we become who we are today, the fact is the world we encounter is of our own choosing. We learn and grow when we are willing to be authentic with others; when we accept and celebrate differences, although self-interest is the essence of the human condition; and by taking responsibility for our choices. Western adults judge their self-worth by four basic elements:

> . Power [the ability to influence or control others];
> . Virtue [adherence to moral and ethical standards];
> . Acceptance [affection and attention from others and self];
> . Competence [successfully meeting expectations for achievement].[14]

1. Power and Politics

The exercise of power, control, and politics that goes on in all human and international relationships is also an ongoing battle between an individual's internal and external world. Human beings tend to project personal feelings and unresolved conflicts, which actually reside within themselves, upon the outside world. Leaders, particularly, must separate out their own internal states and power needs from those existing in the world. For most human organizations, authority is the first agenda item: "Who's in charge?" Most of us function better within well-organized social frameworks; yet, not one of us likes to be reminded that we are answerable to or take orders from another. Power and politics are integral parts of our inheritance, our culture, and our history.

Our educational system, industrial and military organizations, and the majority of our cultural institutions take the view that people cannot be trusted, that they must be led, instructed, rewarded, punished, or controlled by those who are wiser or who have higher status in our system. In our society we say that power is vested in people; in reality, there are two kinds of power: personal power and system power. Personal power is developed inside the self and system power is acquired outside the self. When an individual "becomes more self-aware, more self-acceptant, less defensive and more open...to grow and change in the directions natural to the human organism,"[15] then a personal-powered self emerges. Leaders who have dynamically balanced their personal and system power trust themselves and those they lead.

"Power over others, or authoritarian power, is still the primary political orientation in the world,"[16] in the family, in the schools, and in all American institutions and organizations. We remain dependent and primarily other- or outer-directed if we do not let go of our parental and authority figures, or if we do not learn from experience to trust ourselves as our primary authority. Self-esteem, then, is a political issue. Power hungry people are attracted to running big countries, big cities, big school systems, and big corporations, which are based upon power and control and the methods, tactics, and ideologies for controlling people, states, and governments.

Since both power and control and methods and tactics have positive and negative aspects, the personal empowerment of individuals through positive self-esteem will often conflict with those institutions that practice the negative aspects of power and control and the negative methods and tactics of managing people, individually or collectively. Thus, the resistance to self-esteem by the powers-that-be has much to do with power issues: hierarchically-oriented, power-hungry people are just not going to share power. Their fear-based egos require power for ego building, ego protection, or ego maintenance, which are met primarily at the expense of others or through higher status. Also at issue are a basic distrust of human nature and of the processes of change; hence, authoritarians who need to exercise power and control over other human beings need to maintain their narrow views that some people are more equal than others. Such people are invested in perpetuating the status quo. What prevents societal reforms and political change is not necessarily bad people but their attitude, "It's God's will!" or "That's the way it is!" or "I'm more equal than others!" without a vision of alternatives that does not include holding onto their so-called earned position, power base, or ideology.

In our Western intellectual tradition, we do not teach what we need to know about the fabric of our thoughts or the schemas stored in our unconscious, which govern behavior and control our lives. "We give meaning to life through the pursuit of knowledge, the joyful expression of our artistic originality, and the mastery of the physical"[17] and of our destiny.

The task of everyone in our democracy is to practice responsible freedom and to become a responsible individual. Where do we learn to do all that when there are few models to emulate? They are in the invisible curriculum. If we do not "get it" and practice it, our democracy will not continue to work for all. True, many people do not want the burden of making decisions or having responsibility; they are willing to sacrifice their personal freedom and autonomy. Some of them have learned from experience: *The nail that sticks out is the one that gets hit over the head.* Risk-taking is a decision-making strategy. To make good decisions we need a lot of data. Some of us approach the world with caution; we are low-risk-takers. Some of us engage ourselves with the world as we take our chances and reach out to heal the terrorist within.

"Only when a man makes use of his power of self-awareness does he attain to the level of a person, to the level of freedom. At that moment he is living, not being lived."[18] When we have positive esteem, we use personal and system power wisely: we assert our freedom, we are responsible for ourselves and to others, and we esteem others by acknowledging our interdependence with all living beings and things. Then each of us can truly say, "I am Somebody!"

2. Virtue

Virtue is the second element, listed above, by which people judge their self-worth and self-esteem. It is said that virtue isn't virtue until it is tried. Well, in New York City on September 11, 2001, thousands of people's virtue was tried. And there are hundreds of stories in the media about firefighters, police, office workers, medics, and search and rescue crews from all walks of life who risked their lives to save others' lives. The story of Josephine Harris was especially compelling. She was found exhausted, after walking down innumerable stairs of the World Trade Center, by firefighters who stayed with her as they slowly made their way down to the fourth floor when the tower collapsed, trapping them. Five hours later they were rescued; then they realized if they had not helped her, they would have been killed by the collapse of the floors above and below them. She called her rescuers her angels. She was their angel, too. Crises have a way of bringing out the virtue in Americans, and from now on thousands are going to live their lives differently. All earned our love and respect in their response to the victims of the terrorists' attacks. It recalled being in Moscow in 1991 when Russians were fighting for their freedom: *svoboda*. One defender at the barricades of the smoking "White House" [Moscow] said, "I knew who I was for years but didn't have a place to show it before."

The word *virtue* derives from the Latin *virtus* meaning manliness, worth or from the French *vertu* meaning goodness, power. Being virtuous is equated with having and behaving with general moral and ethical intelligence, or excellence, toward people who are like us, people who are unlike us, and ourselves.

3. Acceptance

Most of us feel that if we are not approved of and recognized as a Somebody, we will not be accepted. John Powell, wrote *why am I afraid to tell you who I am?* about acceptance. He proposed that if I tell you who I am, and you do not accept who I am, that is a fearful thing to do as then I am a nobody in your eyes.[19] Our culture teaches us through songs, "*You're Nobody 'Til Somebody Loves You.*" It takes a person with a keen sense of self to withstand others' critical eyes and judgments. Even in childhood, life is about choices. We choose to fit in and belong to our family and society by adapting or conforming, and those survival choices get us to adulthood.

Adults who become parents do not consider the pain and cruelty they inflict on their children when they withhold love, acceptance, and approval in order to keep their children within the bounds of their comfort zones. Many of us are molded and carry within us who and what we are not. Creating a climate for change to occur in human beings is an attitude of acceptance: unconditional positive regard.

Parents who raise their children with unconditional positive regard or accept them *as is*, without conditional love, create an emotional climate for them to grow and accept themselves. Then they bloom, become their unique selves, and have empathy for others. Most children and adults, though, are judged by their behavior, rather than for themselves, so they get scolded, compared, rejected, or labeled and disabled in the process. Some of us parents love "to control them rather than loving them...People are just as wonderful as sunsets if I can let them be. In fact, perhaps the reason we can truly appreciate a sunset is that we cannot control it...it unfolds."[20]

If conditionally loved children do not learn to accept, love, and prize themselves, they may remain narcissistic and wear a mask of self-importance. Others may be unable to accept any positive feelings aimed in their direction; they find it difficult to let in any warm and loving feelings: "People flatter me just to gain something for themselves" or "They may like what I have done but not me." The narcissist will latch onto any compliments tossed into a room as his own. It takes conditionally loved children a long time to learn that positive feelings of acceptance and love are not dangerous to give or to receive. Some children's only exposure to unconditional love is four-legged, from a beloved animal.

Loved, conditionally or unconditionally, we can learn to accept ourselves. Whether oneself or a situation, accept; then act. "Whatever the present moment contains, accept it as if you had chosen it. Always work with it, not against it. Make it your friend and ally, not your enemy. This will miraculously transform your whole life."[21]

4. Competence

Competence has many faces. There are personal, social, intellectual, emotional, street smart, professional, and leadership competencies. Personal competence (how we manage ourselves) requires self-awareness and self-management. Social competence (how we manage relationships) requires social and intercultural awareness and relationship-management. Intellectual competence is the domain of the neocortex whose specialty is technical and analytical skills; whereas, emotional competence is the domain of the brain's limbic system and prefrontal lobes. Experiential competence (learning by doing and through street smarts) entails intelligences that are not usually the foci of academia. Professional competence requires the knowledge, skills, and experience needed for our chosen work as well as motivation and emotional literacy. While work competence may be technical-, analytical-, experiential-, or relationship-oriented, leadership competence (how we manage ourselves and lead others) requires all of the above plus a vision of and plans for the future of our institutions, organizations, or nation.

Most people consider their careers to be the most important function of their lives. It is an opportunity to exercise power, to demonstrate competence, and to "earn" a self. Hans Selye is known for his work on stress; he viewed work as the place to direct aspirations and to complete and fulfill biological needs. He proposed that individuals must find ways to relieve pent-up energy without causing problems for others and to fulfill their own aspirations.[22] Without the incentive to find his work niche, an individual would likely seek, instead, "destructive, revolutionary outlets to satisfy the basic human need for self-assertive activity. Man may be able to solve the age-old problem of having to live by the sweat of his brow, but the fatal enemy of all utopias is boredom."[23]

The human "mind is not the brain but what the brain does…which makes us see, think, feel, choose, and act."[24] The human mind is a product of evolution and is conditioned by culture; therefore, careers for men and for women have been subject to stereotyping along sex differences. A more modern view of work that suits us best is Gloria Steinem's, "There are really not many jobs that actually require a penis or a vagina, and all the other occupations should be open to everyone."[25]

The question, for Dr. Selye, was not whether we should work but what kind of work would suit us best. However, if our self-esteem is vested in our work and is the source of our power and competence, we are dependent upon the system, just like a dependent wife. Her self-esteem is invested in her children and husband; they are the source of her power, competence, and self-worth. Love what you do and money and success will follow has been touted as the path to earn a life. The facts of life and work are we may not find our ideal job for a long time, if we wait. In the meantime, "We can choose the attitude we bring to our work...There is always a choice about the way you do your work, even if there is no choice about the work itself."[26]

Human beings who do not find satisfaction in their work often lack pride and responsibility for devalued work; then recreation or an obsession with self or illness becomes the main focus of their lives. "Economic rewards, that is, incomes, are not distributed according to the recipient's contributions to economic production...Economic services...are rewarded...according to the social esteem in which the occupant or profession is held...Jobs which are conspicuously in the public eye are equally overpaid."[27] Low status work, despite being essential to our daily existence, tends to be work where lasting evidence of the effort is not easily discerned or destroyed or the work has to be repeated over and over again; therefore, housework, childcare, services, clerical, and farm work receive the lowest value and the lowest pay. Careers requiring talent and creativity (filmmaking, artistic expressions) and skill (flying) are rewarded at the top. At the bottom, many are willing to work for the experience; some can afford to have expensive hobbies; others succumb to the starving-artist syndrome as they pursue their calling.

Research points to a paradoxical situation: people say they would like to work less and have more leisure time. "On the job people feel skillful and challenged, and therefore feel more happy, strong, creative, and satisfied. In their free time people feel that there is generally not much to do and their skills are not being used, and therefore they tend to feel more sad, weak, dull, and dissatisfied."[28]

80

Education used to be the key to gain entrance to a chosen field of work, success, and competence. Not anymore. In our society, contacts rule alongside competition. The late Dr. W. Edwards Deming opposed competition in school and the workplace. "Why produce artificial scarcity [grading and ranking people], when there is no scarcity."[29] He believed that there is no scarcity of good students or good workers; however, treating schools and work as a game implies that there will be winners and there will be losers, and the losers are branded for life as incompetent. The very system that is supposed to draw out and expand upon students' talents often cripples their young minds instead. Both educational systems and parents could heed Kahil Gibran's[30] message, *Your children are lent to you for a little while.*

If competition were balanced with formal mentoring or coaching, the outcome would be finely tuned, competent students and workers. Throughout history, the craft guilds trained young people. Most of us learn better by doing, observing others, working as a team, or following our instincts. A mentoring approach may include the visible academic curriculum and the invisible one. A positive mentoring experience contributes to our loving what we do and to our competence. Work is such an important factor in self-esteem development that it will be covered also in Chapter VII, Personal and Professional Development.

Self-Esteem's Underpinnings: Five Domains

Judging our self-esteem by power, virtue, acceptance, and competence does not include the whole story of self-esteem, what it is, what it is composed of, how to get it, and how to pass it on so we can keep it current. The esteeming process begins with the small self and ends with the larger Self. A useful metaphor is a set of Russian wooden dolls nestled inside each other. In your mind's eye, or if you have a set, consider the largest doll the person we are today; the smallest doll represents the infant each of us once was. In between there are at least five other dolls of varying sizes. Each doll represents, as we grow and learn, a layer of lived human experience:

Doll #1 (smallest)	The human infant
Doll #2 (next size)	Human Development (Chapter IV)

Doll #3 (next size)	Cultural Development (Chapter V)
Doll #4 (next size)	Moral & Ethical Development (Chapter VI)
Doll #5 (next size)	Personal/Professional Development(Ch. VII)
Doll #6 (next size)	Spiritual Development (Chapter VIII)
Doll #7 (largest)	The human adult.

The boundaries of learning are not as distinct or as rigid as the Russian set of dolls since we learn all the time and at random. We are not linear learners; we are pattern detectors, and we have leaky margins, which allow us to make connections and find themes in the disparate data we bring to a situation, so we can solve problems or come up with innovative remedies. We do not exist, live, work, or play in a vacuum; we are all interconnected. We become habituated to our familiar environment; hence, it is important that we seek new learnings and challenges to renew our curiosity, which is the alpha and omega of being human. The self-esteeming process is an interdisciplinary one; it crosses diverse phases of development. When we understand the parameters of each developmental stage, or domain, we grasp the underpinnings of self-esteem, from the impact of human, cultural, moral and ethical, personal and professional development to the ability to pull it all together into a meaningful whole: spiritual development.

About Esteem's Domains: Chapters IV-VIII

The five domains of self-esteem are not to be perceived as stages where one domain has to be completed before getting to the next, but as a continuum or a series where each is simultaneously interacting with the others. During human development, for example, we are immersed in our family's culture and neighborhood culture. We learn about morality — what is considered right and wrong — in our family, at friends' and relatives' homes, in church, in restaurants, on television, and what behavior is acceptable by society for our gender and age. Differences about right and wrong often cause value judgments and divide people into us versus them. Some of us find our passion or calling very early so our personal and professional lives develop in unison; some of us without direction, passion, or guidance take longer to find a niche that satisfies; and some of us settle for jobs or careers that subsidize our hobbies, or satisfy our survival needs.

The word spiritual is often perceived to encompass religious beliefs and practices, and religion can be an expression of spiritual beliefs; however, we may nourish our spiritual domain without adhering to specific religions. The word spiritual, for our meaning and purpose, is about a human being's capacity for love, meaning, purpose, wisdom, appreciation of nature and the arts, creativity, and justice, and practicing the Golden Rule daily. At that point, we have gone beyond the small self to the larger, relational Self, where we know that we are all connected.

As our human development continues on into young adulthood, we act on our own and others' preferences and experiences or choose models to emulate in our personal and professional lives. Many of us may be so busy figuring out who we want to be and how we are going to get there that it may take a while before we spiritually connect with others or find our calling, which usually means our developmental processes have been tampered with by a significant other. If so, it is our responsibility to become aware of our drawbacks and reparent ourselves. After age eighteen or twenty-one, we are the inner terrorists who choose to allow past terrorists to rule us today.

Self-Esteem Assessment: Chapter IX

After grasping the concepts in Chapters IV-VIII, you may wish to see what domains remain as an issue, or are not an issue for you, based upon your current state of esteem. We believe we do not have to dig into our past to uncover the amygdala's content, or our negative experiences, since our current situation, attitudes, behavior, or responses reveal the story of our lives every day of our lives. However, listening (through journaling) to ourselves, and to our reactions to the responses to the statements in the Self-Esteem Assessment, is an empathic way of promoting fuller self-realization, of making ourselves whole, of healing ourselves. A cognitive understanding of our past or a diagnosis of our problem does not automatically transform us or resolve any residual problems. Emotions influence learning in many ways: limit input, interfere with processing data, bias evaluation of perceptions and cognitive data, impair memory, and limit output. Our attitude toward any feelings and emotions that arise in completing the Self-Esteem Assessment is data for exploration. What matters is accepting and affirming ourselves without judgment or evaluation.

The Self-Esteem Assessment (SEA)is not a test; it is based on the data in the five domains that influence the development and maintenance of esteem. SEA contains twenty statements for each of the domains, or a total of one hundred statements. From the scoring, you may determine which domains you have successfully navigated and those you have yet to master to achieve your esteem potential.

An interpretation of the SEA scores appears after the SEA instrument. The SEA scores are not to be considered binding or statistical analyses of our own or anyone else's self-esteem. Instead, SEA focuses our attention on what we have yet to learn and where to start to attain positive or enhanced esteem. Just as we had to learn the letters of the alphabet in order to learn how to read, it is equally important to understand the sources of esteem so that we may pay attention to the details that affect the big picture of self-esteem, represented by the largest Russian doll.

The intent of the Self-Esteem Assessment is not merely to determine a self-esteem score that puts a label on us, as some assessments and tests do. It is intended to utilize the information derived from SEA to help us develop positive Self- and Other-Esteem, through a right- and left-brain journaling technique.

Journaling: A Right-Left-Brain Way: Chapter X

Journaling creates a "buffer" between the mingled data of our right- and left-brains or between self and another by separating the right- and left-brain data from each other in order to perceive objectively and to increase insight and learnings. There are overlaps between the right- and left-brain: the left pre-frontal lobe is positive; whereas, the right prefrontal lobe is negative. The left prefrontal lobe motivates hope, quells frustration or worry, and learns the lessons from the experience of setbacks and failures. The right prefrontal lobe is pessimistic. Through the multiple processes of observing, recording, finding

84

themes, and reflecting, we find our motivations and truths. Journaling is a way to examine the terrorist, pacifist, passivist, and healer within; to illuminate our shadows; to count and live our blessings; and to put ourselves back together again by resurrecting the spirit within us which reconnects us to ourselves, others, and the universe. Journaling offers a daunting transformational process!

No one can teach us anything; someone can impart information to us and guide us, but we teach ourselves. Most of us learn more by doing, interacting, reflecting, and experiencing. Our writing gives us feedback, organizes our complex thoughts and disparate feelings, makes learning visible, and releases inhibited energy to maintain our health and well-being. Our writing may be based upon present and past experiences, new learnings, or the data from the Self-Esteem Assessment.

The double-entry journal method is essential to sort out the doing from the feeling, the descriptive from the reflective, the objective from the subjective, the rational from the emotional, myth from myth, myth from reality, the monocultural from the intercultural, the details from the big picture, and self from non-self or another. Examining our thoughts, feelings, emotions, and actions on paper illuminates our projections onto others, or theirs onto us, and/or how our behavior may be controlled by others; provides answers to who we are and why we behave the way we do; and allows us to take responsibility for what happens to us by our actions or non-actions, so we may strengthen our self-connection and enhance our connection to others and the world: Self- and Other-Esteem.

When we arbitrarily separate, in our journal, the data from the human brain's right and left hemispheres, we learn to value the function of each hemisphere and to give each equal weight. The data are recorded in a journal as anecdotes (a narrative of an occurrence). *Anecdote* derives from the Greek *an* and *ekdotos* meaning "not published;" thus, anecdotes are unpublished stories. With anecdotal evidence in hand, we are in charge of what we think, feel, say, and do and how we behave. The double-entry journal is an empowering way of teaching ourselves to become whole persons with integrated data processing; to understand others *as is* without being tainted by our biases, judgments, expectations, or needs; and to learn not to set ourselves up for others' negatives. When we pay positive attention to people, they usually respond in kind. If they remain negative, we retain the power in the relationship, if we stay positive, thereby not allowing them to control our behavior.

The story of Western psychology evolved from the concerns about the nature of the universe and the nature of man to focus on people's pathological nature and their pathologies: how to label and how to fix them. The primary focus, in education and in therapy, has been on the left-brain's attributes: cognitive, talking approaches. Western "talking" therapies do not work for everyone; some people prefer meditation and hypnotherapy; others may prefer an eclectic approach.

Many Japanese therapists, for example, have "a basic distrust of the intellectual mode of knowledge when not supported by 'taiken,'"[31] which is body-based experience. The so-called quiet therapies emphasize experiential practices rather than theoretical ones. "A book on cooking will not cure hunger. To feel satisfied we must have actual food. So long as we do not go beyond mere talking, we are not true knowers."[32] Talking is a tool to reveal who we are to ourselves and to others; however, it is often used to disguise and conceal our inner feelings and thoughts. Words lipped, but not lived, do not reveal an authentic self.

From working twenty years with American Indians in the American Southwest, Carl Hammerschlag discovered, "Once I was comfortable only with speaking words; I have since learned to sing, to pray, to touch [and to dance]. I reveal [stories about myself] and I listen. There is a world beyond our own awareness."[33] For many, the emptiness felt inside cannot be satisfied by food but by meaning and purpose. Milton Erickson, the master hypnotherapist, knew that when we tell a story, we speak directly to the unconscious — the essence of a listener.[34] There is power in stories, and there are miracles. "No one makes it alone. We must be all connected to something other than ourselves...We each have our own truth and our own power, and that is what we must follow."[35]

It is not only in the writing of the stories of our lives in a journal that most insight and esteem comes but in the rereading and looking for patterns and themes. Journaling is a tool to use during stressful times, to make sense out of events, or to seek answers. In the words of the mystic poet William Blake, "We are put on Earth for a little space that we may learn to bear the beams of love."

A Multifaceted Approach to Esteem

The traditional intellectual approach to life and work is a fragmented one: learn more and more about less and less, so we may specialize in a particular field or find our individual niche in our group or society. That mechanistic, not holistic, approach to raising children and preparing adults for full participation in this world has deprived human beings of their wholeness and of their knowing that everyone and everything is connected in some way to everyone and everything else.

To overcome our fragmented inheritance, each human being's responsibility is twofold: to heal oneself, that is, to make oneself whole, and to become aware of and recognize the blocks — human, cultural, moral, ethical, religious, professional — that lead to perceiving others from a *we* versus *they* perspective. Human beings have come a long way from "the survival of the fittest;" however, we are still engaged in organizing and belonging to groups, sects, or religions that conflict with other equally or unequally matched groups, sects, or religions. Common values and beliefs induce people to cooperate with others, including those unlike themselves, within their group. Like-minded groups, sects, and religions preach cooperation and kindness within the group, but their leaders often fleece their flocks and do not practice what they preach. When one group, sect, or religion believes or perceives itself to be "better than" another, intolerance ensues, often manifested as violence. Today, as never before in human history, the media, trade, international and domestic terrorists with threats of biowarfare and nuclear strikes make us globally interconnected. For better or for worse, it is imperative that we focus on the many external forces that affect our esteem and on the internal forces whereby we esteem ourselves as unique, lovable, and capable without comparing ourselves to others or needing to use others as a foil, and on having esteem for those unlike ourselves.

When we are open to new experiences, we recapture our innate ability to see and hear, with eyes that hear and with ears that see, which involve the heart. Enjoy the process of learning or affirming who you are today and are willing to become tomorrow!

Four

I can't steer my ship by another man's compass.
— Captain Edmund Frampton (1873-1953)

Human Development

UNIQUENESS IS WHAT EVERY HUMAN BEING HAS IN COMMON: from unique life experiences and perceptions to unique fingerprints, footprints, voice prints, tongue and brain prints; and each emits unique scents and sounds. The genome project has produced a book of life: the 3.1 billion chemical "letters" of human DNA — the coded instructions for building and operating a fully functional human being. In the coming years, each human being may have his own customized how-to operating manual.

At this time, knowing the code for a gene does not tell us what protein it produces in the body, what it does, or how it interacts with other proteins, so the next projects are metagenomes, the DNA of ecosystems (microbiol species); proteomics — the molecular underpinnings of life: proteins made according to the genetic blueprints stored in cells — and glycomics — the study of essential sugars that adhere to the cells and promote intercellular communication and enhance the immune system. What we do know now is that while each of us is unique, creating our sense of uniqueness is basic to positive esteem.

Our Inheritance: Patriarchy

The Bible's Old Testament describes the history of the creation of patriarchy and the human family: "The first step was to invent a male God who created the world without a woman's help, a God who created Man first and just threw in Woman as an afterthought."[1] The 19th century Industrial Revolution and the introduction of factories meant fathers were no longer rooted in the family. By the 1960s, many fathers had not been part of family life since the

Great Depression years beginning in 1929. For hundreds of years, each generation of fathers has passed on less wisdom and love to their sons on how to be a man to the point where most fathers became largely irrelevant in the lives of their children.[2] Many daughters learned to be subservient in a male-dominated society.

It began during World War II, and in the 1960s men still wanted the privileges of patriarchy, but some "decided they were by nature chimpanzees and that promiscuity was the natural order of things...they had a sexual revolution that effectively ended the human family by sacrificing marriage to...narcissism."[3] In some areas of our society, "A man's belief in gender inequality and male superiority is going to make him look like an idiot, is going to wreck his marriage, may cost him his career...is going to leave him lonely and unhappy."[4] Due to power and economic reasons, patriarchy has not ceased in our country; yet, the Middle East's militant terrorists are punishing America for threatening their powerful patriarchy.

Mothers

For centuries, women have been the designated caretakers of children and the family; her place was in the home, dominated by a male head of household. Society has changed from some intact, nuclear families to blended families, single and foster parent families; yet children's basic human needs have not changed for love, trust, security, physical and psychological care, and belonging. No child escapes unscathed from divorce, from the limited resources of a single parent to the burden of emotional trauma and antisocial behavior. With 45 percent of first marriages and 60 percent of second marriages ending in divorce,[5] children and mothers are socially, emotionally, and economically challenged.

Women's work as homemakers has been disvalued by society — it was not included in the GNP (gross national product) or in today's GDP (gross domestic product) — for women are not treated as equals to men as bread-winners (equal work for unequal pay, usually), and the majority of women are powerless to change their own and their children's lives for the better. Traditionally, power has been men's domain, and women were socialized and conditioned to live in a male-dominated world so the roadblocks to women's power are internal, external,[6] and historical.

Working mothers are blamed when a child does not do well in school, not the confluence of an antiquated educational system and the absence of fathering in child-rearing. From the 1970s on, research helped mute some of the early child psychologists' and pediatricians' opposition to working mothers.

Fathers

"Bad fathers — violent, sexually abusive, neglectful, alcoholic — now play a large role in the psychological literature, amid wide and growing concern with the ill effects of the absence of good fathers from children's lives."[7]

"Family life in Western society since the time of the *Old Testament* has been a struggle to maintain patriarchy, male domination, and double standards in the face of a natural drift toward monogamous bonding."[8] In our Western society, most boys and many grown men are searching for "the lost father who has not yet offered protection, provision, nurturing, modeling, or, especially anointment"[9] are suffering from Father Hunger:

> All those tough guys who want to scare the world into seeing them
> as men, and who fill up the jails; all those men who aren't at home,
> who don't know how to be a man with a woman, only a brute or a
> boy, and who fill up the divorce courts; all those corporate raiders
> and rain-forest burners and war starters who want more in hopes
> that more will make them feel better.[10]

The media serves up male role models for young men in our culture:

> Neanderthal professional wrestlers; hockey 'goons,' ready at the
> slightest provocation to drop their sticks and pummel an opponent;
> multi-millionaire professional athletes in trouble with the law,
> demanding 'respect' from fans and the press; and angry, drug-using
> misogynist rock stars.[11]

Fathers who participate in their children's upbringing with unconditional acceptance and love, established limits, and realistic expectations, will satisfy hungry egos, offset negative influences, and foster esteem.

The Juvenile Revolution

The Men's Sexual Revolution, the Women's Movement, and women's influx into the workforce were accompanied by a Juvenile Revolution. Between 1947 and today, many children age 18 and under have engaged in crime sprees. In 1947, "only 4 percent of the people arrested for violent crimes and 13 percent of those arrested for property crimes were under the age of eighteen."[12] By 1968, "the juvenile share of arrests had climbed to 22 percent for serious violent crimes and 55 percent for serious property crimes."[13] In 1998, children under 18 were involved in "17 percent of arrests for serious violent crimes and 33 percent of arrests for serious property crime"[14] at a time when there was more crime committed by those over age 18. Therefore, "The cost and complexity of maintaining order [in the United States] increased sharply in the second half of the century."[15]

It is evident from the foregoing that families are not raising humanely developed children. Many of our nation's youngsters are leading lives of violent desperation. Not only are children more violent, they are also more likely to be victims of violent crimes.

American Youth

In America, the most affluent nation in the world, too many children are failing to thrive and strive on their own merits. Love and bonding are not enough; neither are rules or limits alone enough. Authoritarian caretakers of children who are emotionally unavailable, and control their children too closely, raise passive and withdrawn children with negative self-esteem; militant parents' children may emulate their parents' power and control issues, become violent, or rebel. Permissive caretakers who care for their children, but are lax in enforcing rules and indulge them, raise children who are spoiled and lack self-control. Such parents and caretakers think their children's success is ensured by not exposing them to failure; instead they provide material things and success through easy or minimum effort, without perseverance, which does not prepare children to realize there is life after failure.

Indulgent parents or caretakers are more likely to raise manipulative children who learn through threat, dishonesty, or blaming to avoid, escape, get around, or away from situations. They learn what their parents want to avoid, escape, or delay, including feelings that their children may not like them or that they are not good parents. Children who manipulate those around them do not learn how to respond to life and life's challenges and, as a consequence, they earn negative self-esteem, which may manifest itself in narcissism or toxicity to others.

Authoritative parents and caretakers who combine love and limits through consistent rules and judicious discipline tend to raise children who thrive and strive with positive self-esteem. Positive esteem is self-generated and constantly renewed through effort, self-reliance, and perseverance.

Some children do not get in the human development door. The deplorable states of human development and esteem in segments of American society are shameful reminders of the serious cracks in our democratic society. A 1990's study conducted by the University of Minnesota and commissioned by the Indian Health Services found that American Indian youths on reservations are a devastated group of adolescents: one out of six teenagers had attempted suicide; eleven percent reported extreme hopelessness; eighteen percent reported they were constantly sad; one in five teenagers developed drinking problems before the end of high school; and that report did not mention their physical health status, such as diabetes and obesity.

Our government has created and perpetuated structures that do not work for human beings' self-respect and -esteem, from Indian reservations and welfare to educational bureaucracies. An adequate standard of living may lead to better housing but not necessarily to a better life. Private enterprise created Baby College with a *Touchpoints* program to teach child-rearing or human development to poor mothers across cultures. Dr. Brazelton says, "when you give a mother self-esteem [respect and value for good mothering], she passes that along to her children."[16] Effective human development requires the human touch.

The three Rs do not teach or reinforce the basic life skills for Self- and Other-esteem: respect, responsibility, restraint, rapport, impulse control, empathy, and emotional literacy needed for cognitive learning. Instead, children are growing up to be adults who lead wasted intellectual, emotional, and spiritual lives. Why?

Emotional and Cognitive Literacy

For years, the research psychologists avoided human emotions since it is easier to study and document more quantifiable forms of human behavior, from IQ to academic and achievement tests. Anger, though, has become a problem in our society. Violence is the automatic response to perceived slights, put-downs, or "dissing" in school, on the street, in the workplace, or at home. Road rage is rampant. People with short fuses harm not only themselves but also blame and harm others. Type A hostile people are more vulnerable to heart attacks. Anger's source may be chemical, such as caffeine, steroids, diet, pesticides, preservatives, drugs, and antidepressants, or stored in the amygdala as negative experiences. Emotional memories are older than cognitive and symbolic memories: a child's right-brain, the seat of emotions, is operative when a child is in the womb and after birth when he has no voice. Thus, those memories and experiences are out of conscious awareness,[17] are stored as schemas, and can become the underpinnings of later negative life experiences. Schemas run our lives, until we become emotionally literate and learn to manage deficits for our benefit. Hostile people need to learn it is easier to change themselves and their expectations than it is to change the world. Rude people do not affect our responses or equanimity when we have esteem; we do not accept ownership of their problem being projected onto us.

Before the breakdown of the traditional American family and just before World War II, in 1938, a transmittal letter accompanied a commissioned American Council on Education Report from Chairman Prescott, written at a time when Hitler was in power in Germany. Prescott predicted that our country would face a dire future if emotions were not part of the curricula's business of knowledge:

> World political developments, new devices for swaying the emotions
> of entire nations, simultaneously, emphasis on blind mass fervor,
> impatience with the scientific approach to national problems, all

have driven home the lessons that the job of education is not done when knowledge is disseminated and increased. If the scholar, concerned with his primary business of knowledge, fails to deal with the whole man, particularly with the control of passion and the guidance of desire, he [scholar] may properly be charged with contributory negligence when the democracy becomes either a mob or a regimented army, when freedom to learn or to teach disappears, when the neglected emotions submerge the life of reason, and so force recognition of their claim to share in the lives of men.[18]

Japan attacked the United States on December 7, 1941. With our entrance into World War II, Chairman Prescott's letter and Report were shelved and not resurrected. Decades later, the freedom to learn and to teach is compromised by unruly students, the emotions are still neglected in academia, and the Western intellectual tradition survives. We have students who have the intelligence but cannot learn due to emotional problems,[19] are ignored, bored, unmotivated, or angry with insensitive teachers or classroom and playground bullies. The bullied have taken their revenge on innocent classmates in public schools, as in Littleton, Colorado. At the least, schools need to teach students about managing emotional behavior instead of telling them they should not feel angry or afraid while grading their behavior.

Despite our historical inheritance, the state of parenting, mothering, fathering, and the Western intellectual tradition, it is a miracle that so many human beings get out the human development door at all. And all are subject to judgment by the "norms" of the age and stage theories subscribed to by society's institutions and organizations, without attention to gender, maturation, culture, race, and class. We have upper, middle, and poor classes of people in America. In addition, America's middle-class is dwindling, and the poor class is increasing as earnings become more unequal. The windows of opportunity in America are becoming mere peepholes.

Rugged individualists who are left-brain dominant and concerned only with amassing wealth and perpetuating their power and control — even though they may set up foundations to further their personal issues and pet projects — may be more coldly logical and tax-oriented than morally and ethically motivated. Princeton University research demonstrates that the

94

emotional brain drives moral decisions, not the analytical brain. Integrating the emotional brain into the Western intellectual tradition is important because we live our lives as if our moral judgments are based upon reason, and we make up reasons to justify our actions and behavior. However, we act according to our "gut" which includes embedded schemas from our past negative experiences. Brain research illustrates that human beings are positioned to learn and grow to capacity when both sides of the brain — the analytical and the emotional — are developed and dynamically balanced. It is not uncommon for one side of the human brain to dominate the other or for one side to be neglected altogether. Three hundred years ago, rugged individualists were needed to help America grow. Today, the neglected emotions have, indeed, forced "recognition of their claim to share in the lives of men," women, and children.

Age and Stage Theories

Human Development is a process, not a race. Researchers who developed age and stage theories, presumed them to be a sequence of steps whereby males, primarily, develop their concept of who they are and what they wish to achieve in life. The theories begin with the need to preserve the self and end, ideally, with a turning away from the self and merging self's interests with those of the larger community, the world. Not everyone progresses though the stages; many do not get beyond the first stage where self-interest only or having a roof over one's head and food on the table gives meaning to life. Others get beyond self to include the family and settle comfortably there. Few people reach the reflective individual level, and fewer still willingly merge their interests with the larger whole.

Just as we used to accept the societal dictum that children play, students study, adults work, and retirees relax, we now know that work, study, play, and relaxation are equally important to all throughout life. We also know that maturity comes not only with age and education but from lived and vicarious experience as well. Some children are as wise at seven as some adults are at forty. Thus, the concept of human development as stages, age, and maturity is a linear, although spiral perspective; whereas, human beings are nonlinear.

Human Development Models

Our study of human development models of family structure — whether intact, single parent or blended — led us to *power* (from Latin and French words meaning *to be able to*) and to *politics* (from words for *citizen*). The locus of a human being's personal power may be internal and external; whereas, the locus of system or position power, which flows down from the top, is external.

Most families in Western societies, which have been traditionally male dominant, raise their girls to be dependent and their boys to be independent. Few families consciously raise their children to be interdependent. More women than men are raised to be dependent upon others for their identity and esteem — family, husbands, and children — or upon their physical attractiveness and ability to attract a well-to-do husband. More men than women are raised to be independent — to get their identity and esteem through their careers, status, and money. Note that both are dependent: one upon relationships and the other upon the workplace or the system. The interdependent human development model requires developing a keen sense of self and dynamically balancing the need for intimate relationships with the need for meaningful, fulfilling work, and financial autonomy.

The dependent model is consistently lower in self-esteem since the locus of power is external: in others or material things. Dependent women may not like, vote for, or get along with independent or interdependent women who represent what they did not accomplish for themselves through their own talent and efforts. The independent model is similarly afflicted: people who invest their lives in their work or career do not realize until it may be too late that their performance only is valued, not the self, so that when skills become obsolete or they retire or are fired, their self-esteem — bolstered by their role in the workworld — is in jeopardy. Only the interdependent family model of human development is dynamically balanced in that we recognize that two separate halves (a dependent woman and a so-called independent man) do not make a whole person or a whole relationship. Equal partnerships require whole people who can stand alone or together. A combination of personal power and system power is a requisite for human beings to effectively and productively work and relate to one another or to rear humanely developed children.

What gives purpose to our potential humane development is investing energy in developing whatever we were born with to earn a self who is loving, self-reliant, responsible, and conscious of skills, talents, and limitations. We must also "invest energy in recognizing, understanding, and finding ways to adapt to the forces beyond the boundaries of our own individuality...if we don't...we will regret it."[20]

Five Processes of Human Development

Human Development is a complex and all-encompassing domain that is concerned with the inherited genes and the layers of the environment that have a formative influence on children and human beings from an interdisciplinary perspective, such as the physical, psychological, emotional, social, cultural, race, ethnicity, world of work, community, nation, and the world.

In this chapter, we emphasize the importance of five human development processes: physical; psychological; communication — interpersonal and intrapersonal; and the human brain — emotional and cognitive processes.

1. Physical Processes

Human beings are nonlinear; therefore, age and stage theories offer guidelines only. Similarly, it is difficult to separate the physical from the psychological since what harms or enhances us on a physical level also harms or enhances us on a psychological level. Our basic physical needs must be satisfied to attain psychological maturity and vice versa. While the basic human needs are for food, water, sex, elimination of waste, oxygen, and sleep, brain research has revealed the biochemical consequences to infants raised without loving touch and security. They have high levels of stress hormones. Those hormones impair the growth and development of the human brain; so do fast food, cigarettes, and alcohol!

Life begins with our first breath and ends with our last. Breathing in oxygen jump starts our hearts and gets our blood flowing to awaken the cells of our body, carry away the waste, and clear and focus our minds. Inhaling deeply through our noses and exhaling thoroughly through our mouths carries nutrients to every part of the body, increases energy levels, calms us down, and promotes physical and mental health. Breathing deeply releases natural brain chemicals called endorphins; they help us manage pain, ward off fatigue, and feel good. Sleep deprivation and sleep disorders are common since most of us have poor sleep habits or environments.

A common belief is that people require less sleep as they grow from infancy to adulthood. However, studies over the past twenty years of teenagers who begin class at 7:20 a.m. or so indicate that they require more sleep to perform optimally than do younger children or adults. Evidently, teenagers' sleep deprivation negatively influences their management of emotions and behavior, their ability to learn or perform, and their vulnerability to depression and attention deficits. Some U.S. states are considering laws to prohibit school starting before 8:30 a.m. Attention must be paid to our basic physical and psychological needs, at each age level, to protect us from any diseases that undermine the body, mind, emotions, and spirit.

Some of us may be born as princes and princesses; many of us begin as ugly ducklings. We view ourselves through others' authoritarian or critical eyes when people remark, "What a beautiful little girl!" or "What a darling little boy!" If we get no response, if we are physically abused, if we are compared with a disliked or feared relative, or if we are seen through critical eyes as being deficient, then our whole being may become distorted and discolored by our real or imagined view of our physical selves. Therefore, the human body, not the mind, is the primary focus of attention in our material, youth-oriented society where how one looks and what one wears and owns are more important than being good. The multibillion dollar cosmetic, perfume, and clothing industries; plastic surgery field; fitness-oriented businesses; and image-makers reflect society's priorities. The public's perception of beauty, age, and aging is influenced and controlled through the media by advertising dollars. When we think we look good, we tend to feel good. Feeling good is the state most of us want to be in most of the time. That is the criterion most of us use to buy products and services and to judge our esteem and our esteem of others. Feeling good needs to be balanced with being good, for when we "buy" self-esteem our personal power is external, not inside ourselves. Feelings are fleeting; whereas, being good and doing good works can bring us internal personal power and satisfaction.

The body and the mind are one; they interact interdependently, except when they act separately, as in nonverbal language, or when acute, sporadic, or chronic pain expresses psychic pain, which is less acceptable in our society than physical illness. Back, neck, chest and other pains, including migraines with no visible structural damage, may be due to repressed emotional issues which, when addressed, may lead to pain free lives.[21a] Awareness of and a belief in the mind's ability to heal the body, on a conscious level, does not mean it has been accepted by our unconscious emotions where fears reside. Nature provides us with mechanisms to heal ourselves, but we must acknowledge the body-mind connection to esteem and heal ourselves. Edrita Fried observed that underdeveloped, narcissistic, passive, and dependent people are more conscious of their lower senses than of their higher senses.[21b] Our lower senses give us feedback about our body temperature, other body conditions, and sexual arousal. Our higher senses of sound, sight, and intuition—which enable us to be aware of the world around us—are less frequently tapped. When we are preoccupied with our small self's lower senses and less involved with our higher senses, that priority impairs our relationship with self and others and our mind-body integration.

The physical world affects the state of the mind and body. Some people have a low tolerance for a deficiency of light. Depression and fatigue are symptoms of SAD (seasonal affective disorder). SAD affects people in northern sections of the world. The dis-ease may be offset by daily doses of sunlight or full spectrum lighting. Human beings are electromagnetic generators, and our brain cells possess crystals of a highly magnetic mineral known as magnetite, according to recent research. So our cell membranes, brains, and nervous system are not immune to natural and man-made electromagnetic forces, the weather's barometric pressure, or even the moon's influence.

The benefits of exercise, including walking, are not immediately visible to the eye; they are on the inside. Exercise aerates the body. Without sufficient oxygen, glucose is catabolized into lactic acid. The lymph system has no pump other than the heart, so exercise accelerates the disposal of lactic acid and expedites the flow of nutrients and oxygen to the cells. Exercise also maintains good body and skin tone, builds lean muscle, and helps maintain the recommended lean muscle tissue to 25 percent fat ratio. Laughter is internal jogging.

Pregnant women's inadequate nutrition results in "premature birth, low birth weight, and a high mortality rate."[22] An inadequate diet negatively affects the development of the central nervous system of a fetus; it also makes a newborn more vulnerable to diseases. Breast-fed babies get a head start on health. Babies born to alcoholic parents have signs of fetal alcohol syndrome (FAS): "unusual facial characteristics, small head and body size, congenital heart defects, defective joints, poor mental capabilities, and abnormal behavior patterns."[23] Research on mothers who had smoked cigarettes during pregnancy found that, at age four, their children had diminished language skills and cognitive development than those children whose mothers had not smoked. Children whose mothers smoked were twice as likely "to be anxious, disobedient, or hyperactive or to exhibit some other behavioral problem."[24]

Eating disorders are common in the U.S. Most Americans are fat despite the adage, "You can't be too thin or too rich." Our diets are too rich in "bad" fats, trans fats, oils, sugar, and junk food with preservatives. The government's Four Food Groups have been enlarged upon to a Pyramid with too many simple carbohydrates and not enough "good" fats and vegetables. We are inundated with diet books and diet groups; yet, we are overweight and subject to heart disease, cancer, diabetes and other degenerative diseases. Eating is a way to block out negative feelings. Home alone or in solitude is the context for binge eating, bulimia, or anorexia nervosa. Young girls, in particular, and young women are prone to believing they are "too fat." They have episodes of compulsive eating (bingeing), purging after compulsively eating (bulimia), or not eating or eating very little (anorexia nervosa). All are learned disorders that negatively affect the body and its proper functioning, including the brain. The sources of eating disorderse may be cultural (a fast-paced culture produces tension and anxiety so food becomes a panacea, and a fashion industry whose models are undernourished 12- and 13-year-olds!), social (peer group pressure, lack of friends or need for approval), educational (fear of failure or of success), and emotional (sexuality issues, lack of positive self-esteem). Whatever the source of the eating disorders and body distortions, the human body undergoes physical stress, affecting vital organs; sometimes, prolonged damage is irreparable. Healing eating disorders begins with repairing the diet and the emotions that derail self-esteem.

The mind, body, and diet are intertwined in a complex orchestration with the immune system and the emotions. Despite its bad name, we need fats to burn fat and fat is what makes the brain work effectively. The eicosanoids (eye-KAH-sah-noids) were the first hormones developed by living organisms; they use fats as their building blocks; they are the hormones that both heal and harm: the good and the bad. The bad are derived from omega-6 fatty acid, and the good require an acid found in fish oil, omega-3. Good eicosanoids increase the oxygen and blood flow to the brain; the bad ones have the opposite effect. We need both. Insulin is an essential regulator of the enzymes of the body. Good eicosanoids decrease the insulin production in the pancreas; the bad eicosanoids increase the production of insulin. Elevated insulin levels stimulate the production of the bad eicosanoids. When we make excess insulin, we gain weight. Obesity increases cholesterol; both insulin and cholesterol problems are treated with drugs; however, they can also be treated by diet.

A dietary approach that helps shed body fat and balances insulin levels requires hormonal thinking versus caloric thinking, says Barry Sears: "The best way to stop this cycle [insulin and eicosanoids] is to consume high doses of fish oil"[25] Fish oils are critical to our brain function, immune system, physical health, and emotional well-being: to avoid or treat depression and to adapt to stress by increasing serotonin. Sears recommends that each meal consist of low-fat protein (although salmon is fatty, it is an excellent protein), complex carbohydrates — fruits (berries, not sugar-concentrated juices or white-flour desserts) and vegetables (not bread, crackers, pasta, white rice, and white potatoes), and fat — monounsaturated fat (olive oil, avocado slices, almonds). From Sears' diet perspective, liquid fish oil promotes health and deters degenerative diseases. As a child, it was years before Florence realized what orange juice tasted like; hers always had a teaspoon of cod liver oil in it. The scare about mercury, PCBs, and DDT in fish led to a safer but very expensive pharmaceutical-grade fish oil. Hazardous to our physical and mental health are the chemicals, food additives, preservatives, and pesticides in the food we eat, the air we breathe, the water we drink, the clothes we wear, the sprays we use, the furnished homes we live in, and the public places we frequent. Organic foods and natural products decrease toxins in our blood and in our fat cells. A diet of white "food" products (flour, rice, sugar) is a threat to long-term health. The food industry's focus on non- or low-fat products, over the past decades, has increased Americans' obesity. Most low-fat products are simple carbohydrates with "bad" fats. The lower fat ratio is achieved by adding more sugar, or simple carbohydrates; thus, the same amount of fat is in the product, but it seems to be less when compared to all the other ingredients. Figures do not lie, but liars figure.

The Human Genome Project has revealed more about our genes and our blood type's cellular influence in every area of human physiology. Some research has been done on the connection between diet and blood types: "Each blood type possesses a different antigen [self and non-self markers monitored by the immune system] with its own special structure. Your blood type is named for the blood type antigen you possess on your red blood cells."[26] Type O antigen is zero, the base for the other blood types: A, B, and AB. A chemical reaction between our blood and the food we eat is part of our genetic inheritance. That reaction is due to a factor called lectins, which are various and abundant proteins found in foods; those lectins have agglutinating properties, that is, lectins are the glue by which bacteria and parasites are disposed of by the liver's bile ducts; however, bacteria and other germs also have lectins on their surfaces and can attach themselves to the body's mucosal linings. There are lectins in foods that interact with blood types which can interfere with digestion, metabolism, and the immune system; therefore, about "70 percent of all the inflammatory, digestive, or stress illnesses...involve some sort of toxic imbalance."[27] "By matching your dietary proteins to your blood type physiology you can cut down on the level of unabsorbed proteins left in the digestive tract and their toxic byproducts."[28a] From Peter D'Adamo's health perspective, Blood Type Os should avoid wheat, wheat germ, corn, kidney beans, navy beans, lentils, peanuts, and potatoes, plus a long list of other foods. Blood Type A should avoid kidney and lima beans, potatoes, cabbage, eggplant, bananas (80 percent of As), tomatoes, wheat (20 percent of As), corn (20 percent of As), and a long list of other foods. Blood Type B should avoid chicken, corn, buckwheat, lentils, peanuts, sesame seeds, tomatoes, and a long list of other foods. Blood Type AB should avoid chicken, whitefish, corn, buckwheat, lima and kidney beans, along with a long list of other foods. Diet may also be involved in attention deficit disorders (ADD), with different approaches for different blood types.

Human cells are composed of more than genes and proteins since carbohydrates (simple and complex sugars) and lipids (fats) play profound roles. Refined white sugar or sucrose is the worst for our health. Glucose and galactose are oversupplied in our diet: converted from white sugar, fructose, starchy foods, and milk sugar. Maltose in beer causes beer bellies. Other sugars, not readily available in our diet, perform a wide range of jobs: modify many proteins and fats on cell surfaces, are involved in immunity, cellular repair, cell-to-cell communication, and play a part in averting diverse diseases, from viral infections to cancer. Heralded as the missing link in human diets, glyconutrients (Greek *glyco* = *sweet*) are found in aloe vera, garlic, certain mushrooms, yeasts, breast milk, pectins from fruits, and some algae, for example. Those sugars are fucose, mannose, xylose, N-acetylneuramic acid, N-acetylglucosamine, and N-acetylgalactosamine. When absent in the diet, complex chemical conversions are required, which are inhibited by the effects of stress, toxins, and nutritional and genetic deficiencies. Pharmaceuticals are focusing on a particular sugar to manufacture drugs for particular degenerative diseases. Food supplements provide the missing glyconutrients and vine-ripened fruits and vegetables or phytonutrients (Greek *phyto* = *plant*). Since the foregoing nutrients are essential for optimum health, they complement a balanced diet of complex carbohydrates, proteins, fats (omega-3 and omega 6 oils), vitamins, minerals, and water.

One diet does not fit all human beings for health and well-being due to our inherited genes, different levels of development and esteem, and our different lifestyles. Some basic "bad choices" affect all: white flour, sugar, and rice products; preservative-laden processed, junk, fast, and snack foods; "bad" fats; and high glycemic fruits and vegetables, for example, creating the "overfed but undernourished syndrome" and diseases. About one in five Americans are estimated to have prediabetes, that is, they have high cholesterol, high ratio of bad cholesterol to good, high blood pressure, central obesity (mid-section of the body), high triglycerides, and small LDL (bad cholesterol) particles. Those conditions are closely associated with heart attack and stroke[28b] as well. In addition, being overweight does not increase the number of fat cells; they just get fatter, making it difficult for insulin to attach to them properly to transfer the necessary sugars and fats into the tissues. Sugars and fats left in the bloodstream circulate longer and their elevated levels lead to blood problems—prediabetes, heart attack and stroke—and obesity. There is more.

All breathing, eating, moving people produce free radicals (FRs) in their bodies; they are essential to energy production and other processes. However, uncontrolled FRs are terrorists; they are molecules of oxygen with a missing electron, so they steal an electron from other oxygen molecules. Toxic FRs come from the polluted air we breathe, herbicides, pesticides, drugs, sun and

X-rays, microwaves, high tension lines, computers, TV screens, etc., and the foods we eat, especially those that contain rancid fats. Oxidized fat smells bad and tastes bad (like linseed oil), resulting from the rancidity of fats and oils, foods containing oils—such as nuts—and products made from fats and oils—such as chips and baked goods. "Oxidized oils promote arterial damage, cancer, inflammation, degenerative diseases, premature aging of cells and tissues,"[28c] and damage DNA itself. Antitoxidants (AOs) are found in fresh fruits (including dried prunes) and vegetables, extra-virgin olive oil, Vitamin E, and are sold as AO food supplements. AOs support our bodies' natural ability to defend itself from FRs and to heal itself. An optimum diet begins with knowledge, so read the labels and avoid foods that contain the words "partially hydrogenated" and excess sugar (with its many names) and salt/sodium. There is a saying, "Eat anything that will rot, but eat it before it does." Keeping a food/mood log alerts us to allergies. Shopping for food and preparing it with love also give us the opportunity to influence the health of our whole family and to create healthy family relationships and traditions.

When ego, life, health, freedom, or property are threatened — real or imagined — a child or an adult is prepared to fight, flee, freeze, or feign. Stress is considered to be one of society's "norms." Unmanaged stress is a source of sickness. Stress normally occurs in the human body when we walk, talk, think, feel, eat, and relate; it is an interior phenomenon. Even having exciting times can be stressful, but it is perceived by the body as good stress, also known as "eustress."[29] In general, stressors arise from one of the following five categories: **Physical** — trauma, infection, cancer, metabolic imbalance; **Personal** — low self-esteem, unmet needs, chronic illness; **Inevitable transitions** — marriage, child-bearing, death in the family, leaving home; **Unrelenting conflict** — incompatibility with spouse or co-workers, boredom; and **Unexpected events** — losing a job, divorce, accidents, and other stressful encounters.[30]

The mechanics of stress are also activated under circumstances of physiological and/or emotional stress. The key to the proper functioning of the nervous system's two branches (sympathetic and parasympathetic) is balance. Problems arise when one branch dominates the other for a long time. Chronic stress engages the sympathetic at the expense of the parasympathetic. Since health and healing are driven by parasympathetic activity, when the sympathetic is in charge of the nervous system for prolonged periods, it leads, inevitably, to a breakdown. Stress also impairs the immune system, promotes diseases, accelerates the aging process, and influences self-esteem. The body releases cortisol to control long-term stress. Excess cortisol kills off brain cells, especially in the hippocampus where memories are stored, and it inhibits short-term memory. Caffeine promotes stress reactions, which raise cortisol, which raises insulin, which leads to weight gain. Laughter is an antidote to stress: it decreases cortisol production and increases the immune system's natural killer cells and T-cells, or thymus-derived cells.

The human body has a unique way of making emotional memories register with particular potency in the human brain. It utilizes the same neurochemical systems that prime the body to act when confronted with life-threatening emergencies by fighting or fleeing and to also vividly imprint the moment in memory. Research found that "a universal trigger for anger is the sense of being endangered. Endangerment can be signaled not just by an outright physical threat but also, as is more often the case, by a symbolic threat to self-esteem or dignity: being treated unjustly or rudely, being insulted or demeaned, being frustrated in pursuing an important goal."[31] Such perceptions, real or imagined, set the stage for the fight or flight syndrome with attendant adrenal (epinephrine and norepinephrine) and cortical release. One of the hormones provides the body with a fast shot of energy for vigorous fighting or running; another is secreted gradually into the body, which heightens the body's "sensitivity to events, and also makes one hyperalert to any coming danger."[32] The freeze or feign syndrome also alerts the adrenals.

"Yale researchers point out that it may not be anger alone that heightens the risk of death from heart disease, but rather intense negative emotionality of any kind that regularly sends surges of stress hormones through the body."[33] The emotions and the immune system are also linked by way of hormones released while under stress. Hassles, upsetting events, or marital fights show a strong pattern of coming down with colds or an upper respiratory infection "three or four days after an especially intense batch of upsets...That lag period is precisely the incubation time for many common cold viruses, suggesting that being exposed while they were most worried and upset made them especially vulnerable."[34] Research confirms that Type A aggressives are more prone to heart attacks, if they have hostile personalities.

Also distressful are gender attitudes toward the human body. Having a body implies we are sexual beings, whatever our sexual orientation or preference. In a society that equates masculinity with dominance and sex with violence, gang rape becomes one way for adolescents — or adults "stuck" in adolescence — to prove their masculinity both to themselves and to their peers. Rape is about domination, power and control or anger, not love or lust. Anthropologist Peggy Sanday[35] found that male toughness, militarism, and distant father-child relationships are indicators of interpersonal violence, including rape. Men's abuse of women is also an indicator of negative views of women, where women are either madonnas, mothers, or whores, and of negative self- and other-esteem where personal power is manifested by brute force or brawn.

In the 1960s the Beatles sang "All You Need Is Love." Scrawled at the bottom of an "All You Need Is Love" poster, hanging in the hallway of a New Jersey K-12 private school that we visited, was "All You Get Is Sex." A male student in a Human Development class (Physical Processes) spoke, with regret, of his early attitude toward sex, love, and women. His buddies in high school had based their image on "conquests." A prize conquest was their minister's daughter. Each had tried to seduce her, he won, and was highly esteemed by his buddies, until the ante was raised. Sex is a natural and mutually enjoyable physical and psychological process when love and esteem for self and a partner are present. Even today, with rampant AIDS, herpes, and other sexually transmitted disease, the primary emphasis is on condoms and safe sex, not on developing committed relationships and responsibility for self and to others. Young males with raging hormones and narcissism often intersect with females with budding nurturance and fragile, outside-self-esteem, or extrinsic locus of power. Too many people learn too soon that love and sex are not interchangeable words, nor always found in the same place. Without emotional literacy, ongoing adolescent attitudes toward love and sex will interfere with adults' ability to satisfy both needs humanely.

Physical ailments, diseases, or "skin disorders can diminish self-esteem, sometimes wounding the soul more than the skin"[36a] and sometimes deter-mining one's career path. John Updike, for example, suffers from psoriasis; he chose to be a writer, a novelist, so he would not have to see people on a day-to-day basis. Body, mind, emotions, and soul/spirit influence each other.

2. Psychological Processes

The biological and psychological births of an infant are not simultaneous incidents. The latter is an unfolding intrapsychic process.[36b] Brain research shows that the brain's hippocampus — the locus of cognitive processes — is not fully mature at birth; whereas, the brain's amygdala is more fully formed, especially during the first two years of life. Hence, emotional memories and habits, including negative experiences, are stored in the amygdala and are potent later in life because they are out of conscious awareness and are, therefore, hard to understand and overcome. And that is one reason why we cannot rid ourselves of unwanted data; we may learn to cope with or manage them, but we can also learn from them since there is a cognitive component to emotions.

Early childhood is, therefore, the key to understanding an adult's later life. A child is born with a healthy narcissism to be cared for and respected for who he is now rather than for what he does or will eventually be able to do or become. When he is affirmed *as is*, his ensuing self-esteem paves the way to successfully integrate into the larger society, beyond family. There are no narcissistic disturbances when a child's parents or caretakers do not use him or her to fulfill their own unfulfilled ego needs. Both experimental and clinical studies show that people carry ideas about themselves that are powerful factors in shaping their level of aspiration, ways of defending themselves from loss of self-respect, and choice of behavior patterns in many situations. A person's self-esteem influences everything he perceives from his senses and all his choices of action; therefore, feelings about self are as important as ideas about self.

Working with cancer patients informed Bernie Siegel that the fundamental problem most patients face is "an inability to love."[37] Those patients had been unloved by others during some critical part of their lives, usually childhood. At a Korean Shaman Seminar at the Asia Society in New York City, a male shaman and his female assistants performed a mock funereal rite on stage for a deceased man to ensure his achieving Nirvana. A common belief among the Korean lower class is that most people die with at least seven to eleven resentments. Resentments may be unfulfilled needs, wants, or desires, such as, loving parents and loving relationships, good looks, good health, good education, successful children, rewarding career, financial success, long life, or fame. The shamans performed rituals with a long drape of folded cotton with seven half-bow knots. Each knot represented a resentment the deceased needed to resolve on Earth before going to Nirvana. After each ritual of alternately drumming, chanting, or dancing, the shamans would shake the drape, and a knot would unfold. "Aha!" said Susan, a psychologist-friend, "That's what I do! When I help my cancer patients untie their knots, they don't have to die any more. Or they die in peace."

3-4. Communication Processes: Interpersonal and Intrapersonal

The positive attitude people, such as the late Dr. Norman Vincent Peale, offer simple rules for successful living: Tell yourself you can do anything you want. Slap down self-doubt that creeps up on you. Gravitate toward people who believe in you; avoid those who put you down. Find out what you do best, and stick with it. Delight in your work without feeling guilty. Never try to solve a problem by reacting emotionally. Think of everyone you meet as a good person until you find out otherwise. Love yourself and every other human being, lovable or not.[38a]

Fish! is a self-help book to help us find the source of energy, creativity, and passion within each of us and to learn to love what we are doing, even though we may not be doing now what we love to do. The authors suggest, "We can choose the attitude we bring to our work;"[38b] we can play; we can focus our attention "on ways to make another person's day"[39] by being present or totally engaged in what we do and where we are; all promise a constant flow of positive feelings.

All of those rules and ways to recreate ourselves often conflict with our deeply embedded values, beliefs, attitudes, and habits, which are inherited or adopted from family, society's institutions, the dominant culture, peers or life experiences. Changing our frowns to smiles, our slouching posture to an upright one, and wading into action change negative attitudes into positive ones. Emotional literacy is the key for effective communication.

3. Interpersonal Processes (How we get along with others)

> Interpersonal intelligence is the ability to understand other people:
> what motivates them, how they work, how to work with them.
> Successful salespeople, politicians, teachers, clinicians, and
> religious leaders are all likely to be individuals with high
> degrees of interpersonal intelligence.[40]

Interpersonal intelligence begins with listening. Mastery is needed in listening to another's words, listening to what is being consciously hidden by another's words, listening to what another is not saying, listening/observing nonverbal communication, or body language, and listening to the sound of another's voice. A nasal voice or a monotone may indicate a lack of enthusiasm for what is being said or may denote depression. A harsh, guttural voice may reveal a belligerent attitude. A shrill or strident voice may be a clue to tenseness or irritation. When spoken words agree with the nonverbal message, then the total message is easier to understand. If there is a lack of agreement between what we think, feel, say, do, and how we move, a mixed message is sent. Mixed messages are indicative of intrapersonal conflict, which may lead to interpersonal conflict.

Communication is speculated to be 7% verbal, 38% tonality, and 55% physiology. In close agreement is Anthropologist Hall's assessment that words represent 10% of communication, while behavior represents the remaining 90%. Hall questioned, "How is it possible to maintain a stable world in the absence of feedback from the other 90 percent of communication?"[41] When we learn that it is not what people say but what people do that we must pay attention to, and when we recognize the hidden rules [culture] that govern us and others, then we become competent listeners and effective communicators.

A cancer cell was described by a physicist[42] as one with incompetent intercellular communication. The cell's inability to communicate its needs alienates it from the rest of the body. To survive, it feeds on healthy cells, and each healthy cell has a built-in agent, p53, which forces it to stop growing or to "commit suicide" when damaged by a cancer cell. Cancer either wins the battle when there is too little p53, or too much p53 ages the body. Interestingly, human beings who did not experience enough love and caring from their caretaking phase may have incomplete interpersonal communication skills. They may destroy prospective healthy relationships because of their unresolved needs or harm themselves or those whose lives they touch. Communication incompetence affects interpersonal interactions because it may hook into another person's unresolved issues, as illustrated in the following story.

At a psychology study group that met monthly, a young member, a divorcee with children, was interested in improving her interpersonal relationships with men. A particular man in the group appealed to her, so one day she approached him and said, "Where are you going for lunch?" He responded abruptly, "Where you're not!" Upset by the rejection, she began to cry; a woman's group quickly formed around her. After more than an hour of much emotional outpouring with "Men are..." sentence completions and her receiving verbal affirmations and hugs, a member asked if she would be interested in examining her communication process that triggered his negative response. She was. "If you had said to him, 'I would like to go to lunch with you!' [a direct statement] instead of 'Where are you going to lunch?' [an indirect question indicative of passive or manipulative women], do you think you may have received a different response?" "Oh, Florence, you're so clinical!" one woman responded. Another said, "How can you be so rational when she's so upset?" Evidently, they were not ready; however, the teachable moment was lost as well as Carl Rogers' reminder: "This divorce of reason from feeling is one of the first myths to disappear in a person-centered approach."[43]

Communication involves thinking styles that may not be class- or race- or gender- or culture-dependent. Interpersonal conflicts considered personality problems could be disorders of understanding caused by profound thinking style differences. Brain researchers identified two different modes of thought: the left-brain is oriented toward the linear, sequential, symbolic, elemental, and logical. The right-brain is oriented toward the holistic, spatial, structural, emotional, and intuitive processes. In addition, what a person thinks — the content — has two dimensions: concrete and abstract. Concrete thinkers like direct, bottom line, tangible results. Abstract thinkers enjoy dealing with conceptual or theoretical subjects. Individuals have thinking style preferences; however, all thinking styles are equally valuable.[44] It is an advantage to recognize and move from one style to another to communicate with people with different thinking styles. Similarly, learning styles also cross class, race, gender, and culture.

Understanding the "out-of-awareness" aspects of communication requires understanding the different molds into which each of us is cast. Anthropologist Hall treated culture as a form of communication and asserted that "the real job is not to understand foreign cultures but to understand our own."[45] Our embedded culture imposes blinders on us, making it difficult to communicate with different others. He proposed that "human beings live in a single world of communication but they divide that world into two parts: words and behavior (verbal and nonverbal)"[46] with 10 percent words and 90 percent behavior. Both words and behavior depend upon what the brain decides it will see. "We adopt perceptual attitudes as infants/children to maintain our consensus or bond with our parents and later, society."[47] When we realize it is not what people say but what people see and do — or do not see, say or do — that we must pay attention to, then we become aware of the hidden rules that govern us and others to become competent listeners and effective communicators.

4. Intrapersonal (How one gets along with oneself)

> Intrapersonal intelligence...is a correlative ability, turned inward [See Interpersonal intelligence above]. It is a capacity to form an accurate, veridical [genuine] model of oneself and to be able to use that model to operate effectively in life.[48]

It is possible to undergo a magical transformation in perception or attitude which, in turn, changes the way we perceive our situation, ourselves, and gives us the faith to live with integrity. Dostoevsky, the Russian novelist, was of the nobility, a gentleman, who lived in St. Petersburg. Csar Nicholas arrested him in 1849 for participating in a secret group to illuminate the government's faults. After surviving the emotional turmoil of a mock execution, his real sentence was to be sent in shackles to Omsk, Siberia, and to work at hard labor for four years.

In Siberia, his fellow prisoners were criminals, mostly Russian peasants. Since he was of a higher class, they would not accept him so "the thin-skinned and excruciatingly vulnerable Dostoevsky, ready to flare up at the slightest pinprick to his self-esteem, was now caught in a nightmare...from which there was no escape."[49] Prison camp torments included the harsh life, hard work, surrounded by enemies — the peasants' hatred of his class — and the total isolation. The climax came during a rowdy Easter celebration in 1851. He threw himself on his bed plank to shut out the ugliness around him. A memory flashed in his mind of a long-forgotten incident when he was nine years old when he wandered in the forest of his father's small estate. He thought a wolf was after him; he ran, threw himself into the arms of one of his father's serfs, Marey, who stopped work, soothed the trembling, terrified boy, and assured him he was safe. Dostoevsky remembered Marey's face, smiling at him like a mother, and blessing him with the sign of the cross as he sent him home. With Dostoevsky's face retaining "its gentle smile of recollection...his whole attitude toward his fellow convicts...had 'undergone a magical transformation.'"[50] He got out of bed, looked around him, but it was with different eyes: "'all hatred and rancor had vanished from my heart'...Nothing had changed, but the novelist's attitude was transformed."[51] After four years in the prison camp, he served as an Army private before he was allowed to return to St. Petersburg in 1859. Those ten years deepened his insight into human behavior and his love of Russia. His prison experiences were the source of his genius; he died in 1881. "Where a man's wound is, that is where his genius will be."[52]

While teaching people to play tennis, Timothy Gallwey[53] discovered that an individual has two selves: a Self 1 and a Self 2. A useful metaphor is to perceive Self 1 as an instructional, critical voice that treats Self 2 with disrespect, demonstrates no trust, and calls Self 2 names. Self 1 is also the rational, thinking, detailed, trying, unsure, scared, egotistic and terrorist mind; whereas, Self 2 is innate wisdom, free, relaxed, effortless, exhilarated; a rhythmic, powerfully experienced, moral and ethical self. When Self 1 mistrusts Self 2, Self 2 becomes anxious and worries; it thinks it has to instruct the body on what to do, how to do it, and urge it to "try harder." The harder Self 2 tries, the more uptight it gets, and the worse it performs. Thus, the inner obstacles which prevent us from doing our best are fear, shame, self-condemnation, lack of self-confidence, poor concentration, being too willing to give up, not willing to try hard enough, trying too hard, perfectionism, self-consciousness, frustration, anger, boredom, too high or too low expectations. We often play out a split in consciousness leading to possibly arguing, accusing, and discussing the management of self. The intimate terrorist at work!

A similar Self 1 and Self 2 interaction occurs in any learning or business situations, where we may not trust our first impressions or our instincts, with similar negative outcomes. Positive self-esteem reduces the tension between and unites the body and mind. When we see more clearly what our intimate terrorist is doing to us, from either habit or an unfamiliar context, then we can choose to make positive interventions to dynamically balance Self 1 and Self 2. An imbalance accounts for losing our rhythm (on the tennis court or as a manager or group leader) in responding to a cerebral question, "How did you do that?" is similar to the centipede's dilemma:

> *The centipede was quite happy*
> *Until the toad in fun*
> *Said, 'Pray, which leg comes after which?'*
> *Which brought its mind to such a pitch*
> *It lay distracted in a ditch*
> *Considering how to run.*

Psychological states color our perceptions of the external world; therefore, the quality of our performance reflects our emotional state as we perform. The ability to change is called "mental toughness."[54] When we change from anger to happiness, from boredom to excitement, our biochemistry changes. Even more revealing is the work with people with split or multiple personalities. Not only does their personality change from personality to personality, but their allergies, food preferences, physical diseases, and biorhythms and circadian rhythms also change. Thus, what the mind perceives has much more to say about what is real or not, rather than the external world.

For the average human being, not magic, but practice, attitude, optimism, motivation, and talent determine how well we perform. Emotional control cannot replace talent or the skills developed through practice. Emotional control gives us the stamina required to practice and the staying power necessary for achieving our goals, along with the attitudes required for performing at the upper levels of our abilities.

In the study of emotions, a child's emotional responses are his first and only mode of communication; thus, the importance of an adult's perceiving emotional responses as signals from a child of his/her internal state. The transition from early childhood to adolescence will be successful if the youngster develops emotional tolerance. Emotional tolerance is an individual's ability to tolerate and/or modify the intensity of his emotional responses. Competent parents help their children to practice emotional tolerance, just as they help them learn to walk or swim. The Don'ts (*Don't cry!*) or *You do like your sister/brother/aunt/uncle!* teach children to suppress emotions. Parents who allow their children to bear intense emotional tension, but step in and comfort them before their emotions overwhelm them, teach them to bear their emotions with increasing comfort and security. However, "Adolescence is not the last opportunity, or crisis, for the emotions...Every life crisis presents opportunities; calamity is opportunity in work clothes."[55]

Emotional control includes not taking things personally. Taking others' words, slights, or actions personally, instead of systemically, distorts our perception. We can counter habitual negative responses or actions by observing our reactive impulses — including hidden fears, suppressed anger, and self-abusive (Self 1) feedback — while breathing deeply, meditating, or counting to ten to center ourselves and regain control. We can also counter others' negative responses with humor or phrases (such as, "Thanks for sharing!" or "I believe you believe that!") as a way to heal our programming and to avoid undue stress. When we can acknowledge what we feel without being overwhelmed by it, we can focus on others' positive intentions and use our feelings as data in our whole brain response. We cannot change anyone but ourselves. When we change the way we perceive things, or change from a negative to a positive attitude, the possibility exists that others may change as well when we respond positively instead of negatively. Journaling as a change agent is outlined in the last chapter.

In the study of winners, the essence of the "X" Factor is: (1) "a kind of singleness of purpose...the capacity to focus;" (2) "unselfishness...The capacity to give when other people won't or can't...to create the win with absolutely no concern for who gets the credit...to convey a sense of family and caring and concern with all different kinds of personalities...being willing to make himself the last...he does unselfish things;" (3) "Toughness...being honest in your effort when other people are not being honest, sticking to the principles of fair play and ethical behavior and out-conditioning, out-thinking, out-working your opponent rather than finding ways to bend the rules;" (4) "all champions are smart. It has nothing to do with IQ, with education...it's street smart, country smart...they just know their business...It's partly intuitive, but it's also part training;" and (5) "Champions never quit."[56]

This experience of the X Factor is not unique to athletes; it happens to all of us. The Russians call it "the white moment," in Japan "ki," in China "ch'i," in India "prana," and for Mihaly Csikszentmihalyi[57] it is "flow." He explains flow as experiencing a special state of involvement and concentration that makes an activity worth doing for its own sake rather than as an end in itself. We do not consciously go into the flow state in order to accomplish something; the flow state occurs when we are totally absorbed in what we are doing. To be in the flow state all the time is possible only when our personal and work lives merge into one. To achieve flow we cannot be self-conscious; we have to be willing to take risks, to stretch, to put ourselves on the line, and to be positive.

Finally, the keys to intrapersonal competence are the ability to have access to our feelings, to know the difference between one feeling and another, anger and fear, for example, and to find the cognitive meaning of the feeling. Then, we may integrate all the data to communicate authentically, from both hemispheres of our brain.

5. The Human Brain: Emotional and Cognitive Literacy

The human brain is complex; there are diverse opinions about how it processes data and how it works. The brain is a three-pound universe and is an organ heavily dependent upon embedded data, environmental stimuli, meaning and context. Scientists believe we carry human evolution inside our brains, for the structures within the brain appear to have been built in different eras and areas. The brain may be divided into three parts: the hindbrain (the oldest), midbrain, and forebrain. The hindbrain includes the brain stem, which controls basic automatic processes necessary to remain alive. It is the home of the "fight or flight" or "freeze or feign" response. The hypothalamus, the size of a peanut, sits at the base of the forebrain. The hippocampus and amygdala are in the forebrain. The amydala is part of the emotional brain, the limbic system, which used to be considered the seat of emotions, but it appears there may be more emotional systems in the brain, not just one.[58] The left and right prefrontal lobes, for example, are involved in the emotions.

The human brain has two hemispheres, right and left, which are separated by the corpus callosum. The left side of the brain is more concerned with language and is logical, analytical, linear, rational, sequential, detail-oriented, and unemotional. The right side of the brain is more concerned with spatial matters, emotions and feelings, recognition of faces, visual patterns, music, songs, art, reflection, the big picture, intuition, stored negative memories, and body or nonverbal language. The brain's division is an incomplete one in that the main connection between the hemispheres is a bridge. That bridge, or corpus callosum, has millions of nerve fibers carrying information back and forth between the two hemispheres. Music, for example, enlarges the thick cable of neurons in the corpus callosum, increasing the interconnections between both hemispheres. Thus, the brain operates as an intricate system, like a committee, but each half appears to have a different assignment, with some overlapping, and to be further differentiated by right- or left- handedness, gender, inheritance, and experience. Even an adult brain can reconfigure itself.

The word for *left* in French is *gauche*, meaning *lacking social grace, awkward, crude, tactless* — even in our own language — long before it was known that human beings are asymmetrical. In right-handed people, the right side of the brain controls the left side of the body and the left side of the brain controls the right side of the body. The valued thinking skills are in the left-brain and the disvalued emotions are in the right-brain. If we are left-handed, or are predisposed to be left-handed even though we are right-handed, the possibility exists that our thinking skills could be in the right-brain and our emotions could be in our left-brain. We cannot see clearly or behave congruently when one hemisphere dominates the other.

Referring to the brain's right hemisphere as the emotional brain and the left hemisphere as the cognitive brain does not tell the whole story of how the brain works since there is overlapping. For example, the prefrontal cortex consists of a left lobe and a right lobe. The left lobe has a positive-orientation;

the right lobe has a negative-orientation. Therefore, pessimistic feelings originate in the right prefrontal cortex, and happy feelings originate in the left prefrontal lobe. Education and training can change or regulate negative and positive emotions in the prefrontal cortex, which is linked to the amygdala. That "open-loop" aspect of the emotional centers of the brain relies on connections with other people for emotional stability; "it allows people to come to one another's emotional rescue — enabling, for example, a mother to soothe her crying infant."[59] Exercises for the brain will be in our future.

Human beings have separated reason from passion, thinking from feeling, and cognition from emotion since the time of the ancient Greeks. Since then, cognitive science emerged, but emotions keep emerging too, so "cognition is not as logical as it was once thought and emotions are not always so illogical."[60] Further, "our genes give us the raw materials out of which to build our emotions...But the exact way we act, think, and feel in a particular situation is...not predestined by our genes...emotions do have a biological basis, but social, which is to say cognitive, factors are also crucially important. Nature and nurture are partners in our emotional life."[61]

Cognitive scientists have observed the mind at work and report that the data from our senses lead to cognition — a thought about what we sense — and to feeling, our emotional reaction to what we sensed, felt, or evoked from past experiences. These thoughts and feelings are translated into intentions and plans to take action. Neuroscientists have also observed the mind at work and report:

> whenever we sense something, that information goes immediately from eye to ear to the thalamus, a relay station [in the brain] that translates raw physical waves into the language of the brain. From there the information is shunted to the neocortex, the thinking brain, as well as to the amygdala, that storehouse for negative emotional memories, such as the things we fear. If the amygdala recognizes an emotionally potent stimulus similar to something we reacted strongly to in the past, it unleashes a flood of emotions and a fitting action.[62]

Brain studies show that "a highly activated — or hot — amygdala impairs our ability to turn off our negative thoughts and emotions."[63] A hot amygdala "floods the body with high levels of cortisol...It turns out that the hippocampus is thrown off-kilter by the flood."[64] In his research, New York

117

University's Joseph LeDoux found that in survivors of trauma that the hippocampus is shrunken. "It seems clear that adrenal steroids account for these physical changes in the hippocampus and in the memory problems that result."[65] Emotional pain that is not acknowledged or resolved may manifest itself as physical problems. In some cases, physical diseases, from asthma to cancer and heart attacks, have been found to have emotional roots.

Many scholars concur with "The future of teaching and learning lies in the study of the brain."[66] Human beings have genetically transmitted programs and traumas. Some scholars use the term schema to denote the presence of accumulated data in the amygdala which drive human psychological behavior; other scholars use the term *schema* to denote *schemata* for humans' inherited generalized tendencies and patterns of physical behavior; for example, a newborn who does not have a program for sucking would have a feeding and a survival problem. The presence of schemata is indicated by babies' interest in human faces and voices. More important than terms is the knowledge that we do not come into this world with clean slates or erasures, and all lived experiences in the womb and early years are saved for later processing.

According to Erik Erikson's[67] age and life cycle theories, a much loved and well-cared-for child will grow up to trust his world and to have a highly adaptive schema. A child who does not get adequate love and caring or who is abused will grow up to mistrust his world and to have a maladaptive schema. Five of the common maladaptive schemas are primarily shaped by our earliest experiences with our parents and family are: Abandonment (reaction to loss); Deprivation (misunderstood or not cared for; needs won't be met); Subjugation (by controlling parents); Mistrust (people can't be trusted); and Unlovability (feeling flawed: shame and humiliation). Five more of the common maladaptive schemas are due in part to experiences within and beyond our family are Exclusion (outsider); Vulnerability (loss of control); Failure (not worthy; a fraud); Perfectionism (trying to win love and approval); and Entitlement (feeling special; conceit).[68]

The schemas are presented, one by one, but in reality we may be plagued by several, which may become operative in some close relationships but not in others. The positive side of schemas is they protect us from what might be overwhelming at the time, but we ultimately pay a price for living our lives by unexamined, self-defeating, distorted beliefs, feelings, and reflexive reactions.

Schemas may be identified, challenged, and healed when we keep a journal, as suggested in Chapter Ten.

Learning used to be perceived as a function of time; tests still are. Fortunately, children learn to walk before they go to school; otherwise, if they were subjected to learning to walk the same way they are subjected to learning to read, write and do math, there would be fifteen-year old students in remedial walking class.[69] So there is much more to learning and the human brain's capacity for intelligence than analytical processes. Our traditional educational systems persistently reinforce the perception that knowledge is the accumulation of facts. Few educational approaches legitimize all aspects of human intelligence and human learning beyond the logical-mathematical. At the end of his life, Albert Einstein concluded, "Knowledge is experience. Anything else is just information." Older traditions taught, "Knowledge is wisdom," which gradually transformed into "Knowledge is power." Knowing something is one thing; knowing how to apply it, when and where, is another thing. Wisdom comes from integrating data with experiences.

The human brain is not organized or designed for linear, one-path thought; it operates by simultaneously going down many paths. Traditional educational systems demand that the human "brain meekly put aside its mighty resources and go step-by-step down one path is to cripple and inhibit it."[70] Boring! Educators may learn some day what most businesses know: "Businesses are not paid to reform customers; they are paid to satisfy customers."[71] We have two brains, each with different kinds of intelligence: rational and emotional, and our mind is what those brains do. "How we do in life is determined by both — it is not just IQ, but emotional intelligence that matters...each is a full partner in mental life. When these partners interact well, emotional intelligence rises — as does intellectual ability."[72]

Learning research indicates students cannot learn well when they have negative self-esteem, their emotional state is unstable, and they are in environments they perceive to be ego threatening. To stimulate students, to heighten brain activity, content must be introduced in an interesting, fascinating way. Dull, repetitive situations or presentations lead to boredom, drowsiness, and sleep; thus, learning is reduced to a chore instead of an adventure. About 95 percent of today's teaching at elementary and secondary schools tend to lower mental processes — rote learning of grammar, multiplication tables, scientific and historical names and dates. Few teachers spend time on the higher mental processes: problem-solving.

Utilizing data about how the brain and mind work and applying different thinking and learning styles allow teachers the opportunity to reach seventy-five to one hundred percent of their students. Different people perceive the world in different ways: most people have learned preferences for one sensory mode — visual (seeing), auditory (hearing), or kinesthetic (touching or feeling). When we use one sensory mode more than another, all available sensory data are not utilized, so the missing data may have a negative impact upon our thinking, learning, and behavior.   Many professionals, from scientists to engineers, may succeed in their fields without high quality interpersonal skills, but their employees and families may suffer. Insecure people are not good thinkers; they do not entertain different thoughts, ideas, new approaches to life, or people, thus avoiding the risk of greater insecurity. Fear, being afraid to take a risk, is the source of an unwillingness to change. With increased self-knowledge, though, we can loosen the control of the ego, and fears are decreased when their sources are understood. When we understand the workings of our own mind, we can better understand the workings of other people's minds as well.

How does memory work? That's a question still in need of a good answer. An individual selects data for retention in short- or long-term memory, and some out-of-conscious awareness memories are retrievable. Through hypnosis, people are able to recall more than they can otherwise articulate. Music helps Alzheimer patients' recall their memories. "Absentminded" means: the mind is occupied elsewhere. Stress is memory's worst enemy. Retrieval problems are called "blocks." When we relax or "free associate," it is possible to recall lost data. And sometimes we have to sing a song (right-brain activity) to access and articulate its words. Physical blocks may be due to an inadequate diet, toxins, illness, fatigue, anxiety, a head injury, alcohol or drugs. We put up emotional blocks to protect ourselves from unpleasant things or memories. Rote memory skills are valued in our society as intelligence.

Critical thinking is not the same as disagreement or judgment; nor is it just logical thinking. Critical thinking requires sensory and perceptual data, experience, ideas, logic, creativity, and innovation. It is a process that emphasizes a rational (to measure out) basis for beliefs and feelings and offers procedures for analyzing, testing, and evaluating them. Critical thinking is employed to understand and work with others' positions and to clarify our own. Intuitive, creative thinking is the process by which there is a period of incubation — letting go, relaxing, moving on to something else — and then comes the illumination or an Aha! which may be verified by logic.

Innovative, creative thinking is the process whereby new value is created and a contribution is made by converting a material into a resource or combining existing resources into a new configuration, that is, being opportunity-based or perceiving problems as opportunities. For example, shipping companies' high cost of transporting goods — from breakage to pilferage by longshoreman — led to preloaded containers and container ships.[73] The September 11, 2001 hijacking of jet liners by the suicide-terrorists has already led to changes in security checks and baggage handling. Some creative individuals will find ways to make people identification easier and transportation safer than before the terrorists' attacks on New York City and Washington, DC., hopefully without compromising any freedoms. Necessity is the mother of invention.

The human brain may not be the sole domain of our thinking processes. New research has discovered that neurons are not only in the human brain, but also in the heart and in the solar plexus (gut).

A healthy society has a genuine sense of community, a place where people care about one another and are not afraid to talk about their fears and joys, their disappointments and achievements. The opportunity to integrate the emotional and analytical sides of ourselves and to work on becoming whole people and a healthier society was presented to us on 9/11. Instead, our U. S. Government chose war against the International terrorists (Al Qaeda, Osama bin Laden, and the Taliban) in Afghanistan and against the tyrant Saddam Hussein in Iraq. Our wars have erased the majority of the world's 9/11 empathy for America and Americans. Peace in the world is in ruins for our leaders remain hawkish, the terrorists continue their terror, and the Israelis and Palestinians continue to terrorize each other. Many human beings are seeing clearly that history is repeating itself as masculine energy prevails with the left-brain's coldly logical, black or white thinking, expecting unquestioned patriotism, blind belief in government, support of an infallible military, and sacrifice of freedoms for the illusion of security. The right-brain's values of

121

tolerance, caring, and respect for all nature are missing. Until human beings and their institutions and organizations evolve to a more integrated way of thinking, feeling, being, and doing; war, violence, and misogyny will continue, for "As a culture ages, its wars become increasingly explicit symbols of its growing death-impulse and reversion to nature"[74] and to new paradigms.

Human Redevelopment

Once upon a time, in preliterate societies, the right-brain's attributes were integrated with those of the left-brain. However, around five thousand years ago, literacy became manifest. Research indicates that learning to read and write influences the way the brain's hemispheres work, which formed the basics of Western civilization. The evolution from an oral tradition to one that is alphabet-driven reinforced the left-brain's dominance, leading to the degradation of the right-brain. In *The Alphabet Versus The Goddess:* The Conflict Between Word and Image, Leonard Shlain asserted, "Writing of any kind will realign the gender politics of any culture...a shift in which men appropriate power."[75]

The language we use also reinforces gender politics. European languages — not English — divide things (nouns) into masculine and feminine. The term *masculine* is used to describe the energy or attributes of the left-brain (logical, quantitative, task- versus people-oriented) and *feminine* is used to describe the energy or attributes of the right-brain (emotional, qualitative, people-oriented). While each of us has both brains, when one dominates the other, our responses and behavior become somewhat fixated. For human beings to be dynamically balanced, a whole-brain approach is desirable for responding to diverse situations, not fixations.

Metaphors may also be used to describe the hemispheres: the color blue for the left-brain, for it is logical and cool, and the color red for the right-brain, for it is subjective and emotional or hot. An integrated, dynamically-balanced human being "thinks purple." For centuries, the color purple (a mixture of red and blue) has been worn by royalty, church officials, rulers, and others to denote their higher status and imperial authority, which is not learned or earned wisdom.

The perceptual biases whereby the left-brain suppressed the qualitative judgment of the right-brain is beginning to shift because of the influence of TV, film, video, photography, and even computers. "The integration of alphabet [West] and ideographics [East]...and left and right awaits the next stage in human evolution."[76]

Human redevelopment is upon us as the neuroscience revolution is changing the way we perceive and understand ourselves, our relationships, our reality, and our world. The prevailing view we inherited from past thinkers — a mechanistic, reductionist, parts mentality — has kept us in an adolescent stage of human development and has led to divided selves, divided people, and divided nations. When our head, hearts, lips, hands, and feet are out-of-sync with our possible selves, we exist on a lower plane of human consciousness, which often includes humans' acts of violence to other humans, all living things, and the Earth's resources. When airplanes crash, the "black box" is sought to determine why the accident occurred. Today, our black box (the human brain), can be examined by high-tech machines that monitor the brain's activity while talking, thinking, feeling, and relating, for example. The recorded data provide insights about human behavior and why we do the things we do despite our good intentions. The discovery of the plasticity of the human brain means we can change our present modus operandi and our future. Therefore, each of us has the ability to transform ourselves to a higher, more mature plane of human development.

We are on the verge of a paradigm shift in thinking, doing, being, and relating that has already been embraced by 21st century thinkers, philosophers, some psychologists, and others in disparate disciplines. Our concept of reality was challenged on 9/11, and only through a critical dialogue with ourselves and others will be able to live in this world as fully functioning whole-brain human beings. Hamlet's statement (William Shakespeare) is relevant today: *To be or not to be, that is the question.*

Human Development and Beyond

Human Development is an academic discipline that covers more than the physical, psychological, and socialization (interpersonal and intrapersonal aspects) processes covered in this chapter. The Human Development field may include cultural and moral and ethical processes and aspects of other personal, professional, religious and spiritual processes.

Keep in mind that our book is a multifaceted approach to esteem. To achieve esteem, we need to be aware of and accept the impact that culture and other developmental forces play in our self-, group-, and global-esteem. We choose to attend to cultural, moral and ethical, and spiritual developmental processes as separate chapters to emphasize their importance to self- and other-esteem. Cultural Development, for example, impacts individual lives below the level of human beings' conscious awareness.

Five

Cultural Development

THE CULTURAL DIVIDE BETWEEN EAST AND WEST is far greater than the geographical one. The transnational terrorists came from middle-class homes in the Arab world; they were not poor; they were educated; then they went to Europe or America to study. They encountered closed European and American cultures that clashed with their own culture; the Western values and customs were the antithesis of their own. As outsiders unaccustomed to adapting to new rules and social customs, they preserved their dignity by insulating themselves and adhering to their roots. As "outcasts," they became more religious, and they were easy-pickings for militant fundamentalists. The players in the foregoing East-West encounters were ordinary people, not government agents or bureaucrats. Defusing cultural chemical reactions between East and West is the key to future international terrorism, and it must begin at a grassroots level.

Human beings are, by nature, social animals since the survival of our species has required an infant to receive prolonged postpartum care and a parent's willingness to provide it. The human infant is programmed to grow and develop, to learn a language with complex grammar, and to develop habits and preferences that make each unique. Individuals differ: some are sociable; some are not. Temperament is under some genetic control; however, with personality appearing later, it is difficult to determine if a child's behavior is the result of his own or his parents' experiences, actions, and environmental influences. Children acquire their beliefs and standards by intuiting who cares for them and who regards them as a nuisance and by observing the behavior of others. We presume, though, that there are certain standards and values common to all humanity, especially among those of us who have been civilized into believing in the essential goodness and beauty of human beings.

The term *culture* is defined as *the qualities in a person or society that represent the best in the arts, manners, and the improvement of the human mind through education and training.* Yet, human beings have the potential for and demonstrate their inhumanity. The term is also used to mean the *sum total of the ways of living built up by a group of human beings and transmitted from generation to generation,* which may be the best and the worst qualities in a person and in society.

An African tribe — the Iks, the Mountain People — were forced, before World War II, to give up their hunter-gatherer nomadic ways; they were banned from the mountains now known as the Kidepo National Park. Over a period of three generations, the Iks became dehumanized: from industrious families and daunting hunters to scattered bands of starving people who preyed on each other, even their own children.[1] They abandoned their humanity, and their descent represents how fragile society's structures can be.

Hitler's Nazi Germany abandoned its humanity and millions died because of his madness. Today we have the right-to-lifers who kill to save a life; the warring religious and ethnic factions all over the world; Iraq's Saddam Hussein used biowarfare against other Iraqis, the Kurds. The Taliban in Afghanistan put women in their place: home. Osama bin Laden, his ilk, and the Islamic-extremists cultivate terrorists by deifying martyrdom. The warriors and martyrs are men and boys; however, a few Palestinian girls martyred themselves. Militant Islamic-extremists, radicals, and martyrs believe they are purifiers and saviors; yet "everything the world has learned in the last decade about why some countries develop and others stay mired in poverty shows that women can make all the difference...women can help increase economic development and stability."[2] Throughout the world, individual, social, cultural, and economic practices that perpetuate adversarial attitudes and behaviors have increased as the technological advances, from nuclear to biochemical weapons, have also increased and are available to terrorists.

The U.S. government appointed a highly qualified Arabist as ambassador to Iraq in the 1980s. The Arabist is a woman. That was a problem for the Iraqis since in Iraq, and in many Arab nations, men look down upon women, so our sending a woman to do what they perceive as "a man's job" may have been construed as a sign of our nation's weakness and naiveté or as an insult. The Gulf War proved otherwise, but Saddam Hussein remained in power. Our ambassador to Saudi Arabia was recalled, since the Gulf War, at the Saudi's request; he is a man. He is also fluent in Arabic so Westerners' fluency in their language may be as big a problem for those nations as gender.

Under the Taliban rule in Afghanistan, women were degraded, abused, and perceived to be competitors for low-level jobs usually filled by lower class males. Culture was subverted by raw egos' interpretations of the Koran to enforce their moral code. For years, we knew through e-mail and the media about the plight of women, especially educated women, in Afghanistan: doctors, lawyers, and other professionals had been stripped of their status, stoned, starved, and murdered. The film made by an Arab-British woman, *Behind The Veil*, chillingly portrays what women were up against in Afghanistan. Mavis Leno, wife of the host of TV's "The Tonight Show," has been working for the Afghani women's cause for the past five years, but it was not until September 11, 2001 that their freedom and rights were taken seriously. Embedded culture, even in abused women, is difficult to confront for they fear a Western-cultural assault on their traditional ways; therefore, not all Muslim women oppose the Islamic-extremists. A thirteen-year old Pakistani girl, wearing a chodor, during the Afghan war, said, "I have seen Western movies and their clothes are their fashion, but this is an Islamic country, and Islam doesn't allow us to wear such clothes. I think they look bad."[3] The fashions the Arabs see are those worn by our Hollywood icons and rock stars, not those worn by ordinary and extraordinary Americans or Western women. Power over and control of women are recurring themes in culture and religion throughout the world's history.

America's lesson to learn from the sorry state of nations who degrade women is to increase women's influence while preserving the positive aspects of their culture. Women are needed to balance and strengthen moderation in all cultures, and the Arab culture, as in Iran and Iraq, to improve standards of living, education, nutrition, family planning, and family income. America's choices are to make life worth living for all in the Middle East and other struggling countries or to collude in excluding women in rebuilding governments, education systems, or economies. Social and cultural survival are as important as individual survival; however, *any* culture that denigrates women and limits their freedom and rights is fearful of change. We have women in our country who do not want to be "liberated" either; however, it is their individual choice and not a governmental or religious mandate. Americans' greatness lies in preserving and living our vaunted democratic principles and human values instead of sacrificing our humanity or our diversity.

Culture's Origins

From history and experience we learn that some nations are composed of people who are united by a common dislike of its neighbors and by a common myth of its origins. A nation's cultural mores are man-made and "what gives man his identity no matter where he is born is his culture."[4] "It takes culture to create self and self to create culture; they are the yin and yang of being human. There is no self except in interaction with a culture, and no culture that is not made up of selves."[5] Culture and socialization go hand-in-hand. The warrior culture emerges where the moral code is weak, the legal system is ineffective, bureaucratic systems and structures are missing, and women are male dominated with little paternal involvement in childcare.

Our culture determines what we pay attention to and what we ignore; it also reinforces our learned or inherited belief that something or someone different is either better than we are or inferior to us, or primitive. In psychological jargon, to be socialized means we learn to want what our society expects us to want, which is different for males, females, and children of different class, race, and ethnic origins within the same society. To be acculturated means we inherit, absorb, or consciously and unconsciously act on what we learned from our ethnic origins and religious, spiritual or philosophical exposure and from our environment. We soon learn when we go to pre-school, kindergarten, or other public places that there is a dominant White culture in America into which we either fit or do not fit. Culture's function also provides us with a screen to separate us from them: those who are unlike us.

Cultural Glue: Sports and The Arts

One of the many functions of sports and the arts in our society is to remove the cultural screens that separate us by removing internal and external boundaries. Then we realign ourselves according to preferences for teams, appreciation of talent and skills, and the joys of music and art. Self-restricting self-images disappear when we ignore the old programming or beliefs about self and others. The majority of Americans, of all colors and creeds, revere Black athletes, musicians, and performers. Talented people, from sports to entertainment, were the first to cross the old U.S. color lines.

Each of us has an Inner Game[6] dilemma due to negative self-images, beliefs, or others' ways of operating that limit our experiencing life's possibilities beyond culture. Jeanne joined the Black Gospel Choir at Yale and attributes that relationship to her ability to complete a year of study she felt was destroying her creativity. A trainable retarded class in a Pennsylvania elementary school made huge academic strides when they were taught to play the harmonica by a volunteer; they received recognition and respect from the rest of the school for their concerts. Religion is supposed to be the glue that binds different cultures together; however, in the U.S. with its multicultural and multiracial diversity and the haves and have-nots, we have no unifying theme or myth that suits all, except for the American dream to be upwardly mobile. Individuals' and our government's responses to 9/11 have united many Americans and alienated others.

Hidden Culture

People do not exist apart from their individual cultures, especially the hidden constraints of covert culture, that is, the undercurrents that structure our lives below the level of conscious awareness — from the way we think, talk, act, walk, and communicate — verbally and nonverbally. We assume that our way of being and doing is natural or God-given and that different ways of being and doing are unnatural or wrong. Most people of all nations experience differences on emotional rather than on rational or goodwill levels.

We assume, because we are Americans, that we share a common culture. Shared meaning is the essence of culture. We tend to think that people from

129

other nations who emigrate to our shores are underdeveloped Americans and that as soon as they learn our language and laws, they will then act like "Americans" and will fit into and abide by our society's established structure, rules, and mores. That is a misperception. Most immigrants settle where they have relatives or fellow countrymen and retain their language and cultural identities, which are familiar; some feel that to do otherwise would betray or destroy their own roots. America is large enough to be home to all cultures, races, and creeds.

Most nations share a common culture and shared meanings; therefore, foreigners find it easier to label Americans collectively. America is unique. Despite the "Mayflower people" and their ancestors, we are a gathering of people of different cultures and races from all parts of the Earth. Our institutions are run, though, as if we are a monocultural nation. Our popular culture, as portrayed by the media, influences the world's perception of us and our values and ignores the cultural diversity that makes this country unique.

Why are human beings so hard on themselves and/or so hard on other human beings? One answer is that we are not sufficiently in awe of ourselves. Our bodies are about 70 percent water; so is the Earth. We are made of stardust: over 60 percent of a human body's atoms were once part of the Big Bang; we are radioactive; our bodies contain more cells than there are stars in the galaxy; our hearts beat about 4 billion times in an average lifetime; our circulatory system is 60,000 miles long![7] Culture is so imbedded or imprinted within all human beings that many cannot tell the difference between innate and acquired characteristics. In fact, most do not even know who they are or question how they became the way they are.

The hidden dimensions of diverse cultures' nonverbal communications are rarely perceived to be the source of racial and interpersonal problems in America. It is easier to label intercultural conflicts as racism, anti-Semitism, anti-Muslim, or anti-American because that is what people see. What we do not see are the cultural undercurrents that steer behavior. "Like the invisible jet streams in the skies that determine the course of a storm, those hidden currents shape our lives; yet their influence is only beginning to be identified."[8]

The out-of-awareness cultural nonverbal communications sent out and received by Whites, Blacks, Asians, Jews, and Arabs are misread and acted upon consciously. Early researchers revealed that when people talk, their bodies also "talk:" hands wave; fingers point; eyes blink, roll and shift; eyebrows move; heads nod and turn; and faces may wear masks, but the whole body dances. When individuals' movements are synchronized, they get along despite their verbal messages; however, when their movements are not synchronized, they do not get along at all. When we react from our nonverbal, emotional brain, if our rational brain disagrees, we send mixed messages, and then what we say and do are not in sync. Adults and children can be made aware of nonverbal communication so they may be more receptive and responsive to people unlike themselves. We need to be in charge of the responses we give and get. We absorb individual differences within cultures without talking about them, playing one-up games with our knowings. An illustration:

Michael traveled frequently to Japan on business, and on each visit he ate the raw fish offered by his Japanese associate. Michael does not like sushi, but he ate it each time to be culturally correct. Finally, his associate came to New York, accompanied by his camera. Michael offered to take him on a private plane ride up and down the Hudson River for a rare opportunity to photograph New York City at 1,000 feet. He fell for it. When they arrived at the private airport in the suburbs, Michael introduced his wife Kelly, at the controls, as the pilot of her plane. She was seven months pregnant. After a pregnant pause, Michael's associate said, "When baby come?" Satisfied with her answer, he boarded the plane. They spent over an hour sightseeing over Manhattan while the associate exposed rolls and rolls of film. Back on the ground, Michael's associate turned to him and said, "Michael, no more raw fish!" Each knew the other was playing the cultural game of one-up-manship, and they both knew how to level the playing field.

At lower levels of human development, the outcomes of cultural differences and ignorance of them are tragic. "Unpopularity, poor grades and a host of other problems that afflict school children may derive from an inability to read the nonverbal messages of teachers and peers."[9] Adults' inability to read the emotions revealed in tone of voice, body language, or how close to stand to someone while talking, to recognize happy, angry, or sad faces, and most of all the ability to send such messages are skills that most children learn naturally, until they are socialized. Other children feel powerless to manage how other people respond to them or treat them so they get labeled or are avoided. Evidently, the less our emotional state is preoccupied with problems, the more clearly we can see and read others' nonverbal signals. Our choice of words and how we pronounce them also betray our state of esteem, our class, education level, and determine how we are perceived.

Nonstandard English

The only way we can understand the hidden constraints of culture is to actively participate in the very parts of life that we take for granted. The not-so-hidden constraints of culture are our accent and dialect. When we open our mouths to speak, our accent, dialect, and proper usage of the English language come across faster than our content. Our audience attempts to classify us as a native of a particular geographic area, as educated or uneducated, and as lower, middle, or upper class. Americans are intrigued by accents. Receptionists with English accents are in demand; the corporate image is perceived to be enhanced by a "cultured" voice, where culture is synonymous with "upper-class."

Black English exemplifies the fact the "Language is a curious and mysterious phenomenon."[10] Black English is considered a careless way to emulate Standard English patterns. Since Black slaves came from different parts of Western Africa, where a myriad of different languages are spoken, they were forced to speak a pidgin English to communicate with each other as well as with their owners. In Black English, English roots and African roots coexist. When Black and White children and adults say, "He crazy" or "Her my friend" and "Nobody don't know it" or "Don't nobody know?" the speaker is judged as language deficient. Most of us learned to use the helping verb "to be", such as, "I am not" rather than "I ain't!" and that two negatives make a positive statement, such as, "I didn't do nothing!" instead of "I didn't do anything!" In Old English and in Middle English...and even in Shakespeare's time, two negatives or more served to intensify the negative quality of a sentence, not to delete it."[11]

Black English has roots in West African languages as demonstrated by African words that are now part of our Standard English vocabulary: "tote, okra, yam, banana, cooter (turtle), jazz, banjo, juke, jive, jam, boogie, rap, and dig."[12] Black English is ingenious when linguistic reversals are employed to achieve complexity of meaning, such as *a mean dude* means *a good man* or *a bad momma* is *a good woman*. Metonymy — the use of part for the whole — is another way to achieve complexity of meaning when *threads* refer to *clothes*. Toni Morrison's main characters in *Song of Solomon* have pun names: flaws, mistakes, yearnings, gestures, which is a way of utilizing another culture's language and customizing it. Brother and Sister are used in the Black Church to address their religious families. The Feminist Movement adopted the term *Sister* to unite women in a common cause; yet the more universal term *brotherhood* presumes to include all human beings when it does not.

Native American: Navajo Code Talkers

The importance of Native American languages to our country was discovered during World War II in the war against Japan in Southeast Asia. The Japanese were able to break any of our codes devised to communicate with other U.S. commands. In 1942, several hundred Navajo Americans were recruited as Marines and trained to use their language as code; then Navajo servicemen were strategically placed to talk to each other in Navajo. Information was immediately transmitted and understood without the delay of human decoders or machines. The Navajo code was the only one never broken by the Japanese, which was a key to our winning the war.

It took a long time for the American public to learn of the Navajo culture's special contribution to winning the war. *Windtalkers*, written by John Woo and starring Nicolas Cage, is a movie about the Navajo code and World War II. The MGM film was released June, 2002. Navajo code talker Lloyd Oliver received a Congressional Medal of Honor for his service in World War II in 2001.

Americanisms

Our American language has its idioms, accepted colloquialism, and tortured grammar. When we resist and insist that others accept phrases as "He don't" instead of "He doesn't" or "He axed me" for "He asked me" and "You ain't" for "You aren't" or "All's I want..." instead of "All I want..." and many similar examples, we must accept responsibility for how we may be perceived (uneducated!) beyond our immediate social group and within our culture. James Joyce's *Ulysses* is an example of stream-of-consciousness writing. When some students in a seventh grade English class wanted to write creatively, creative to them meant paying no attention to grammar, spelling, sentence structure, and punctuation. They were disappointed when they learned that James Joyce knew the difference; he knew the basics of the English language, and he chose to innovate.

Knowing the difference and knowing how we are being perceived, if we choose to be different, are forms of intercultural literacy. Speakers' over-usage of "You know" and "like" and "Uhs" or "Ers" and persistent profanities are usually out of their awareness and habitual; however, they are also used as a means of monopolizing the air waves while they think. A reliance upon meaningless words avoids silence, but an aware listener may disregard the message; whereas, profanity may shock, silence, or turn off listeners. During World War II, there was a saying, "Loose Lips Sink Ships." Today's loose lips "sink" relationships, destroy positive first impressions, indicate faulty thinking or emotional immaturity, and show little sensitivity or regard for other people, so we lose prospective relationships or, at the least, their positive regard.

The Profane

Standard English and Black English are not the only languages to make use of the senses, context, obscenity, and profanity. Obscene and profane languages are sprinkled throughout most communications among males and females of all nations. While they are used to attract attention or shock, they are also expressions of frustration, disappointment, or disgust. They are also used as an assertion of dominance. Carl Sagan[14] discussed sexually obscene utterances, used as verbal aggression in our language and in other languages, which are examples of sex terms being used as an attempt to dominate. F—- you! is a common utterance. Note that the "I" is understood in the complete statement. That common utterance probably derives from a Germanic and Middle Dutch verb *fokken* meaning *to strike*. The word is reminiscent of the German aircraft, the World War I Fokker, built by the Dutch. Note that F—- you! and rape have nothing to do with sex but with power, dominance, emotional illiteracy (anger, violence), and shock. However, negative terms capture the brain's attention and become a ready response for suppressed emotions and feelings of inferiority and frustration, which are inevitable when ignorance of and intolerance for cultural differences produce students who are undereducated, making them prone to cults, violence, and dis-ease.

Sensory Modalities

Miscommunication often results when people try to communicate using different sensory modalities and the many words pertaining to each modality, from *see* and *hear* to *touch, feel,* or *intuit.* Highly visual people (I see) do not like living in untidy spaces; highly kinesthetic (I feel) people do not like sleeping in a bed full of crumbs. For auditory (I hear) persons who primarily respond to words, illogical reasoning is as unpleasant as a Coney Island roller coaster ride is to a kinesthetic person or throbbing psychedelic lights are to visual people. Most people have a preferred sensory modality. We gather more data when we are attuned to them all.

The ability to recognize and to translate one sensory modality's words into another creates understanding. We are taught to listen to content, but we also have to be aware of the context of the content. When we use all modalities to relate or teach, we increase our chances of being heard and understood: the basic premise of communication. Hearing what is not said, reading between the lines, seeing the invisible, or coming up with innovative or creative ideas involves intuition. Intuition is not necessarily "extrasensory," it is a natural outcome when both the left- and right-brains work in unison and we are not contaminated by too much rote "education" or too many "can'ts." It is based on having the knowledge, the ability to get out of our own way (of thinking, believing, judging, feeling, and assuming), and "letting go," so both the intellectual and emotional brains can work together: to do the impossible, we must see the invisible.

It is possible that we are never more real than when we are asleep. A lot of problem solving goes on subconsciously. Daytime dreams are considered thoughts; whereas, nocturnal dreams are often disregarded or misunderstood. Otto Loewi,[13] a German physiologist who escaped the Nazis, settled in America, and died at the age of 88 in 1961. He fell asleep one day in 1921 while reading a novel. He had a dream or was experiencing nocturnal mentation (thinking); he awoke, wrote it down, and went back to sleep. He could not decipher his cryptic note, so he went to bed the next night hoping the dream would recur. It did. He awoke at 3 a.m., went to his lab, and proved that a chemical messenger (acetylcholine) slows the heart rate (and facilitates dreaming). He went on to prove that epinephrine or adrenaline speeds up the heart. Dreams' meanings, if any, are usually hidden in symbolism, metaphors, non-sense or nonsense.

Subliminal Imprinting

Culture may be imprinted subliminally in the brain. We do not have to consciously pay attention to be conditioned. Advertisers and brainwashers have known for a long time that the brain is susceptible to its environment. Fleeting images on a television screen, words flashed before our eyes, hidden messages embedded in songs, barely audible taped messages in our language or in a foreign language get the brain's attention even while preoccupied with other tasks. It means the human brain is susceptible to conditioning through exposure to stimuli even at imperceptible levels. Subliminal learning has been controversial and considered a gimmick, but Boston University's research is finding ways to detect such learning even when it is subtly absorbed and out of awareness of the learner. The next step is to utilize subliminal learning for real learning in the classroom and the workplace.

Education as Cultural Transmission

Education is one of America's biggest businesses for transmitting our nation's culture; yet public schooling is the only business where many of its customers try to get the least out of it for the money spent by taxpayers, parents, and government. Why? Our school system is modeled upon the factory system of the Industrial Revolution, which was modeled upon the Prussian Army. In early America, public school schedules followed farmers' needs for their children to work the fields; the cities followed suit in the belief that much schooling damaged children's brains without attention to children's needs to constantly move, even in school. At school and at work, the focus is the curriculum or the job — the content — and not upon instruction — the process by which to teach or manage different kinds of people at different levels of development. Context and meaning are also missing.

The educational system does not take into account that we are born with intrinsic motivation and the capacity and eagerness to learn. Infants' curiosity is believed to be an inborn instinct. Those traits may have been enhanced or tampered with before we reached school or are stifled in school. People of all ages have the capacity to learn naturally. Each human being has multiple intelligences. Howard Gardner calls them *Frames of Mind*: Linguistic, Musical, Logical-Mathematical, Spatial, Bodily-Kinesthetic, and Personal (self-knowledge or self-esteem) Intelligences.[15] Intelligence has much to do with making adaptive responses; the Latin verb *intelligo* means *to select among*. Some Native American Indian cultures have a different notion of "teaching" and rearing children, and they value nonverbal communication more than most Westerners:

> Children are expected to constantly observe the world around them
> and learn from it. From this, it can be seen that one does not 'teach'
> a child to learn...intervention in the child's autonomy would risk
> forever destroying the child's ability to observe and learn from his
> own motives. The child is encouraged only to seek out knowledge
> of human experience and skills by being present in their practice
> or their telling.[16]

Most Native American Indians do not learn as well when material is presented a little bit at a time, in an analytic, sequential but fragmented manner. Sequential, incremental learning must be preceded by an overall picture or global view of what to expect. That is how the human brain works; it perceives wholes; it simultaneously processes disparate data.

In our culture, children and adults learn by observing what other adults practice: they compete with each other and work for grades, positions, titles, and money, not for knowledge or for inner gratification. People learn to constantly compare themselves to others; therefore, the opportunity to work with intrinsic pride and joy is replaced by extrinsic stimulation or by rewards. Most learn what is modeled: not to value knowledge and wisdom over grades or people over profit.

Once upon a time, teachers expected their students to learn traditional subjects in a one-room schoolhouse for all ages and at all levels of ability. Those who caught on more quickly also learned from the higher grades' lessons; those who were slower had the opportunity to catch-up, if they were motivated to do so. There was also the opportunity for students to hide learning deficits since each student was given less visibility and more time so they were less likely to be labeled because they eventually learned what they needed to learn to pass the tests. From the foregoing, it can be deduced that test results need to be perceived as what has yet to be learned.

Students are segregated by age, grade, and sometimes ability, teaching is geared to tests, and knowledge is poured, to borrow a metaphor from Carl Rogers, out of the teacher (jug) into the students (mugs). Academic achievement is thought to depend upon innate ability, as demonstrated by IQ and readiness tests. Parents hold teachers responsible. Teachers blame the child's IQ or behavior when they fail. Research demonstrates, "The best indicator of academic success is how parents interact with their children...Parents who are quick to praise, spend time with their children, set high aspirations and use consistent discipline are the parents who turn out scholars."[17] Schools and work are not central to children's lives, despite the fact that American parents know that to become an Olympic athlete or to perform at Carnegie Hall, it takes years of daily practice. They seem not to make the same connection with success in academics as in sports or music. Negatives are used to control children "for their own good:" "Don't fall!" "Don't be naughty!" "Don't cry!" and "Don't fail!"

The burgeoning usage of standardized tests in most academic disciplines in America, Japan, Britain, and other nations is creating human beings with artificial or rote intelligence. "By-the-book-smarts" is emphasized instead of actual applicable intelligence, which is acquired through integrating book learning with experiential learnings mediated by the emotions. Once we incorporate emotional literacy, initiative, and meaning into the current K-12 curricula, children and schools will stop failing each other.

Low IQ scores or poor academic achievement have more to do with emotional literacy than with intelligence, race, class, or gender.[18] For many children, IQ scores have more to do with time than with real intelligence; those with higher IQs make faster decisions and complete more test questions.

By adding a few extra minutes, New York City public school children's reading scores were notably improved. Nevertheless, IQ scores create and maintain class and caste systems with self-fulfilling prophecies "growing out of teachers' expecting less of some children; thus, tacitly treating them in ways that underestimate the potential and ability of poor kids generally and caste-like minorities in particular."[19] Many scholars and scientists know that people's low IQ score or academic achievement "has little to do with their race or their genes: it is a consequence of the structure of society as a whole."[20]

Since World War II, urban sprawl has led to suburbs becoming bedrooms of larger cities; people spend hours commuting; large complexes of schools and shopping malls have been built on the outskirts of towns with less open and shared community spaces, such as parks, community centers, or outdoor meeting places so popular in European cities or in old-fashioned, established American towns. It was a setting ripe for children's demands for television, video games, computers, and cell phones as they coped with being isolated and unable to develop relationships or self-reliance, while relying upon school buses to take them home after school or upon their mothers to transport them to after-school activities.

The bigger the school, the more alienated students become. Most children are treated without respect in most public school systems. Instead of reforms to alleviate "understaffed, boring, authoritarian classrooms...the schools turned to psychiatric diagnoses and treatment as a solution to 'behavior' and 'learning' problems."[21] It is a sad commentary on our culture, ten years later, when such practices continue to be widespread, when dominance-submission patterns exist throughout our culture, and when success worship leads to thinking human beings are commodities.

Our educational and social systems are still hampered by cultural stereotypes and low expectations for minorities, even though they were disproved sixty years ago. Prodded by his wife, Eleanor, Franklin D. Roosevelt helped thirteen Blacks break the color barrier of the U.S. Navy in the 1940s. The Navy had kept them segregated and allowed them eight weeks instead of the normal sixteen weeks of training. The thirteen men banded together and taught each other. Their examination scores were so high, a retest was ordered, resulting in higher scores: "3.89 out of 4 —- the best class score ever recorded there. No graduation ceremony was accorded the men, but they were commissioned as ensigns on March 17, 1944."²² The 1988 movie *Stand and Deliver* was based on a true story of the value of studying: Hispanic-Americans' superior high school math test results were deemed to be "irregularities" until the tests were retaken under rigorous conditions, and the excellent test results were affirmed. In the U.S., there are pockets of schools where minorities are unquestionably excelling, but those schools are not the traditional run-of-the-mill schools of the Western intellectual tradition. Those special schools work with the whole person.

A backlash from our traditional intellectual approaches to teaching and learning became apparent in the late 1980s when research found that some students who do poorly "saw being studious as betraying their racial identity — by 'acting white' in the students' words...they identify achievement with betraying their roots."²³ Their rationale is culture, identity, and self-esteem are preserved when they choose to fail, which is a subcultural response to an insensitive dominant culture that is not attuned to most of its own members' needs either. It is not surprising that it is *cool* to fail oneself before being failed by teachers. Not studying and not doing homework are ways some students rebel against controlling authority figures who are quick not to trust them, judging them by their behavior versus stimulating them to learn.

Schools are not the best places to learn the basics or how to live in society for those students who do not have a keen sense of themselves. Schools are not even career- or job-oriented when the personal skills needed to "sell" oneself and to get along with other people are not in the usual curriculum. A university used to be a place to study, seek wisdom, and experience ourselves in the universe. Today, most of us channel our energies in one discipline to master it to become a specialist while we learn more and more about less and less. With a fragmented or parts mentality, we rarely get a glimpse of the bigger picture, so it takes several years to learn how to read. How to read may be taught in one hundred hours.

A common academic and social response to "remedy" underachievement in the public schools is a "back-to-basics" curriculum approach. That approach does not acknowledge that there are multiple intelligences operating in each classroom that are not being serviced. The rote-lecture method of teaching does not work in a society that has become visual- and action-oriented due to television, video games, comic books, and the movies. To be a couch potato is also learned in the classroom! Another common academic response to "upgrade" achievement in the public schools is standardized testing. What is needed, however, in the teaching-learning process is a refocus on interactions between students and teachers.

The old saying, "Give me a fish, and I will eat for a day. Teach me to fish, and I will eat for the rest of my life," is premised on the assumption that teachers or governments know all about how, what, when, and where to fish, teach, work. Eating for the rest of one's life requires more than specific job training, it requires continuing education to upgrade job and communication skills, and it requires learning to fish or work from each other in changing times. The teacher becomes the learner and the learner becomes the teacher. Initiative is developed in adolescence, and it is not happening when a surprising number of youths are bored, unmotivated, and unexcited by their lives. There are few appealing images of adulthood for them to admire, and the initiative that is motivated by the process is preferable to those of anticipatory rewards. Initiative comprises three elements:

> intrinsic motivation, the experience of wanting to be doing an activity and being invested in it...concerted engagement in the environment, with exertion of constructive attention in a field of action involving the types of constraints, rules, challenge, and complexity that characterize external reality...this motivation and concerted engagement occur over time. Initiative involves a temporal arc of effort directed toward a goal, an arc that might include setbacks, re-evaluation, and adjustment of strategies.[24]

Such initiatives are provided by structured youth activities and structured voluntary activities, such as art and drama groups, sports teams, Boys and Girls Clubs, YMCA gang intervention programs, and other community organizations.

When creativity, initiative, and meaning are not considered valid or part of the basic curricula in our educational systems, people gravitate toward the popular culture to express their felt lack of creativity and freedom. Young people whose sense of self derives from belonging to a gang or group make public statements by their like-minded behavior. They see the latest violent or science fiction movie, listen to rock and rap music, wear designer, black leather, retro, or "kinky" to sexy clothing, flaunt punk hairstyles, body piercing, adopt the "in" words and profanity, and overuse drugs and alcohol. When inner needs are not met, outer ones become the focus of young people's attention. Suppression of emotions and negative injunctions instill fear and pessimism and interfere with natural and academic learning. Insecure people are not good problem-solvers because they will not allow disparate thoughts to coexist and to recombine as new ideas and new approaches to life. Fear, being afraid to take a risk, is the source of the unwillingness to change as well as the fear of success or of failure.

When the schools fail to adequately educate the majority of its population, they do not go out of business; nor do they recall students to correct functional illiteracy. They rarely improve their delivery systems or examine and update their mission. Other social systems inherit their failures: social service, welfare, and prisons. Federal and State prisons are booming. People's intellectual and emotional illiteracy, negative esteem, and crime are intertwined with culture's impact on esteem.

Culture's Effects on Esteem

Many Americans do not feel good about themselves, even when their basic needs for food and a roof over their heads are met or when they have an abundance of material things. Drugs, alcohol, and depersonalized sex are used as temporary escapes from unwanted feelings and situations, creating, instead, long-term physical and psychological negative effects. The economic impact of self-defeating actions, unhealthy lifestyles, antisocial, and criminal activity is leading to individual, family, and national bankruptcy. Learning from experience provides wise individuals with new start up "capital." Mark Twain realized that in some cases, experience may not be the best teacher. He said, "A cat that sits on a hot stove once won't do it again, but it probably won't sit on a cold one either."

Alcohol is one of the socially accepted means of escape. Babies are born physically and mentally disadvantaged by addicted mothers and psycho-logically challenged because addicts and/or alcoholics are generally unfit parents. Hospital and social services are overburdened, and the middle-class

142

pays the bill. America is still considered the land of freedom, but it is a land where some people exercise more freedom from responsibility than others.

Handing out money rather than utilizing the human touch is society's response to cure everything that ails us. A 1970's *New Yorker* cartoon comes to mind. A woman is in the water, drowning, yelling, "Help! Help!" A man on the pier, with briefcase in hand, says, "I can't swim but would $10 help?"

Money is not always the answer, but it will buy a life preserver, a rope, or swimming lessons. Learning to swim is a self-reliant way to navigate cultural waters, if we are aware of the cultural waters in which we swim. Bureaucrats, though, are difficult to deal with because their regulations are written for each other and they are insensitive to the public's contextual needs. The laws are designed to operate apart from the rest of life. "The common inadmissibility of contexting testimony, including hearsay, sets our courts apart and frequently makes them harsh, inhuman, and impersonal."[25] Yes or No answers in the courtroom and True or False in the classroom! Numbers are easy to read, but they objectify us and leave us faceless.

When we cannot rely on ourselves or on our systems, we rely on isms. Isms are about the lack of esteem. Terrorism, fundamentalism, capitalism, consumerism, feminism, sexism, and "any ism you care to name, really — are all attempts to create meaning for human beings who, if they had not suffered some sort of primary loss early on, would not need it."[26] Isms flourish when self- and other-esteem are missing.

Isms are also about nationalism and idealism. The 1960's Bay of Pigs (Cuba) was a political disaster on land. The explosion of the Challenger Space Shuttle in the 1980s was a national disaster in the air. The Challenger was intended as a national bonding event, with Americans aboard of different races and creeds and a teacher representing children. Instead, it turned out to be a needless tragedy. Those in power did not listen to the voices of technicians. The Columbia was also a tragedy of human error; some administrators would not listen to the engineers. The terrorists' attack on September 11, 2001 was another opportunity to unite Americans by focusing on a common challenge to confront terrorism in all aspects of our lives.

Cultural Harmony

Human beings are the most vulnerable of all the species on Earth. Ordinary people are elevated to larger-than-life status to run our social and business institutions and organizations. We have the democratic infrastructures and people who value freedom and human rights, and we also have massive bureaucratic hierarchies that are so big, like the Titanic, it takes a long time to veer away from a collision course. When individuals become roles, not persons, they collude in ensuring an institution's survival instead of responding to needed changes.

Aside from the possibility that world leaders play out their unresolved familial conflicts on perceived adversaries and that men feel more alive, real, and connected to other men when they are "in the trenches," the fact remains, as General Omar Bradley, said, "We know more about war than we do about peace — more about killing than we do about living." We know how to grow humanely developed human beings, but many human beings are emotionally illiterate, so self-interest feeds deficit egos.

The Western world ideal is to develop a harmonious multicultural and multiracial society; however, integration does not usually take place between unequals. The challenge of culture is to develop its intercultural capability to sustain and hold together a nation attuning itself to needed changes in content, context, and processes. Different cultures have a way of keeping groups from working together; the tendency of subcultures is to pull apart. To achieve high performance, the process requires collaboration. America is not alone in its cultural diversity and intercultural problems. Immigrants' transition from one society to another requires extra effort since the immigration of groups of people without problems does not exist. The mental and material baggage, the characteristics, idiosyncrasies, and education of the immigrants determine their starting position in their new country.

At a seminar at The Royal Tropical Institute in Amsterdam, Dr. Jongmans related stories of working with several Moroccans who had problems in Dutch society. He was the cultural interpreter for worker who were not receiving justice in the Dutch system because Moroccan values were such that to defend themselves would violate their values. He informed us that the Moroccan culture is based upon pride and shame, and many young men leave Morocco to find jobs in Holland; they send money home to the father to keep the family together. In good times, they are able to fulfill their family obligations by living in cramped quarters and being frugal. When jobs are scarce, living expenses in Holland eat up their earnings so there is no money to send home. The father is shamed when his son does not send money home; the son knows this so eventually he gets sick and has to go on disability. Even those who continue to send money home may become ill from the stress of living in a society where they are excluded, or exclude themselves by their priorities. Dr. Jongmans estimated it took about seven years for a Moroccan to become physically unfit to work, to succumb to the pressures of living as a "guest worker."

Developing intercultural awareness and cooperation needs to be an ongoing priority. The democratic infrastructure of our civilized society will be eroded by misreading and overreacting to isms that will not go away peacefully. This decade we have terrorism. Nationalism divides nations and peoples. Only a dynamic balance of larger economic interests mutes many nations' disputes, which is similar to what holds many families together. The real question is, for better and for worse, not whether the other person or nation or sect is good or evil, but, "How can we live together?" or "How can we coexist?" First, we must defend our right to live and then we must learn to live with ourselves. "We [Americans] need to encourage habits of flexibility, of continuous learning, and of acceptance of change as normal and as opportunity — for institutions as well as for individuals."[27]

Culture divides us, and a continental divide facing West and East today is gender. Even in America, the California Gold Rush attracted mostly single males, any family life was male-dominated, prostitution was rampant, and life was lawless and short. Only the Appalachian gold rush was civilized with Cornish miners and their families. Males and females differ in temperament; males are more difficult to socialize; however, today's young girls are joining gangs, and the moral gap is lessening between the sexes. Single-parent families are not an American phenomenon; however, the presence of male and female parents, or caretakers, appears mandatory for the optimum development of both young males and females.   The Bible tells us to "love thy neighbor as thyself." How about the family? The Koran tells us that "human beings are worthy of esteem because they are human." How about women? In the West we have the democratic and bureaucratic infrastructures that guarantee women their freedom and their culture. Progress is being made in Middle East governments to ensure women's rights and esteem. It is a truism, that when people are alienated, the easier it is to keep them divided and to conquer them. None of us is a prisoner of the past or of our culture. We can change "what is" by learning about what we can change and how to make that change. Optimism, the conviction that we can change, is the first step within our reach.[28]

Global-Esteem to Global Village

The late Canadian media theorist, Marshall McLuhan, forecast the homogenization of the Earth into a global village. The melting pot theory did not work in the United States; neither did the salad bowl. While we do have a global media system, it is more likely that one global village will not be in our future, especially when there is so much resistance to the West from the Middle East. Beyond culture, wars, religion, terrorism, persecutions, and greed, there is human nature. To heal the terrorist inside and outside ourselves, we must emphasize the better side of our nature to avoid becoming less than human. It is possible that a multiplicity of global villages, each representing its cultural, ethnic, national, and political individuality will evolve, if self- and other-esteem or global-esteem are fostered. Several peace-oriented global villages with equal freedom and rights for men, women, and children would allow each of us to be proudly different in our mutually esteemed villages on Earth.

War Departments exist in most nations. Until Departments of Peace are a reality, nations' politicians and United Nations representatives will be power-oriented; they will not heed, "Let all the nations be gathered together" (*Isaiah* 43:9, *Holy Bible*) to air their grievances and resolve them humanely. Only when men, women, and children have enough to eat, a roof over their heads, some education, and a future can they consider the effects of their actions on the rest of the world. Esteem is the moral road to ending global poverty, economic self-interest, and messianic intolerance. The Golden Rule is a prerequisite for practicing morals and ethics.

Six

Sail forth — steer for the deep waters only...
For we are bound where mariner has not yet dared to go...
Tying the Eastern to the Western sea...
are they not all the seas of God?...
Nature and Man will be disjoin'd and diffused no more...
— Walt Whitman *(Passage to India)*

Moral and Ethical Development

WE LEARN FROM CULTURAL EVOLUTION THAT HUMAN BEINGS evolved from hunter-gatherers to planters. Tens of thousands of related and unrelated people living and working in close proximity, in agricultural communities, necessitated creating a moral and ethical framework to bond people together with a common moral code, stories to interpret the mysteries of life, and a shared view of the common good, if they did not have a God or gods to follow. Without a belief in a God or gods, for a morality and/or a mythology to work for all — including those who deviated from the code — it may have been necessary for human beings to invent a God: "for believers to project morality onto a divinity...something higher than and outside themselves"[1] to provide the enforcers with the additional powers of a divinity, a good force.

Ancient cultures had their gods, goddesses, mystics, and pagans. Paganism ended around 1000 A.D. in Europe. Yet, there are residues of ancient practices that influenced today's religions. Four thousand or more years ago, Judaism evolved with a God, a Bible with the Ten Commandments, and a Torah. Over two thousand years ago, Christianity evolved from Judaism's Old Testament (Bible) with Jesus Christ's birth and the Bible's New Testament. Some three thousand years ago, in India, the Hindu scriptures, Vedas, celebrated a popular god, Indra. China's religions are Confucianism (500s BC), Taoism, and Buddhism, which are also practiced in Japan. The Buddha formulated his techniques, especially for those in India, some twenty-five hundred years ago. Mohammed's schools and teaching (the Koran) were formulated for the

147

Middle East around thirteen hundred years ago. *Islam* means *submission* in Arabic; Mohammed is the final prophet, and followers of Islam are Muslims. Islam inspires intense commitment; it has spread to Africa and America. Those are just a few of the many peoples and many faiths on this planet Earth.

Down through the ages, the conflict continues between the perceptions that there are good and evil forces on Earth and within human beings. Those perceptions have cast historical shadows on whether or not we can save ourselves, America, and the world by becoming better people. St. Augustine, a Christian bishop, viewed human nature negatively. "Humans, he concluded, are not merely fragile or wounded, they are debased, wicked and ruined. Only an act of divine power can save them from utter and eternal destruction."[2] Freud, too, had a pessimistic view of human nature, of human beings' ability "to find real happiness, to behave selflessly, or to use freedom effectively."[3] Freud chose anxiety as the model affect, not love.[4]

A less than idealistic view of human potential is that human beings have both evil and good potentialities. Machiavelli asserted, "A man who wishes to make a profession of goodness in everything must necessarily come to grief among so many who are not good. Therefore it is necessary...to learn how not to be good, and to use this knowledge and not use it, according to the necessity."[5] We are egocentric when we perceive ourselves to be the center of the universe. In actuality, we are part of the overall ecosystem and are not separate from the rest of nature. "Philosophy has totally evaded the problem of man's conduct toward other organisms."[6] So did Rene Descartes' philosophy that animals "have no souls and are mere machines"[7] which he probably learned from the Old Testament of the Bible. In Descartes' view, mind and body were separate, not one entity. To reform our Horatio Alger myth of every man for himself, we could replace it with a new view toward nature, including human nature: cooperation versus exploitation.

A contrasting view of human nature is optimistic. Carl Rogers, a humanistic psychologist, was convinced of the fundamental goodness inherent in human beings, of their power and ability to change for the better, to achieve authenticity and freedom, and to integrate positive values. Rogers' experiences with encounter groups, large workshops, and person-centered therapy throughout the world, informed him that when people are entrusted with the power to make decisions and to be responsible for themselves and to others, remarkable positive results occur. He discovered that when hierarchical authority was abandoned, individuals exhibited enormous capacities for uninhibited learning, creative problem-solving, and self-disciplined efforts. He knew that his political stance was both idealistic and radical, and he believed in the constructive power of human potential.

America's narcissistic culture has been blamed on humanistic psychology for its emphasis upon individualism, a hierarchy of inner and outer needs, and self-fulfillment. Americans who had struggled during the Great Depression in the 1930s and had sacrificed during World War II in the 1940s wanted to have some security and material prosperity, after forging their identities through scarcity and fear while neglecting their emotional needs. Some of their offspring, though, became disillusioned with their parents' neglect of their inner lives and respect for the status quo, order, success, and material things. They opted for personal success through new ways of thinking, knowing, and being — social consciousness and antiwar movements — that led to the focus on the self, the popularity of exotic gurus, hot tubs, and drugs. Their actions also led to changes in our laws: freedom, and equality for Blacks and women. Other offspring opted for professional success based on modern technology and bigness: big government, big business, big school systems, and big media. Their actions also led to changes in our laws that favored big business. The cultural schism continues as power brokers, money lenders, and narcissistic people profit from the powerlessness and ignorance of human beings.

Humanistic psychology, self-esteem, and personal power are perceived as a threat to the power and control of institutions and organizations that rely upon a minimum wage and submissive working class, so the financial barons may continue to maintain themselves in the style of excess to which they have become accustomed in our so-called democratic society. Rather than focus upon the financial excesses of bigness, the corporate scandals, and emotional illiteracy demonstrated in confession boxes and the Oval Office, Joyce Milton[8] in *The Road to Malpsychia* attributed America's social problems to Carl Rogers and humanistic psychology. Simple solutions to complex problems do not heal emotional, spiritual, and financial sickness; nor does it divert blame from the shoulders of those who worship money and things and do whatever it takes to win more money and power, for most problems begin at the top layer of society.

People get stuck in narcissism when they only value themselves in proportion to the amount of money, power and control they have over others. They compensate for their felt lack of esteem by overvaluing money and what money can buy. Their worth is invested outside, not inside themselves. They are in a similar psychological position as emotionally immature people who base their self-worth upon the number of their sexual conquests. Humanistic psychology is a threat to the establishment, for it encompasses a wider view of humankind than the lone self-centered, narcissistic individual. An infant's necessary narcissism leads to survival. With adult caring, the infant learns to care for himself and to shed his narcissism; then he is able to love others. He is then emotionally literate. When we do not learn — *Do unto others as you want done unto you* — we have been damaged by our life experience — we fail humane development — then we are toxic to ourselves and others and are morally and ethically illiterate. When we project our tendencies toward narcissism or evil on our culture or psychology, we do not experience the blow to our narcissism or evil that owning it requires. Humanistic Psychology begins with the individual (the small self) in order to become the kind of person (the large Self) who can live with others in a world where we are all interconnected.

The Cultural Creatives[9] are revealed by Sociologist Paul Ray and Psychologist Sherry Anderson. Their research is based upon 100,000 responses to questionnaires and hundreds of focus groups. They have found what is missing in our society at the beginning of the twenty-first century: a dynamic balance between preserving and sustaining life on planet Earth and tending to human beings' spiritual and psychological malaise. Cultural Creatives number in the millions in America and may be identified by their positive responses to the following three questions:

1. Do you dislike all the emphasis in modern culture on success and 'making it,' on getting and spending, on wealth and luxury goods?
2. Do you care deeply about the destruction of the environment and would pay higher taxes or prices to clean it up and to stop global warming?
3. Are you unhappy with both the left and the right in politics and want to find a new way that does not simply steer a middle course.[10]

With the new millennium, Positive Psychology was introduced by Martin Seligman and Mihaly Csikszentmihalyi "to begin to catalyze a change in the focus of psychology from preoccupation only with repairing the worst things in life to also building positive qualities:"[11]

> At the individual level, it is about positive individual traits: the capacity for love and vocation, courage, interpersonal skills, aesthetic sensibility, perseverance, forgiveness, originality, future-mindedness, spirituality, high talent, and wisdom. At the group level, it is about the civic virtues and the institutions that move individuals toward better citizenship: responsibility, nurturance, altruism, civility, moderation, tolerance, and work ethic.[12]

All human activity can have a self-perspective or a broader one, or a combination of both. We hope that positive psychology, with an emphasis upon positive emotions, will lead to acknowledging and building positive esteem that allows individuals, communities, and societies to flourish with a balance of esteem for money and for people.

The U.S. is science-driven in all aspects of our lives. Dr. Leon R. Kass, who heads Republican President Bush's Council on Bioethics, believes that, "Science has become so dangerous…because it is a powerful force, yet one that has been deliberately stripped of moral values by scientists who are trained to pursue the truth objectively."[13] While he is a stern moralist, and he has many colleagues who are critical of his views and polemical writings, he cautions us about fully understanding the powers we are acquiring: genetic engineering, for example. He invoked Greek mythology to make his point: "Prometheus, the giver of fire, shared a second, less celebrated, gift with humankind, the gift of blind hope, meaning not to despair at knowing one's own fate."[14] From Dr. Kass's moral perspective, biomedicine's technologists' narrow view of human beings will result in remedies that violate human nature. His overall mission is to include soul in science. Soul is not the sole domain of any one religion, truth is subjective, not objective, and the Golden Rule works for all.

Beyond Good or Evil: Legal or Illegal

The moral and ethical dilemma confronting us, today, is not only the conflict between good and evil or right and wrong, but diverse interpretations of our actions as legal and illegal in our adversarial and litigious-oriented society. Overt injustice and covert justice are inevitable in a society when decisions are made between extremes of either guilty or not guilty or good or evil. Moral anger leading to violent acts does not right moral wrongs; nor do moral wrongs eliminate responsibility for one's actions.

Our rights laws, independent of responsibility, allow all — the guilty and the not-guilty — to plead "Not Guilty!" in a court of law after being sworn in "to tell the whole truth and nothing but the truth." Our laws also encourage the irresponsible to blame and to sue others for their own irresponsible actions. *Innocent until proven broke* is not a joking matter. In addition to lawyerly histrionics, many case outcomes perpetuate a pessimistic view of human nature and an immoral attitude toward responsibility, for ourselves and to others, as well as for human rights and wrongs.

Right and Wrong Conduct

Being moral is concerned with right conduct or the distinction between right and wrong and with the principles or rules of right conduct. Ethical pertains to or deals with the morals or the principles of morality, to right and wrong in conduct. The two terms appear to be interchangeable, but the term *moral* is generally used in connection with the specifics of personal conduct. The term *ethics* generally pertains to moral principles, usually in professional, societal, or national contexts.

Different cultures and different religions have different moral and ethical practices, values, and customs, particularly with respect to business dealings and human rights. Some people are presumed to be more valuable and more equal than others, especially in families where males are valued more than females. The results of such attitudes and practices eventually lead some people to bypass their self-affirmation processes — a prerequisite for loving oneself and others — and move directly from powerlessness to resentment, hostility, and aggression with dire effects for themselves and society. Belonging to a sect, cult, or extremist group bypasses self-affirmation in favor of group association and martyrdom.

Morality: From Childhood to Adulthood

Children are taught right and wrong, good and bad, and to please others through punishment and obedience by their caretakers. In school, children are taught through rewards (grades) and punishment. Children are expected, around age twelve or earlier, to obey authorities and to observe the social and moral rules that govern human behavior. Those children, who successfully integrate familial, religious, and societal teachings, may graduate from a self-centered to an other-centered orientation. Responsibility for self and to others involves doing right by others. Traditionally, women have been taught by our society to take care of others; whereas, men are taught to financially provide for others. Sexist approaches to morality are based on both historical and nature and nurture theories; they do not account for individual differences, especially in transitional times with the breakdown of the American family and the legalization of the equality of the sexes. In theory, people are expected to step outside their personal views and to see others' viewpoints and to operate from a universal moral and ethical perspective.

In practice, the Golden Rule, *Do unto others as you would have them do unto you*, is a solid framework for moral and ethical development. That rule presumes that people feel worthy of respectful treatment. Clichés, such as *Honesty is the best policy* or *Crime does not pay*, have been disproved in the U.S. bottom-line, materialistic, litigious society. Unethical practices ensure that those mercantile sins (sloth, individual failure, and poverty) are avoided. People who have positive self- and other-esteem have the wherewithal to expect respectful treatment and to withstand external pressure to do what is right, rather than what is expedient, lucrative, or accepted. Unfortunately, in competitive business and school settings, it takes but one "bad" apple to override the Golden Rule and to contaminate vulnerable people.

From Self-Denial to Self-Fulfillment

During the early part of the 20th century, "Americans believed that self-denial made sense, sacrifice made sense, obeying the rules made sense, subordinating the self to the institution made sense."[15] In the 1960s, the self-denial tradition was replaced by the self-fulfillment era: the freedom to direct our lives according to our own design. "Each American could, by pursuing his private ambitions, satisfy his sense of moral rightness as well as his purse, pride and comfort."[16] The seven deadly sins — pride, covetousness, lust, anger, gluttony, envy, and sloth — were mainstreamed. Replacing self-denial with a duty-to-self ethic reduced self-fulfillment to free-to-be-me self-indulgence. A society of self-denial or repression will be poor in spirit; although, for the whole of society to prosper some desires must be managed. If a society condones whatever people desire to fulfill themselves, a moral society will not survive very long. The duty-to-self ideal "gives moral sanction to desires that do not contribute to either the individual's or the society's well-being."[17]

Since a viable social ethic is one that bonds the individual with society and synchronizes society's goals with individuals' goals, it is necessary that societies respond to changing times. When there is conflict between the two, there will be visible conflicts. "It is when the two are aligned in mutual reinforcement that civilizations glow with vitality. The genius of a great social ethic is neither to suppress desires indiscriminately nor to endorse them indiscriminately."[18]

A needed viable international ethic is one that bonds nations with nations, East with West. To start changing hearts and minds, we cannot change what has been experienced, but we can change the curriculum to include intercultural literacy and attempt to ameliorate the hate for differences in race, gender, or faith that is being taught by default. Political leaders who are ready to look their own nation in the mirror, not just use the mirror to deflect anger onto another nation or group, may be ready to provide ideological alternatives to the politics of power and hate and martyrdom. "People feel good about themselves when they believe what they are doing is good for others as well as for themselves — when they believe it is morally right."[19]

Problems in relationships arise when we are "confirmed only with strings attached" which leads to two types of community: "the community of like-mindedness" and the "community of otherness."[20] Like-minded communities are composed of people who "huddle" together for security. They think they are safe because they have the same ideals, slogans, and language, but it is a false community: they "feel secure because they are so afraid of conflict, of opposites"[21] or of being a nobody. The community of otherness, on the other hand, "is not where people are alike but where they have a common concern"[22] which is articulated through different voices and often in different confronting ways, but they trust the process. As Martin Buber said when he received the peace prize, "the alternative to war is meaningful dialogue, in which you certainly cannot overcome human conflict entirely, but you can meaningfully arbitrate it by confirming the others even in opposing them."[23]

Modeling Morals and Ethics in the Family

Over the past several decades in the U.S., probably as a reaction to Victorian authoritarianism in bringing up children, permissiveness has characterized the majority of parent-child relationships. The positive side of permissiveness has been children's freedom, but the negative sides outweigh the positive: children's decreased responsibility coincides with a structureless family and decreased limits, which are the antithesis of developing positive esteem for self and others.

In children's early years, before the capacity for language develops, most infants sense their mothers as all-powerful, although mothers may not be aware of their power. As children grow and become cognitive, they begin to see that their fathers, or men in general, wield a form of power; so they usually perceive men as all-powerful instead. Mothers who do not have positive self-esteem or do not feel valued for their role as a woman, within or outside the family, and fathers who believe their primary roles are breadwinner and disciplinarian are modeling gender behaviors that interfere with their children becoming whole persons. Children of mothers with negative self-esteem tend to have problems with esteem, too. Parents' attitudes toward their spouses and the opposite sex affect whether or not their children respect their parents or other adults. Children and adults tend to impose their learned right and wrong conduct on others.

When parents and adults do not confuse love with power, and perceive them as essential states of being human, then they do not have to repress their moral power in the mistaken belief that demonstrating love to children means no feedback about their behavior. "But the parent...who tries to continue showing love on the assumption that love is the renunciation of power will be manipulated by the child."[24] And, the child loses respect for his parents as well. Unconditional love requires specific feedback and feedforward about unacceptable behavior. Behavior is akin to a test that reveals what has yet to be learned; it is not the final product (a humanely developed human being) but a work in progress or process.

Why do kids lie? For the same reason adults do: lies are told to avoid punishment, to get what they think they cannot get otherwise, to avoid hurting someone's feelings, or to win the approval and admiration of others.[25] Lying is a crucial family issue; some lying is part of normal development, but children learn to lie at an early age from their parents. Chronic lying is learned and leads to social maladjustment and distrust, which was demonstrated in the story of the boy who cried "Wolf!" so many times that nobody believed him when he was in real trouble.

By age four or five, children know that unkept promises are a form of lying, but they also need to know the difference between forms of lying. The so-called "little white lies" are encouraged by society to avoid hurting someone's feelings or to protect oneself from strangers at the door, on the street, or on the telephone. However, they are also used to manipulate people. Punishment for lying should not be a priority, but more important is learning the difference between lies and truths — knowing that lying has consequences and does more harm than good in the long-run — and practicing alternatives to lying.

Lying is an attempt to misrepresent ourselves; it indicates that we do not accept self or our circumstances *as is*. Thus, we present a fabricated reality rather than an experienced one. Parents and teachers can teach their children and students how to be truthful not by lectures but through everyday experiences of their own honest and trustworthy interactions. Sometimes it is difficult, but important, to let people know we know when they are being dishonest; otherwise we collude in their dishonesty. For example, a regular customer at a diner observed that each time another regular customer paid his

156

bill, he pocketed a chocolate bar from the display. One day, when they were at the cash register together, he said to the thief: "Thank you for showing me what honesty is not!"

Our moral and ethical development process begins at home: as children we learn from what we live, what is taught, observed, and heard, and from how we are treated. This is expanded upon in churches and schools, on the street, at other institutions and organizations, through relationships, and from exposure to the media, especially television. Experts propose that a child's sense of morality begins after age five and that there are learned, hierarchical differences between males and females. Carol Gilligan's research led her to assert that men's moral development depends upon a "rights morality." Men relied upon abstract laws and universal principles to impersonally, impartially, and fairly resolve disputes and conflicts, or to administer "blind justice." Women, on the other hand, usually rejected blind justice and impartiality; they operated within a "morality of responsibility and care."[26] From a 1992 survey of 126,000 teenagers, ages 13-18, the younger teenagers were found to have stronger values than the older ones, indicating peer pressure is a problem if a keen sense of self is missing.

The ongoing controversy of whether or not religion and values have a place in public education has led to two extremes: moral absolutism and moral abdication. When families fail to inculcate core values, the schools are society's last opportunity to teach and model what's right and what's wrong.

Stories, Fairy Tales, and Reality Models

Morals, ethics, and values are taught through children's stories and fairy tales. Fairy tales of Russian czarist times rarely promised rewards for hard work; instead, they emphasized tricksters who got what they wanted without working. Since the 1920s, Russian tales emphasize discipline and hard work; however, everyday Soviet life contradicted the morality tales. When everyone is promised a job, but there are no promotions or raises and there are few goods to buy with the money earned, why work? Living by one's wits, in such situations, becomes the criterion by which to exist. People also become addicted to hedonism, substances, or other excesses when the creative impulse or the authentic self is stifled or thwarted.

157

A parallel exists between the Soviet experience and the changes that have occurred in our U.S. high technology society where illiteracy and high school dropouts have escalated since World War II. The incentive to work is also eroded when the excessive salaries and "perks" for corporate chief executive officers and upper management lead to the public's perception that they run the company not to be competitive in the global market but solely for their own benefit, and not for its customers or employees either. Government's frame of reference for justifying its high salaries and perquisites (perks) is the corporate world model. Neither is doing a good job of serving America or Americans. Both are in need of a major overhaul.

American businesses have been concerned with the bottom-line, primarily, but some of its top managers and leaders wish to be remembered for ethics, for having never cheated anyone. There is a built-in conflict in being a CEO of a bottom-line-oriented corporation and in wanting to be perceived or remembered as ethical or as honest. Biographies by top businessmen, from Jack Welch (General Electric) and Bill Gates (Microsoft) to Harold Geneen (ITT) are examples of men with yen. Gates is sharing his wealth with humanity through his foundations and in person.

American businesses are also in trouble due to management's short-term focus on dollars: more for themselves and less for everyone else. Emphasis upon competition as the American way of life, work, and play has led to mistrust, suspicion, and scorn; hence, cooperation is driven out. Psychologist Erik Erikson gave the competitive process a name: *pseudospeciation*, which was defined as "A group driven to dominate its rival as though it were a different species, less than human, therefore not deserving normal human consideration."[27] A power hungry boss driven to dominate his employees also treats them as though they were a different species, therefore, less than human and subject to inhuman treatment. A form of pseudospeciation is operative when the transnational extremist terrorists wish to exterminate America and Americans. It is also operative when one culture, race, or gender believes it is more equal than others.

158

The Protestant Reformation and Capitalism

The Protestant Reformation in the 16th century paved the ground for capitalism. "With its stress on the mercantile virtues of industry, individual attainment, and wealth — and conversely on the mercantile sins of sloth, individual failure, and poverty,"[28] extravagant greed has emerged throughout history. "The single greatest engine in the destruction of the Protestant [work] ethic was the invention of the installment plan, or instant credit...with credit cards one could indulge in instant gratification."[29] From the Bible, we learned that the moneylenders were thrown out of the temples for lending money for a steep price, known as usury. Shakespeare's *The Merchant of Venice* is a dramatization of unethical, disrespectful relationships between borrowers and lenders in earlier centuries. For today's haves versus the have-nots, the producers versus consumers, the homeless versus the homed, and we versus they, whether the issue is about money, oil, values, religion, or lifestyle, there is room for an ethic of commitment to the business of mutual survival.

Since World War II, the business world has become the new authority over moral and civil authorities, such as family, church, and social organizations, in our culture. The decisions of corporate officers and managers, and the values that drive their decisions, determine where we drift as a society. Since the 1950s, television has been transmitting Corporate America's values to us. In the 1990s, many young men and women lawyers were dismissed for alleged lack of merit when, in fact, less prosperous times were the cause. Those law firms chose to malign those they fired rather than acknowledge their internal economic problems. They chose to be unethical rather than ethical in the firing process.[30] In the aftermath of the September 11, 2001 terrorist attacks, one hundred thousand people have lost their jobs, and the naysayers have created a psychological climate that is fear-based so that officers of brokerage firms, airlines, and other companies that were in trouble due to poor management and top management excesses before the terrorist attack have found an "out" to downsize, cut their losses, and ensure their golden parachutes. As in the past with the savings and loan debacle, the U.S. Government is bailing out corporations or giving them long-term tax rebates without requiring its top managers and CEOs to cut their exorbitant salaries.

Violence: Our Inheritance

The birth of our nation, under God with liberty and justice for all, was the collective response of individuals to economic, religious, and royalty's persecution, according to our history books. Yet, our forefathers' devotion to human rights and freedom may be considered self-serving when men became the beneficiaries of their political foresight, not women, children, minorities, and Native Americans, and not our history books. Columbus' 1492 invasion of the Americas was the beginning of violence against Native Americans. The Indians of the Caribbean were destroyed within two generations by the Spanish.

Our nation's first citizens' systematic violence toward America's Native Indians, their condoning the importing and dehumanizing of nonwhite slaves from Africa, their presumption that women were not the mental equals of men, and their allowing the labeling of women as witches and burning them at the stake in Salem, Massachusetts, were not Christian acts. That violence was a re-enactment of religions' historical record through the Crusades and the Inquisition. "So successful was the Church's proof of 'moral' right by might that until the Renaissance, over a thousand years later, any artistic expression or pursuit of empirical knowledge that was not 'blessed' by the Church was practically nonexistent in Europe...so thoroughly was the systematic destruction of all extant knowledge, including the mass burning of books, that it even spread outside of Europe, to wherever Christian authority could reach."[31] During that time, millions of enlightened women — midwives, herbalists, anyone who had perceived power — were burned as witches. The witches' cats were also considered witches and destroyed. The rats multiplied and the bubonic plague raged and decimated millions of people. The ensuing Dark Ages engulfed the European continent and the world.

Pseudospeciation is invoked to denigrate human beings and entire cultures to the point that one culture does not regard the members of another culture as really and truly human. Pseudospecific names identify an enemy as dog, swine, tiger, snake, or cattle. Derogatory or invented names for different races and nations and a host of other negative labels are intended to demean human beings and to rob perceived enemies of their human rights, making it fair game to kill, destroy, or, at the least, assassinate their character. Women, too, are similarly dispensed with when they are characterized as bimbos, sluts, whores, "the little woman," or "the wife" and depersonalized when their given names are avoided. Some negative value issues and trauma are embedded in psyches from generation-to-generation.

The cultural war about values goes on and on. The value issues in the U.S. used to be slavery, temperance (alcohol), religion, race, prostitution, and illegitimacy. While there are vestiges of those values present today, the issues are single-parent families, illiteracy, physical and white-collar crime, and the media's obsession with sex and violence. Violence in our society today is celebrated, romanticized, and eroticized in the movies and on television. "In 1996, handguns were used to murder 22 people in New Zealand, 15 in Japan, 30 in Great Britain, 106 in Canada, 213 in Germany, and 9,390 in the United States."[32] Some school children express their anger and resolve their conflict with other students with weapons, not words. They are emotionally illiterate.

Emotional Morality

The sexual double standard, a different one for men than for women, is alive and flourishing in the U.S. A NYC Protestant minister asked his congregation to forgive the five young men who, in 1989, allegedly beat and raped a woman jogger in Central Park; they were later convicted. His rationale was that the young men were no different from the story of the woman [in the New Testament] caught in adultery: Jesus forgave her and told her to go and sin no more.[33] Through preaching, the minister sought to make the rape and violence less severe by equating it with a Biblical sexual act between two consenting human beings. Fourteen years later, NY prosecutors reversed their convictions despite the unsupported but graphic confessions of the young men's "wilding" in Central Park and eight other victims. There is doubt that Matias Reyes, who recently confessed to the assault on the Central Park jogger, acted alone. He was convicted in 1989 of raping another woman. With a reversal of their conviction and immunity from other crimes, emotional preaching, emotional confessions, and emotional convictions are colluding in a miscarriage of justice for both violent young men and their female victims. When plea bargains, attempts to be a witness instead of a defendant (by implicating others), and constructed confessions are standard procedures for lawyers and the courts, morals and ethics are not practiced and "the neglected emotions submerge the life of reason." Emotional illiteracy undermines morality in people and in Western intellectual institutions.

Celibacy is a requirement of some religions. Celibacy does not cause aberrant sexuality. The development of paraphilia (perversion) may be traced to pre- and post-natal factors, family conditions, and other social and cultural factors. Celibacy-havens and anti-women policies and practices do attract those who abuse their status and power by acting out their sexuality problems against innocent children or by abusing women. Stories of the sexual abuse of children by Roman Catholic priests, Boy Scout leaders, foster parents, incestuous parents, and other adults have led many concerned people and teachers not to hug or touch children for fear of being accused of or sued for being molesters or abusers. While there is heightened awareness of the sexual abuse of children, those children who are most vulnerable to sexual abuse are those who have had the least amount of affection in their lives. Emotional literacy is also a deterrent to abuse and moral depravity.

The family, culture, and religious institutions used to be the inculcators of moral behavior in the young. Their methods, based primarily on guilt, were to control human beings. Salvation from sin and hell was supposed to be achieved by adhering to religious principles and commandments. The fear of God was usually instilled rather than the love of God and the love of self, despite the Biblical commandment: "Love Thy Neighbor as Thyself." A sense of shame, unworthiness, fear, and loss of pride — a loss of self-esteem — resulted from any transgressions. Too many people, especially women, practice "Love Thy Neighbor Instead of Thyself." Human beings' self-esteeming process would benefit from universal commandments that close the gap between the diverse cultures and religions.

Religion divides us; spirituality unites us. "The preacher's fire-and-brimstone warning that death will bring a dire judgment for moral wrongs is a masterful psychological ploy."[34] When people are confronted with the thought of their own death, it tends to evoke their moral and judgmental principles. People who are more open-minded judge others less harshly and are more accepting of differences than are those people who are more authoritarian and dogmatic. Interestingly, all religions and cultures emphasize what people *should* do on Earth in order to be protected from a tragic fate (hell) or to gain immortality; thus, death is a central issue in religious and psychological life. People's anxiety about death intensifies allegiance to moral beliefs; however, a number of people are afraid to live and afraid to die, and "Everybody wants to go to heaven, but nobody wants to die!" Except *transnational* terrorists!

"Native peoples [American and Canadian Indians] teach that the ultimate norm for morality is the impact choices have on people living seven generations from now. If the results appear good for them, then the choices are moral ones. If not, they are immoral."[35] That is self- and other-esteem!

The Valuing Process

In the beginning, we value ourselves according to the value placed upon us by others. As we grow and develop, we value and judge ourselves according to how much or how little we are in control of our life and work. If we have little control over our lives, then we may have a problem with positively esteeming ourselves. And we may value others too much. Values and beliefs are analogous to a building's unseen beams that hold up an entire structure. A value is something we prize and cherish; however, many of our values have been inherited from our family, peers, and culture at a time when we were dependent human beings with underdeveloped self-esteem. People value themselves according to the number of situations in which they are in control;[36] therefore, most people have a problem with their self-image because most of us are in charge of so little.

Values are largely embedded in the unconscious, and they are what we move toward or away from. Our values reflect our true outcomes. Conflicting values are the source of life's deepest frustrations when we attempt to satisfy conflicting needs, such as assertiveness and passivity. When we have positive self-esteem, we are able to satisfy polarized needs more appropriately. When our behavior matches our values, we probably experience ourselves as happy, content, fulfilled. Successful people have clear and specific values. The people who impact our culture appear to have values that match those of the majority of our culture's members. However, when we have feelings of dissatisfaction, guilt, distrust, or anger, our values probably are being violated by ourselves and/or by others.

163

When we find out we are not satisfying our highest values, we can take action based upon our responses to the following questions: "What is the one thing that I cannot live without?" "What is the one thing I will do anything to get?" "What is the one thing I will do anything to avoid?" "What is the most important thing to me in my career?" "What am I willing to give up to get what I want?" After answering those questions, the next question is, "How do I know when I'm getting what I say I want?" Once we have articulated our values and reality-checked them, we will find that we have a hierarchy of values at any one time. That is, one value may be prized and cherished over another. Then we can prioritize. What's more important? "A career that is only financially rewarding?" Or, "A career that makes me feel good about myself and is financially adequate?"

Beliefs

Entrenched beliefs, attitudes, and habits get in the way of change and positive action. A belief is our opinion, conviction, confidence, or faith in the truth of the existence of something not immediately susceptible to rigorous disproof. Attitudes are habits of thought formed by our perception and interpretation of life events, other people, and cultures, or the world. For example, our most important beliefs are:

> Belief in self: positive self-esteem;
> Belief in people; a sincere interest in people;
> Belief in and enthusiasm for our services or products;
> A spiritual belief (not necessarily religious).[37]

Habits are difficult to overcome and are best erased by instilling new ones as a substitute. Habits, though, have a way of revealing our emotions and feelings about others and ourselves. "The Broken Window" theory became popular in the 1990s when one tolerated broken window led to other broken windows, the breakdown of community discipline, and to neighborhood decay. That theory equally applies to developing human beings if their caretakers, teachers, or other adults do not model and practice behavior that promotes respect for self and others. When we do not pay attention to neglect, or ignore the little offenses, or require people to be responsible for their actions — from littering the streets and highways to blaming others for their problems, stealing from or harming others — we help create the monsters in our society. Repairing broken windows, picking up litter, jailing offenders, and failing students treat symptoms of human problems. Healing broken communities and broken human lives and spirits fix real human problems.

Moral Tasks

Our intellectual, left-brained culture does not help us make moral judgments since morals and ethics have values underlying them. Morals and ethics are exercised by the right-brain. As our old societal values collapse, they are not being practiced or taught, but new ones are not being inculcated, except by the media's preoccupation with sex and violence. If we do not value something then it is more difficult to get involved, from personal and social responsibility to keeping our own nests and the environment clean.

Children's moral development often runs behind their physical development. The litter in the hallways of her school aesthetically offended a master's student, an elementary school teacher. She began to pick it up and take it to her classroom's wastebasket. She asked her students to do the same on their way to class, and she praised those who participated. Her plan seemed to be working until the custodians complained to her that her students were taking the litter from their bins and bringing it to her class. The students' short-term goals of gaining the teacher's approval as effortlessly as possible did not discriminate between right and wrong and are examples of doing whatever it takes to win approval, status, or lucrative jobs. The teacher used her students' behavior as a teachable moment in the classroom.

The highest moral and ethical task for human beings is self-development so that the fully developed self adds up to more than the sum of body, mind, emotions, and spirit. The task begins with self-development but does not end there; it must be made visible through action, behavior, performance, and modeled as a standard for others.

Self-Actualization versus Me-ism

Human beings' lower order needs for food, shelter, and economic security take precedence over and must be met before we may seek higher order needs: self-actualization. A "starving artist" painting in an attic may be more attuned to self-actualization than professionals who have bought the psychology of affluence and can afford to "buy" self-actualization.

Abraham Maslow anticipated the "Me generation" when he discussed those who seek peak experiences as ends in themselves. He saw the danger of turning inward and away from the world in the search for peak experiences.[38] Self-absorbed people who seek their own personal salvation, often at the expense of others' well-being, run the risk of not only becoming selfish but evil as well.

Moral Sense

Psychopaths lack a conscience; they have no guilt, shame, love for others, and no inhibitions or control. Morally self-righteous people, bigots, and zealots have little love for other people either, except for like-minded associates. On the other hand, many moral and ethical people are so moral and ethical toward others that they are fair game for those who perceive them as "easy marks." Women, particularly, fit this stereotypical role. Highly moral and ethical men and women do not do as well in the fast lane or on the fast track of the workplace as less moral and ethical people. Highly immoral and unethical men and women embrace raw ego, envy, avarice, and ambition as they trade their souls for today's definition of success: money, status, power over other human beings, and materialism. Most human beings, though, have a moral sense; it is activated in times of stress, crises, or challenge.

When we hear or read about an injustice, we feel enraged and that means our moral sense is operating. People inside large organizations become morally frustrated because they do not have the freedom to act morally; people outside the organization are equally frustrated. Smaller organizations with fewer people may respond with moral intelligence. Moral understanding results from self-consciousness: the emotional brain is concerned with morality. Self-consciousness is awareness of one's distinctiveness apart from all others and an awareness of the power of choice.

166

Moral theory, a concern with why we think right is right and wrong is wrong, is indistinguishable from ethical theory. The simplest ethical theory is the Buddhist and Hindu teachings of the Law of Karma: the total accountability of every person on Earth for what he does, at every level of his being. From that perspective, a human being's present is the product of his thoughts and actions in the past, and his future is the result of what he thinks, feels, and does in the present.

Whose Life Is It Anyway?

Whose Life Is It Anyway? was a Broadway play and movie about a paraplegic, the result of an accident. His mind was intact, but he knew that too would deteriorate with time. His well-meaning doctor insisted on his taking Valium to ease mental distress, but he resisted with, "It will do more for you than it will for me." He wanted to be in charge of the only things he had in life: his mind and his death.

Death is a natural part of life, but it is also unpredictable; therefore, many of us do not or cannot prepare for it. However, if we wish to die well, we must learn how to live well and not be afraid of living or dying. When asked by a parishioner about the distinction between religion and spirituality, a priest responded, in effect, that religion is for people who have a fear of dying and going to Hell; whereas, spirituality is for those who have already been there on Earth and have learned that the only fear is of fear itself. In Chapter VIII, we illuminate the evolving force of human conduct — spirituality — which leads to an active sense of concern for all beyond the personal context of self, religion, morals, ethics, and values and to creative aging.

The technology that gives life to sick and premature babies, comatose accident victims, and the dying becomes their captor. Laws protecting life do not discriminate between the quality of life and the quantity of life, thereby prolonging people's hope or their misery. As the U.S. aging population rises, perhaps we will find more humane and dignified ways of dying. The right to die is becoming synonymous with human rights and freedom. However, it appears to be a moral, legal, philosophical, and sociopolitical issue that, so far, has no absolute answers and many moral and ethical questions that involve others human beings' good and evil intentions.

Life, though, is for the living and is to be lived. In the next chapter (VII), we present our case for integrating our personal and professional lives since each influences the other. It is in the personal and professional domain that we play out who we are and what we have experienced, learned (consciously and unconsciously), and not learned. The visible curricula do not cover the learnings, motivation, and perseverance necessary to be a successful human being in life and at work. Too visible are the people who are financially successful at the expense of those whose lives they touch at all levels. Mastering the invisible curriculum makes all the difference in how we esteem others and ourselves and in how we demonstrate our uniqueness and humanity in our personal and professional lives.

Seven

Personal and Professional Development

THE ONGOING STRUGGLE FOR THE MINDS OF HUMAN BEINGS, for what kind of minds they shall have, began centuries ago. Someone realized that human beings' attitudes and behavior are not determined entirely by instinct but by what they have felt and learned, primarily through experience. There are people in the world who want human minds to be directed by and subservient to the voice of authority. Totalitarian regimes are dangerous. Totalitarian people are under the influence of fundamentalists and dictators who are armed with dogma or with the scientific knowledge and technical skills for exploiting the Earth's and human beings' resources. They satisfy selfish goals without regard for the common good. They turn against, hurt, or humiliate those who are perceived to be different; they have distorted or myopic views of the world. There are others in society and the world who want human beings' minds to be curious, logical, questioning, creative and their life goals to be determined by themselves and by group processes in which all have a voice: the stated goals of a democratic society. Thus, human minds and behavior "can be controlled from without; or human minds can participate in shaping their own behavior and destiny"[1] if they have the capacity and the motivation to do so. A favorable environment is helpful but not necessary for becoming all we can be.

Among the first to investigate the effects of different kinds of leadership upon individuals' minds and actions were Kurt Lewin[2] and Ron Lippitt.[3] Their comparison of autocratic, laissez-faire, and democratic styles of leadership led to their concluding that the motivations, decisions, actions, behavior, and goals of groups under democratic leadership surpassed those under autocratic and laissez-faire leadership. The Lewin and Lippitt

169

experiments demonstrated how outcomes are determined by human minds' experiences. The implications are that children raised in families, schools, and societies adhering to autocratic, laissez-faire, or democratic principles will become the kinds of people they learned to be through their lived experiences.

Our family and school systems give lip service to being democratic in our society. The reality is, most parents parent as they were parented and most teachers teach as they were taught, despite the large body of scientific knowledge about human growth, learning, emotions, and behavior. Learner-centered education is rare at the junior and high-school levels, resulting in bored, unmotivated students who have fewer opportunities for decision making than elementary students.[4] If students do not experience learning to take the initiative in extracurricular activities, when they enter the workforce (from high school or college), they will find their education did not prepare them for the invisible curriculum, which they must master to successfully navigate their personal and work lives.

The Personal-Professional Relationship

Personal development and professional development are interdependent: each impacts the other. Personal and work lives used to be expected to be separate; however, how we live our lives, how we relate to ourselves and others, and how we work, study, and play are all interrelated. Personal ideology influences the quality of our carrying out those hows. Adults' favorite questions are "What do you do?" and "What do you want to be [do!] when you grow up?" We expend energy, time, and money on learning a trade, responding to a "calling," studying for a profession, or getting a job to make money, with or without career goals. Work patterns and organizations are changing: more people are becoming self-employed, organizations are more brain- than muscle-oriented, and America has become a producer of information and service-oriented, not a top producer of goods. Most jobs require 25 percent task-skills and 75 percent people-skills. This chapter is about the 75 percent! Therefore, how to get along with ourselves and others and how to utilize people and their ideas for the good of all make the difference between success and failure as human beings. There is little correlation between positive esteem and success in Corporate America, for narcissistic or negative esteem people are willing to do whatever it takes to become financially successful. Some get caught. Many do not.

Professional development is a priority for most of us. Personal development — from emotional literacy to knowing how we think, learn, and relate, and about the verbal and nonverbal communication styles of diverse cultures — is not included in the Western intellectual tradition curricula. Nevertheless, the integration of both personal and professional development is required to optimize performance and fulfillment. What we achieve professionally, through our own efforts or through managing others, will rarely be enough or satisfying until positive self-esteem is attained. Knowledge is power in the professional world. Self-knowledge is power in both worlds since a combination of personal and professional or system power supports a positive state of being for consistent action and successful outcomes.

Healthy organizations require responsible people with self- and other-esteem; otherwise they become places where people are unwilling to be vulnerable by speaking honestly. Unhealthy behaviors cost billions. Unhealthy organizations are run to feed raw egos; they use others' resources and abuse people for their own narcissistic purposes. Businesses with poor communications, poor morale, and poor decision-making skills — because they do not seek on-the-job data from their bottom workers — are not humane places to work. They are usually divided within adversarial camps, not unlike the diverse intelligence agencies of the U.S. Government that did not share, consolidate knowledge, take precautions, or protect us from terrorists' attacks. Adversarial departments within companies or governments occur in stifling cultures, when managers or supervisors do not have positive self-esteem and cannot share power and control, or when employees are fearful or narcissistic or are not team players. In a dog-eat-dog world, everyone and everything suffers. Even "the good guys" finish last! With corporate and government cleanups in the offing, the good guys may have the last word about what wants to happen or change to make it more difficult for terrorists to prevail.

Personal and Professional Behavior

The 9/11 transnational terrorists chose the World Trade Center and the Pentagon as their targets: the icons of our financial and military infrastructure.

A coincidence? Hardly! America's financial and military influence is experienced around the world. As a nation and as a people, we are disliked, resented, and, yes, hated for our competitiveness, arrogance, achievements, and entrepreneurship. Our adversaries and some allies do not want their cultures contaminated by ours.

At home and abroad, Corporate America and politicians have financial relationships for their mutual and exclusive benefit. Corporate elites have successfully lobbied for laws that benefit their companies, themselves, the rich, famous, and infamous, not the environment or the country as a whole. Thus, the number of middle-class people is decreasing and the number of lower class people is increasing as vast fortunes are justified at the top as the rewards for achievement. America rewards individual ability and achievement out of proportion to individual effort and hard work. In addition, when achievement and CEOs' salaries are based on false financial statements (which also inflate the value of a corporation's stock) and when their salaries are not tied to actual profits, then stocks have to keep going up and up to keep overpriced and unprofitable corporations looking like they are legitimate and successful. Our democracy and the majority of American workers and investors were paying for corporate excesses (revealed at the end of the dot-com boom) long before the World Trade Center's Twin Towers came tumbling down. Now we know why we are under siege on all fronts. As Walt Kelly's line in *Pogo* reads, "We have met the enemy, and he is us."

America's past industrial robber barons have been replaced by today's financial robber barons. Since the 1970s, top business managers in Corporate America, under the guise of increasing shareholder value, have subverted the existing system. Paradigm shifts occurred. The first: CEOs and top managers have had their compensation indexed from company profits to the value of its stock and to being awarded stock options (not considered a compensation expense); therefore, some corporate priorities drive up the stock's price, cut corners, and manage financial statements, making the company look good on paper and enriching those cashing in options. The stock market is easily manipulated; corporate profits are not as manipulatable; they leave paper trails.

The second paradigm shift: After joining a firm, CEOs have undue influence over the nomination of new Board members who will solidify their position, rather than function as independents, which was the original intent of having Boards of Directors. Now, CEOs bring in not only their underlings, their yes-men and yes-women, but also their overseers or directors who approve CEO compensation, stock options, policies, and practices. Many Boards appear to be rubberstamps, as evidenced by companies who have been "managing their earnings:" Enron, WorldCom, Global Crossing, Adelphia, Tyco International, and others. Of course, all top executives of Corporate America are not corrupt, but each takes care of Number One. Our elected politicians count on Corporate America's contributions to keep them in power, so they, too, help create the paper lions.

The third paradigm shift: By using both the consultation and auditing services offered by one firm, top managers engaged in questionable ways of doing business. For huge fees, many auditors and consultants followed sanctioned accounting principles to create fraudulent accounting and management practices to produce inflated and misleading financial statements. Financial statements are the basis for stock analysts to evaluate and make buy or sell stock recommendations to investors; only a few analysts questioned high stock prices and low profits. The overhaul of corporate accounting and management practices will be necessary before investors regain confidence in the analysts and in the stock market.

Since the early 1980s, America's top ten CEOs' earnings have risen by 4,300 percent![5] The values of the companies they manage have not fared as well. Of those top ten CEOs, one has been indicted for fraud and at least three others are under investigation. Those ten are just the tip of the iceberg as individual ability, access, achievement, and dishonesty mean upward mobility while individual effort, hard work, and honesty mean downward mobility. One of the debacles, Enron, is symptomatic of white-collar fraud of epic proportions (billions!). By buying influence, via subsidizing Democrats and Republicans to have laws amended for their own benefit, the Enron old-boy network also used numerous fraudulent, offshore "subsidiary" or private companies to avoid paying U.S. taxes. They also "paid for jobs" in India. Enron employees and stockholders are victims of Enron's top officials, directors, and their culpable Board members who out-Ponzied the old Ponzi scheme: they bought energy companies, fabricated financial statements, and hid debts and losses to keep the price of Enron's stock high and the bubble afloat.

Bubbles burst! Disenchanted American workers and ordinary stockholders have legitimate axes to grind against Enron, similar corrupt corporations, accounting-consulting firms, and politicians who sell America's business soul and our future. Americans lost their jobs, life savings, investments, and pensions, but they will not become terrorists because that is an anathema to the average American. However, those top executives, auditors, consultants, and other power-mongers who get rich by making a farce out of our democratic systems and industries are the real terrorists. They are domestic terrorists: adversaries of the American people and of our country.

For years, American companies have shifted their manufacturing plants to foreign countries to take advantage of cheap labor. The fourth paradigm shift in the existing system is American companies that move their headquarters to foreign shores, to Bermuda for example, to pay less taxes and, ostensibly, to increase shareholder value. Shareholders in foreign-based companies generally have fewer rights than in those based in America. We vote for Washington politicians, congressmen and senators, but we are saddled with their baggage, namely, teams of industry lobbyists, lawyers, and accountants whose campaign dollars fight against regulations that benefit the public and fight for deregulations that benefit insiders. Laissez-faire economics does not work in a democracy when some people make themselves more equal than others by buying favors. In addition, the corporate elites take their cut before driving the company out of business or into bankruptcy. Others just move to foreign shores, which are out of reach of America's laws. Influence peddling, insider trading, and self-interest or narcissism have at least one of the seven deadly sins (pride, anger, envy, greed, gluttony, lust, sloth) in common: Greed!

The four paradigm shifts that have changed the way corporations are allowed to do business in this country are destroying our democracy to the point that America could become another second- or third-world country. Third-world countries are burdened with too many haves who "milk" their countries' assets, too many have-nots, and not enough productive people or exports to sustain a balance of trade with other countries. The middle-class in America sustains our economy and generates the bulk of the taxes for the IRS to pay for the country's upkeep. We are experiencing the dire consequences of the concentration of wealth and of negative-esteem people at the top of our corporations. There will be further dire consequences and a higher concentration of wealth at the top because of the Republicans' income and estate tax breaks for the ultra rich. Why are we not outraged? Are we so focused on security, Iraq, North Korea, the transnational terrorists, and the few American citizens who joined Al Qaeda that we are avoiding the domestic terrorists who are selling our birthrights? Rome burned while Nero fiddled. King Louis XVI wrote "Nothing!" in his diary on July 14, 1789, the day the French Revolution began. Evolution is more our style, but more voices must be heard for our dissent to be acknowledged. Fear of being labeled a "traitor" is a deterrent.

Healing The Terrorist Within not only applies to the intimate terrorist but to the diverse domestic terrorists within our country and to those transnational terrorists whose goal is to destroy our country. Healing begins with esteem, respect, regard for self and others that is based on the inner qualities of being human — integrity, honesty, equality, love of humanity — and not on the outer trappings of material things, status, power, and money. While our highly overpaid movie and rock stars, athletes, and their promoters may not be terrorists, many of them are narcissists, and their obscene salaries are making a farce out of our democratic and economic systems. One percent of Americans holds forty-eight percent of the wealth, and twenty percent of U.S. children live below the poverty level. Corporate America treats its U.S. workers as badly as it treats the environment: as expendable resources. How do foreigners perceive Corporate America? The tumbling Twin Towers could be a metaphor for what the transnational terrorists want to have happen to America and for what needs to happen to our inhumane institutions and organizations. Are we willing to take "a fall" for America's corporate elite terrorists? Is there another Franklin Delano Roosevelt — who revitalized the American Dream and reaffirmed our Four Freedoms (freedom from fear and want and freedom of speech and religion) by rescuing us from the Great Depression of 1929 — waiting in the wings to breathe new life into our republic and to rid us of the financial robber barons?

Ideology

What we think is as important as how we think. Attitudes, beliefs, values, theories, concepts, doctrine, dogma, ideals, political, religious, and economic philosophies may be called our ideology. Personal ideologies combined with schemas affect how we think, feel, learn, relate, work, and behave, and they influence our esteem for self and others. In a multicultural society, we are more likely to live and work with those whose ideologies differ from ours. Even within monocultural societies, different ideologies exist, particularly political, religious, economic, and moral and ethical ones, but they are not tolerated as well as in America.

When we find it impossible to accept or tolerate others' ideologies, we may find ourselves in a fundamentalist position: I am right, and you are wrong; God is on my side: a Zero-Sum perspective. Inflexible and intolerant ideologies undermine our ability to make room for differences, to work productively, or to get along or live with others. If we are interested in understanding or accepting ideologies different from our own, we must examine our own conscious ideology and then uncover our unconscious one. We can begin by asking ourselves, "Who am I?" and "Who am I not?" within the context of our family of origin. The responses to "Who am I not?" may surface our disowned ideology that we attribute to another.

Our family of origin is the place to begin to find the interface between our personal and professional lives. Our work family is a place to learn to coexist with differences in an objective way when the work/company is our common focus. It is not a fundamentalist position when we are confronted with personal ideologies that are immoral, such as a Hitler or a terrorist of any nationality, including white-collar criminals. Motives become distorted in morally and spiritually bankrupt people. Ethics, for example, rarely or no longer play a role in business decisions: primarily, competitive pressures are evidenced. Our culture's emphasis is upon "more:" money, possessions, power and control. There is little encouragement to stop, think, reflect, and ask the question, "Is *more* masking a deeper need?" *More*, in the form of food, drink, drugs, power, status, or money, does not fill or replace a felt emptiness that gnaws at our being. People who confuse wants with needs have an esteem problem. How many wake-up calls do we need before we make accountability and responsibility part of the curriculum, life, and work by making it harder to bankroll anti-democratic ideologies?

From Family Role to Work Role

We are all products of a "family orientation," and we have imprints from those early years. Each of us experienced how it felt to have, or not have, a father, mother, sister, brother, grandparents, aunts, uncles, cousins, and extended family members. We learned to love or hate them, cope or fight with them. We may have been the Good Child who obeyed parents and teachers, the Bad Child who resisted authority, the Responsible Child who took care of others, the Chameleon who did whatever was necessary to maintain family order, or the Mediator who tried to settle family quarrels to achieve peace.[6] Our role in our family influences our role at work to a great extent. "If we do not work out our relationships with significant people in our lives...then these relationships have a way of being played out at work"[7] for the people at work become the family members with whom to settle old scores or continue old connections. Dysfunctional and nonstructured families may result in individuals' insatiable compulsion to be fulfilled through status, power, and material things to compensate for missing human development basics: unconditional regard. We may use our jobs to mask ego deficits by demanding or commanding high salaries and expense accounts. It is useful to identify the roles played by self and others since "many of us work as children under the direction of children."[8]

Some people are drawn to particular professions that match their own known and unknown ego deficits. When social or childcare workers apply their whole selves (intellectually, physically, emotionally, and spiritually) to the work environment, they may become conscious of their own recurring behavior patterns played out while working with others' problems.[9] Insight and change are not synonymous, but when we separate out our problems from another's, we begin to behave differently which, in turn, allows others to respond differently. The public arena, especially on-the-job, enables us to see ourselves more clearly and to complete unfinished or unresolved human development processes. As adults, then, we are able to change our childhood roles to better serve ourselves. We can create entirely new different patterns of behavior.

The conventional idea of what work is about may be rethought in terms of work as a form of self-exploration and redevelopment. We work best at jobs that match our thinking and learning styles[10] and values, but many of us select jobs for the money, status, or power. For women, minorities, and immigrants, their jobs used to be the ones that were disvalued by society's norms. However, when we perceive work, even in traditional systems, as an opportunity to apply our emotional and intellectual capacities, we may also complete any gaps in our own human development. Then work may become a productive means to participate, share, collaborate, and communicate with others instead of a four-letter word with money, power, and status as the main reward.

All institutions and organizations are peopled with imperfect human beings, and the task is to make imperfections workable and to take into consideration the differences that make each one of us unique. It has been demonstrated that "No institution can possibly survive if it needs geniuses or supermen to manage it. It must be organized in such a way as to be able to get along under a leadership composed of average human beings...an institution is like a tune, it is not constituted by individual sounds but by the relations between them."[11] Corporations do not survive and thrive in the hands of narcissists, whose behaviors and attitudes trickle down to employees.

Public Schools

Our culture used to consider the term *average* to be good enough or a normal goal for human beings. Today average is a sign of failure. Nevertheless, average human beings are becoming a rarity: many young people are not getting educated the first time around in the public schools. At a basic level, the skills for successful work and successful living are the same. Despite the intimate link between life and work, our educational systems have not been paying attention to our overall development. Absorbing information to pass tests and get into college is emphasized, not on learning how to live and work in a world where political, social, economic, gender, racial, ethnic, religious, and environmental problems are now center stage.

Traditional educational systems, from daycare centers and public K-12 schools to colleges and universities, are traditional places for children to learn, from around age three on. Many public schools are not producing well-rounded people who are ready and able to attend college without remediation, enter the workforce, or navigate our multicultural society. The problem is systemic: public education is controlled from the top-down and by public dollars; schools are inundated with rigid rules, regulations, and policies without a mission statement that puts students' minds, bodies, and spirits first. Students as a priority would be a bottom-up approach. When "real changes are proposed they are attacked by those who perceive an assault upon their way of working, or their knowledge or power bases. The status quo destroys school autonomy and with it, the foundation for effective learning."[12] The old social-teaching-learning order prevails!

Despite the retention of the Western intellectual tradition approach to teaching and learning, a negative paradigm shift has also occurred in public education on two fronts: in administration and in students' behavior and attitudes. The fabled New England spinster schoolteachers ran their schools without the aid of a top-heavy bureaucracy; they produced educated students. Since World War II, education has become one of America's biggest businesses. Our love affair with bigness led to the consolidation of school districts with professional administrations, resulting in thousands of students under one roof in elementary and high schools located on the outskirts of town, insulated from the life of communities. Many school districts have administrative staffs that outnumber the teaching staff. Education has become secondary to bureaucracy. Teaching and learning have become secondary to mandatory testing. Individual students get "lost" in a bureaucracy. Several of them commit antisocial acts that are possible under crowded conditions or anonymity. Bureaucracies do not attract leaders who are risk-takers. Some principals are prone to taking students' and parents' sides against teachers when parents threaten to sue for passing grades or "As" for their children. Children learn they can have teachers fired, so rudeness and disrespect reign; they also learn to manipulate the educational system, which eventually is played out in the workplace. The result of this paradigm shift in public education is a manipulatable power base has been introduced into the teacher-student relationship, which makes teachers responsible without the power to have students responsible for their learning or their behavior. Young people without "Clearly defined limits, goals, and relatively high demands and expectations for performance" have no esteem or respect for themselves or for adults who cannot or do not stand up to them.

Since the 1960s, public schools have become "one of the most potent breeding grounds of alienation in American Society."[13] Apathy is visible due to the separation of education from real life: (a) discipline by others is substituted for self-control and the innate drive to learn; (b) grades are more important than learning how to think, learn, solve problems, get along with others, and how to live; (c) work is synonymous with money and drudgery, not with the inner rewards that come from knowing we did a good job and enjoyed doing it; (d) doing one's best is futile when abusive power, corrupt politics, payoffs, and contacts command the rewards; and (e) "beating the system," that is, passing by not doing the work, can be achieved by threats, litigation, and abusing competent but powerless teachers. "No society can long sustain itself unless its members have learned the sensitivities, motivations, and skills involved in assisting and caring for other human beings."[14]

The public school setting is the primary one for preparing young people to participate as adults in society. Their failures can be measured by the number of students who drop out, get into drugs and alcohol, join gangs, lack respect and social skills, identify with designer labels, require remedial courses to get into college, party instead of studying, and expect to be millionaires by age 40 by doing whatever it takes to accomplish it. Even at higher education levels, students and their parents threaten to sue professors when scholarship is deemed to be below minimum standards. Litigation teaches students there is an easier way to get education degrees than to earn them. Some people inflate their resumés. All demonstrates the lack of esteem. It seems that schools are becoming breeding grounds for Corporate America's financial robber barons.

Why are the U.S. public schools failing the majority of its children? Our Western institutions and organizations are products of a historical consciousness that created rules based upon Ptolemaic, Newtonian, and Cartesian teachings that led to the separation of human beings from nature, mind from body, personal and social responsibility from private and public accountability, math and science from art and literature, personal life from work life, and work from play. The visible curriculum teaches us to be objective, without compassion, and to not only ignore but to disown the subjective, emotional, intuitive, and creative sides of ourselves. The price is the loss of our sense of wholeness and the alienation not only from self, but also from others and the larger community. Schools are failing to teach students' whole brains and are failing to protect them from bullies, assaults upon budding self-esteem, and from themselves and their parents' belief that threats, pressure, power, and money are the keys to get what whatever one wants. Administrators who cave in to students' and parents' demands compromise teachers' integrity, academic standards, and themselves when they make exceptions to the rules and set precedents.

Good schools do not need new buildings, more money, a longer academic year, a national curriculum, or national testing. Good schools are peopled with an administrative staff that creates a democratic, respectful, non-threatening, and safe environment for serving a team of esteemed teachers. It means they are willing to confront those who use fear to intimidate or coerce schools into passing students who do not do the work and to discipline rude students who demonstrate no respect for teaching, learning, rules and regulations. Teachers who stimulate students to motivate themselves to be responsible for their learning are those teachers with self-knowledge, love for their subject and for people, the freedom to adapt the curriculum to reflect the larger picture or the real world, the power to make room for individual initiative, curious and excited learners, and the commitment to reaching students where they are so they will progress. In teach-to-the-test environments, conformity and competition impede real learning. A combination of pressure and boredom stifles the curiosity and motivation of teachers and students.

Individual uniqueness counts and students become responsible learners, players, and participants when all students in a school are randomly assigned to one of four houses or teams, which are creatively designed and implemented with student participation. Each team member's academic, athletic standing, or extracurricular activity is recorded for his or her team. Team members root for their own houses or teams and students have been known to tutor those who are failing to help the team's average. The concept works to reduce individual competition, increase appreciation for individual's talents and abilities, instill a sense of belonging so outsiders become insiders, and discover the personal link between work, study, and play.

In public school systems, we have tenured teachers. Some have taught for twenty-five years: one-year, twenty-five times. They are bored and are boring! Most teachers, though, are as bright-eyed and bushy-tailed as when they got out of college with a "save the world" attitude. Two NJ teachers who were Human Development students in the master's program succeeded in turning negative attitudes into positive ones in their public school by sharing their learnings and refusing to collude in the gossip in the Teachers' Room. Not weeding out the plateaued or burned-out teachers perpetuates a negative environment: they become toxic to themselves, colleagues, and their students. Labels, such as Nerds, Jocks, Bullies, prevail when schools have no strategies for respecting children, honoring their unique talents and capabilities, teaching them respect for differences, and initiating ways for students to benefit from each others' uniqueness.

In every public school system, master teachers go to class each day with the attitude that inside every child there is a smart student yearning to get out. Many students do not know how due to living under ego threats or life-threatening situations, while others live with pressures to succeed. Many students are not properly motivated to learn or are not being taught in a way that is congruent with their thinking and learning styles. On a learning scale beginning with boredom and ending with high anxiety, the research shows that impoverished learning environments are boring, and those that are too challenging cause high anxiety so the human brain downshifts into the innate modes of fight, flight, freeze, or feign. The fight or flight response is excellent for physical survival, but it thwarts the brain's operation and coherent thinking when blood and oxygen are diverted to muscles. When a response is inhibited or frozen or when we have to make believe that we are unaffected (*Cool!*) by what is happening in our surroundings. The body's response to the freeze or feign syndrome also affects the ability to think, learn, work, and relate.

After creating a learning environment between the parameters of too boring and too challenging, teachers who wish to reach a high percentage of their students adapt their teaching methods and lesson plans to at least four different ways that human beings take in sensory data (see/observe, hear, touch, feel/intuit). There are also at least four ways that people think, that is, right- and left-brain dominant people process data[15] in different ways (people- or task-oriented and long-run or short-run/bottom-line, for example). Teachers' classroom judgments are influenced by their concepts of how children develop and how they learn. When people understand why children behave as they do, they perceive behavior through the eyes of the "behaver:"

1. Behavior is caused and is meaningful...
2. The causes which underlie behavior are always multiple...
3. Each individual is an indivisible unit...
4. The human individual develops...it is the interaction between the organism and its environment over a period of time that develops the individual personality...
5. Every human individual is a dynamic energy system, not just a machine acted upon from without...
6. Dynamic self-actualization is made possible to an individual by the existence of an organizing core of meanings (values) at the center of the personality...
7. Each individual is different from every other.[16]

The primary creative outlet in the public school — the arts and arts education — is and has been perceived as a frill by educators. The role of the arts in the overall learning process has been undervalued and ignored since it is the first budget to be cut. The studio approach to art maintains that students learn best by participating in art; the discipline approach asserts that students should learn art appreciation through history. Studio arts involve artistic expression, which is difficult to test and to time. In a master's class held after school hours in a northern New Jersey public school library, a student — a shop teacher — voiced a dilemma: what grade to give to one of his shop students who had "quietly fooled around" most of the school term by walking around and admiring other students' projects. Yet, in the previous three weeks, the shop student had designed and completed an excellent project but not in the expected lock-step way from day one of class. That 1980's day, *The Wall Street Journal* had carried a full-page IBM advertisement decorated with butterflies. Florence, the teacher-facilitator, fetched it from the rack and asked him to read the ad to the class:

183

DREAMERS, HERETICS, GADFLIES,
MAVERICKS, AND GENIUSES

> The story goes that Henry Ford once hired an efficiency expert to
> evaluate his company. After a few weeks, the expert made his
> report. It was highly favorable except for one thing. 'It's that man
> down the hall,' said the expert. 'Everytime I go by his office he's
> just sitting there with his feet on his desk. He's wasting your money.'
> 'That man,' replied Mr. Ford, 'once had an idea that saved us
> millions of dollars. At the time, I believe his feet were planted right
> where they are now.'

> At IBM, we have 46 people like that, and we don't worry about
> where they put their feet either. They are IBM fellows. They
> earned the title by having ideas that made a difference. Their job
> is to have more ideas like that, but under a very special condition.
> It's called freedom. Freedom from deadlines. Freedom from
> committees. Freedom from the usual limits of corporate approval.
> For a term of at least 5 years, an IBM Fellow is free to pursue any
> advanced project of value to IBM, even if chances for success may
> seem remote. As a result, some of the great innovations of our
> time have come from IBM Fellows. We may not always understand
> what they're doing, much less how they do it. But we do know this.
> The best way to inspire an IBM Fellow is to get out of the way.[17] IBM®

After the shop teacher read the ad, the class asked him, "What grade are
you going to give your student?" "An A!"

Artists and other seemingly nonconformists or freethinkers are more
concerned with seeing, hearing, and expressing the visions, perceptions, and
realities within and outside themselves than in being followers. Because of this,
the leaders of every man-made society fear their artists, poets, and writers;
artists threaten the status quo. Why does the creative impulse within us wither
and die? One answer: "The English teacher who wrote fiercely on the margins
of your theme in blue pencil: 'Trite, rewrite' helped to kill it. Critics kill
it...Families are great murderers of the creative impulse."[18]

"If there are faults, or rather inadequacies, in some of our teachers, they are the result of inadequate and inappropriate training rather than of lack of devotion to the task or to the limitations of capacity."[19] The faults lie, not in our nation's teachers, but in a system where teachers are caught in the middle: a powerless role between the administration, policies, and regulations and the parents and students. Parents' faults lie in trying to overprotect their children. All parents want their children to achieve and to fit into society; otherwise, their lives will be problematic. Children's lives could be more rewarding if they learned how to educate themselves, which is a learner-centered approach to education. The failure to learn is due, primarily, to emotional illiteracy, which is not included in schools' curricula.

Our educational system is based on and dominated by public schools with school boards elected by communities or appointed by city officials; they are rarely educators. Input from students at board meetings is rare. It is a big impersonal business and a big bureaucracy with multi-levels in conflict with each other; yet so powerful that unions, associations, and parent groups have to defend themselves against the undemocratic monolith. However, when unions are used to protect the weak from their own weaknesses or the entrenched and complacent from upgrading their skills and human relations, then they, too, no longer adhere to democratic principles. While unions and tenure were intended to protect people from oppression and unfair labor practices, and to cope with top-down power and control, sometimes they attract the unqualified, unmotivated, connected, or dishonest (or those who like the security, money, or the hours but not the work) people who use their union, association, PTA affiliation, or governmental connections not to overcome oppression but to become the oppressor. Their victims are those whom they are supposed to educate, service, or rehabilitate.

Society's large bureaucracies, from public school systems to Federal and State social agencies and prisons will be the last to change for the better in our society. Too much money and power are at stake. It takes positive self- and other-esteem teachers, principals, parents, and administrators to continue to feel effective in captive environments where those who truly want to lead, teach, and learn are intermingled with those who do not. The schools have lost sight of their primary reason to be — developing people to potential — and of their responsibility to make schools and society safe for America's future citizens to live, work, study, and play together.

The U.S. public schools have not changed their course since the 1960s, but community colleges with learner-centered classes are places for students, even those who are bored in high school, to enroll for a quality education. Prescott College (Arizona) has accredited learner-centered undergraduate and masters' degree programs. Union Institute & University (Cincinnati, Ohio) has accredited learner-centered doctoral, masters' (Vermont College), and undergraduate degree programs. The University of Phoenix has already accomplished a paradigm shift in learning by offering higher education courses in many fields on-line and world-wide.

Money

In the free-enterprise (capitalist) system, there is a strong tendency to believe that the more money one makes or has, the greater the genius to account for the achievement. There is no correlation between the accumulation of great wealth and great intellect. The top ten CEOs whose compensation increased by 4,300 percent over the last twenty years are not role models for America's youth. The affluent, in general, assume an air of self-confidence, self-approval, and competence. Too often, an ego that is supported by money and power is unsupported by positive self- and other-esteem or by integrity. Inheritance and indifference to legal constraints do not denote mental acuity either. Either way, money may mislead us. A person who has a lot of money is generally confused with having high self-esteem when, in fact, the rich have problems with drugs, and immoral behavior, as do poorer people in society. Their negative behavior betrays their lack of esteem.

Since the early 1970s, the business, knowledge, and entertainment workers and their CEO and CFO elites (including sports, movie, and TV figures) have far surpassed the earning power of service workers and the moral economy (teachers, child-caretakers, maids, cleaners). The wage inequality is a national crisis; so is the gap between the haves and the have-nots; we are no longer a true middle-class society. Decades before 1970, the U.S. Government's political decisions — throwing people out of work and using interest rates to fight inflation — led to the current pay inequality.[20] Our economy was in trouble before the 9/11 terrorists struck. For more American workers to become middle-class and achieve the American Dream, the U.S. government will need political voices and clout to reinstate commonsense policies to prevent us from becoming a second if not a third-world country.

Our individual relationship with money is usually unexamined and remains an emotional issue since most of us swing between worrying about having enough and impulsively spending it: "a penny-wise and dollar-foolish mentality." Some of us who have lived through hard financial times have a "poverty mentality," even in better financial times, and feel guilty about spending money. "Money hoarders [and penny pinchers]...tend to hoard feelings and thoughts as well as money, and generally seem more 'withholding' as personalities than spenders."[21] Money, esteem, and personality traits converge (a) when the "freeloader" disappears as soon as the check appears at the restaurant or when he orders the most expensive item on the menu because someone else is footing the bill, (b) when the "big spender" has to pick up the check or tip beyond his means, (c) when employees pad their expense accounts for whatever reason, (d) when the "deal-maker" needs a discount or nickel-and-dimes a seller, (e) when the Ebenezer Scrooges (Charles Dickens' *A Christmas Carol*) of this world are so miserly that they squeeze the life out of their employees, and (f) other examples of people valuing money and things more than people's well-being. Most people are unaware that their emotional relationship with money is visible to others and what it reveals about their character and state of esteem.

In changing and recessive times, we cannot avoid financial problems since "Money is a huge, driving force in our lives. It determines where we live, how often we move, and what food is on the table, what expectations to have."[22] Money is an easy substitute for love, respect, and personal and professional success, but it is no guarantee since the money field is a competitive one and is subject to inflation, stagflation, comparison — keeping up with Joneses or the competition — and bankruptcy. The love of money is said to be the "root of all evil," for it attracts to us those who live by their wits, do whatever it takes (lie, steal, kill) to acquire it, and sell their souls for money. Money divides us into economic classes (low, middle, upper), without attention to the qualitative aspects that make each human being unique.

Competition

Competition may be normal or natural in human beings. Aggressive competition is learned in society and practiced by adults. There are two kinds of competition: "that which is sick, neurotic and aggressive...that which is at times useful, healthy and assertive."[23] Competitiveness is taught in the schools, but it can be the kind of competitiveness where medical students destroy peers' experiments or it can be taught as working together toward solving human medical problems.

Competition in international markets requires a long-term outlook and the infusion of investment capital to stay on the cutting edge of research, development, and better products. A competitive workforce requires motivated individuals with knowledge and diverse skills to work smart and the positive self- and other-esteem so that money, status, and power are not needed to feed inflated egos. Because of the perceived discrepancy between the quality of our public school system and our university system — which attracts students from all over the world — America is "not likely to be competitive in the world economy of the future because we are failing to educate our youth."[24] We are creating a nation of haves and have-nots in the educational system as well.

Our educational and work systems are based upon competition. The wrong kind of competition! If competition were balanced with formal mentoring or coaching, the outcome would be finely-tuned students and workers. Mentors and coaches have experience that is meaningful to new employees or students who are otherwise left to make it or break it on their own. Coaching approaches help fill the void between the visible academic curriculum and the invisible one needed to be a professional. A positive mentoring experience contributes to our loving what we do and how well we do on the job and is a long-term investment in human resources.

Play

Games and other occupations of young children have been intensely studied by scientists who seek to uncover what is needed for academic achievement. "When a person acts because his behavior is motivated by the enjoyment he finds in the behavior itself, he increases his self-confidence, contentment, and feelings of solidarity with others; if the behavior is motivated by external pressures or external rewards, he may experience insecurity, frustration, and a sense of alienation."[25]

There is a deeply entrenched dichotomy between work and play that stems historically from the Puritan work ethic, which defined work as the primary purpose of life. Play was conceived of as a waste of time and a sin at worst since it brought about no visible or concrete results.

Play versus Work and School

The real difference between play, games, learning, and work is that "in recreation goals are clearly defined...the score keeping is better...feedback is more frequent...participants feel they have a higher degree of choice...they don't change the rules in the middle of the game"[26] and we know why we are playing the game. Most of us will pay for working harder at play than we will for work that we are paid to do. Ideas for becoming a winner at work are borrowed from winning at play: in games, the feedback is immediate, and we know how we are doing compared to others; at work we may be given a job description and expected to perform without ongoing or subsequent feedback.

Most managers dislike giving feedback; usually it is negative, and it comes too late to change. Many teachers use tests to manipulate and punish children for their behavior. People who are perceived to be unimportant, such as students or hourly workers, are told how to work. However, important people are treated differently: we explain to them why they or we have to do something. The fields of play in business and in schools are not clearly defined; in play we know where the out-of-bounds markers are. People who get involved deeply in games forget hunger and other problems; for some people work or study does the same thing. Students are not in one classroom long enough to get deeply involved; they are constantly interrupted by bells, so we either learn to play the game of school or work, or the game plays us. When we apply the intrinsic rewards of enjoyment of play to learning, working, and other activities, we rely on our own feedback to tell us how we are doing.

Short- and Long-Term Learning

Through learning, playing, and working we find that personal and professional processes are intertwined. The Western intellectual tradition's (TWIT) well-established ways to teach and learn have put teachers in an untenable position: held accountable for learning results but lack the means to measure the learning. Learning has two dimensions: short- and long-term. Waitresses who remember what we ordered until they deliver it are similar to students who cram for a test, regurgitate it, pass, and forget the data the next hour, day or week. TWIT's subjects in the curricula are fragmented into little bits, which are presented to a student bit-by-bit, over a period of time. The student is expected to logically assemble the bits and make a whole out of it, even though he is not given an inkling of the whole. The lock-step logic of the curriculum-builder (the textbook writer) and of the teacher's lesson plan is invisible to the student because the human brain does not process data in a sequential logical manner.

The brain is a simultaneous processor of incoming data by comparing it with old, stored information to extract a pattern. Without a file, frame of reference, or the big picture in which to store incoming data, fragmented data get scattered. Thus, learning may be defined as "the extraction from confusion of meaningful patterns."[27] Learning is obstructed when there is no grasp of why to learn something and when there are constant interruptions or confusion. People learn best experientially, by doing, and we are our own best teachers. After we have learned the skills (25 percent) we need to be a professional, then learning how to market ourselves becomes a number one priority.

Pygmalion Principle

Our language and our metaphors define our experience of life and our reality. We remove ourselves from nature when we believe we make (industrial: manufacture) versus grow (nature: agricultural) ourselves: we say we make love, babies, friends, time, money, a living. In our impatience, we ignore or overlook the ecology of all living things and do not learn that we are on Earth to transform ourselves first, then to transform the world by making it a better place than when we found it.

Americans are entranced by the Pygmalion Principle: people are made into and marketed as media celebrities.[28] Well-knownness is valued more than substance, good deeds, or accomplishments. Many people achieve on their looks, intelligence, talent, or personality and get rave reviews for twenty-minute performances. Athletes get famous for their performance in a variety of ball games, from football and basketball to golf, and become good or poor role models for America's youth and America's image portrayed to the world. When the spotlight is on the highly visible through television coverage of Hollywood stars and sports' athletes, other people in society — those of us who keep the goods and services flowing in the commercial economy or are in the moral economy doing the nurturing (society's mainstays) — become invisible.

Our society rewards the visible, not the invisible. In our institutions and organizations, the powerholders reward themselves handsomely, believing they are worth it and better than their subordinates and the front-line workers. We learn their names only when they fall, such as the Enron executives, so their invisibility is akin to the terrorists in our midst. "'Who Wants to Work for an SOB?'...They drive away talent. The best people in any field — the talented few who contribute greatest business value — simply don't have to put up with the misery perpetuated by a bad boss...The SOB leader must reform or go."[29] The motivating emotion driving a SOB boss is fear: of scarcity and of others.

In our human world, as in nature's seasons, there are times of feast or famine, scarcity or abundance, good or bad economic times, and war or peace. Since 9/11, Americans are more aware that change is a constant. Security lies, not in a manufactured image, or in the old competition-scarcity paradigm, but in being an authentic, flexible human being who can respond to rapid changes, anticipate changes that are coming, and connect and collaborate with others on personal, professional, or humanitarian issues. In the 1700s, a small band of revolutionaries in this country created the United States of America: a new form of democratic government for the people and by the people; they disconnected from the power of kings. However, the conflict between wealth and democracy has been a problem since America's founding. Many of the signers of our Declaration of Independence were from America's richest families. The rich continue to profit while workers experience economic hard times.

Today. we are in the midst of a global transformation, enabled by the World Wide Web and affordable technologies. These times of international and domestic terrorism are ripe for change, to disconnect from our inherited pre-democratic institutional and organizational systems that allow the exorbitantly wealthy — *the corporate aristocracy* — the divine right of capital.[30] Many of the "privately-owned" but publicly-traded companies are "buying" government favors and creating a huge gap between haves and have-nots. In his book, *Wealth and Democracy*,[31] Kevin Phillips informs us that the unhealthy relationship between government and the rich and powerful undermines the democratic process. They work together to create privilege at the expense of national interest, especially middle and lower class Americans. In addition, the U.S. is the wealthiest nation with the largest percentage of the world's richest people, but we also have an ever-widening gap between rich and poor. The concentration of wealth in the hands of the few is anti-democratic in design and practice and must be reined in. There are more authentic Americans than those who believe they are more equal than others or who practice fulfilling their wants at the expense of others. Only self- and other-esteem will unite us all: needs will be met, wants will be earned, and people will trust themselves to grow and specialize or generalize versus settling for craven images.

Specialization

In all human, animal, and plant life, cells have the capacity to both differentiate and generalize;[32] however, each develops special forms and functions — such as hair, blood, bone, etc., but each cell retains the capability to change its role. Specialization occurs in all organizations. Specialists, whether managers, administrators, teachers, doctors, lawyers, engineers, or front-line workers, are conditioned by our scarcity-mode of doing and being to taking polarized, adversarial positions with attack or defend attitudes and action. Where there is an excessive narrowness of interests or view, there is usually a lack of awareness not only of the capacity to generalize but also lack of respect for the integrity of another's position or condition and to believe that one's own interest ranks above all others. Such narrowness does not acknowledge the larger, overall purpose for specializing in the first place.

Understanding and appreciating our own and others' diverse roles and responsibilities are prerequisites for learning to manage self well. We need to do that in order to become a life- and work-sustaining worker, team member, or leader of others. When we fully develop and integrate our personal and professional qualities, we may live United Technologies[33] message:

> People don't want to be managed. They want to be led.
> Whoever heard of a world manager? World leader, yes.
> Educational leader. Political Leader. Religious leader.
> Scout leader. Community leader. Labor leader. Business leader.
> They lead. They don't manage.
> The carrot always wins over the stick. Ask your horse.
> You can lead your horse to water, but you can't manage him to drink.
> If you want to manage somebody, manage yourself.
> Do that well, and you'll be ready to stop managing.
> And start leading.

Chaordic Organizations

Disillusioned with hierarchical, power-driven institutions and organizations dominating and failing our society by consuming resources, diminishing the human spirit, and harming the biosphere, Dee Ward Hock[34] coined the word *chaordic* from *chaos* and *order*. *Chaordic* describes institutions that integrate chaos, order, competition, and cooperation with a shared purpose, ethical principles, and responsibility by all for themselves and to others, the organization, and the Earth. In effect, his concept of organizations is to empower everyone to release the human spirit and initiative and to change the workplace from a dictatorship to a democracy.

Everyone is a leader and a follower, Hock says. Our words and deeds influence others, and others' words and deeds influence us. We lose our leadership capabilities when we go to school and are conditioned to be managed: "Our current forms of organization are almost universally based on compelled behavior — on tyranny, for that is what compelled behavior is, no matter how benign it may appear or how carefully disguised and exercised."[35]

Primal Leadership[36]

"Great leaders move us. They ignite our passion and inspire the best in us…Great leadership works through the emotions," say Daniel Goleman and his fellow researchers.[37] In their book, they inform us that *emotional guide* is the foremost job of leadership, from CEO to shop foreman. In all human groups, the emotionally intelligent leader has the power to instill optimism, inspiration, and enthusiasm; whereas, the emotionally illiterate leader may incur antagonism, hostility, and dissonance. An organization and its employees thrive when a leader resonates with energy. If a leader exudes negativity, an organization is more likely to fail. A leader's negative emotions, from chronic anger and moodiness to money, power, and contempt issues, negatively affect his company, employees, and productivity, creating a trickle-down effect.

The problem is leaders usually emerge from having demonstrated their analytic, financial, or technical skills, which are the domain of the neocortex, the thinking brain. Most management training programs are geared to the neocortex, not to the emotional brain where life experiences, habits, and habituated responses are entrenched. With participation in primal leadership training programs, it is possible to change the brain centers that regulate emotions from a negative to a positive orientation. For example, by consciously focusing on the here-and-now, being mindful, a human brain shifts from activity in the right prefrontal lobe (the area that generates distressful emotions) to the left prefrontal lobe, which is the brain's center for positive emotions. Therefore, the plasticity of the human brain is such that it can be reconfigured: we can create new neural tissue, new neural connections, and new pathways to change negative-esteem and emotionally illiterate people into positive-esteem, emotionally intelligent humane human beings. However, all of us need the motivation to change, to uncover the charismatic person we would like to become. It is hard to break the habits of a lifetime stored in the amygdala. It requires courage and a strong commitment to become emotionally intelligent. When we become emotionally literate, we connect with our real self and with others, heal the dissonance inside and outside ourselves in our professional as well as in our personal lives, and live the life we were meant to live.

Courage

To live with sensitivity requires courage. The word courage comes from the French word *coeur*, meaning *heart*. "What masquerades as courage may turn out to be simply a bravado to compensate for one's unconscious fear."[38] While an acorn grows into an oak in concert with nature and a kitten becomes a cat on the basis of instinct, a human being becomes fully human by choice.

We attain worth and dignity by the multitude of decisions we make from day-to-day. Physical courage used to be perceived as the finest kind of courage, but that kind of courage often degenerates into brutality. With moral courage, we take a stand against violence and terrorism. Intimate courage is the courage to relate to another human being with the hope of achieving meaningful intimacy. People with emotional courage are those who undertake development of their whole selves to use all their intelligences. Emotional courage requires self-awareness, social awareness, including empathy, listening skills, the ability to stand in someone else's shoes without losing one's own, and intrapersonal and interpersonal relationship skills.

Technology has changed so that a lone woman can sail a sixty-foot yacht by herself around the world. However, human beings' basic needs have not changed; people need people for many reasons. Emotional courage requires making connections with many people: the more healthy relationships we have, the better we are able to withstand intense stressors and remain healthy; and the more comfortable we are in our own shoes or skin, the more impact we have on people and groups. An ancient prayer asks that we be given the strength to change the things we can and the wisdom to accept what we cannot change, hopefully with a sense of humor.

Humor

Just as nobody wants to be a nobody, nobody wants to be accused of not having a sense of humor. We admit to not being mathematical, artistic, athletic, or having a green thumb, but our hackles rise if someone tells us we don't have a sense of humor. What is a sense of humor? It is easier to describe the humorless types who fit into two categories: the literal-minded who are locked into one perspective, and the paranoid-minded who think the world is out to get them. Beyond a smile or a laugh, there is "a type of stimulation that tends to elicit the laughter reflex."[39] Humans' ability to laugh distinguishes humans from animals, plants, minerals, and the Earth. Laughter helps humans to think and to associate with each other more freely and naturally. Laughter at other humans' expense is learned and is natural when some people believe they are superior to others.

Men have often told women that they do not have a sense of humor. Masculine humor or gags serve that purpose: they shut women up. Humor is powerful. There is a vast difference between humor and saying something funny about someone; it is really a put-down. Many male jokes are intended to evoke laughter at someone else's expense. When your class or group laughs at you, it is totally different experience when you can get them to laugh with you. Women are most conscious of and practice the old adage, *Laugh and the world laughs with you, cry and you cry alone.* The significance of laughter is it provides internal exercise and promotes a positive emotional mode. A negative frame of mind, depression, and scowling impair the body's immune system.

Humor's secret source is sorrow, not joy, said Mark Twain. That statement reminded us of Robert Heinlein's[40] science fiction main character who was considered nonhuman because he could not laugh. He visited the zoo and tossed some peanuts to the monkeys. A little monkey who had happily caught some was promptly beaten up by his fellow cage-mates, and his peanuts were taken. He felt so bad for the little monkey that he laughed instead of crying, becoming human in the process.

Humor is found in positive perception. Humor's overt source is dwelling upon the positive in an otherwise negative situation. Our Uncle Joe and his wife vacationed in Newfoundland, Canada; they rented a car to go "around the bay." Driving down a long hill, the brakes failed; he missed the bridge and went down an embankment into a brook. He was unhurt. Aunt Mildred screamed, "Joe, I'm blind! I'm blind!" Uncle Joe laughed and laughed, with relief: her wig had fallen across her eyes and had "blinded" her.

The crucial difference between jokes and storytelling, folktales, fables, or parables is that the listener is expected to laugh. The purpose of dirty and ethnic jokes is an assault on and the exploitation of the listener. People with positive esteem are able to break the chain by refusing to laugh or by not telling one of their own jokes. Every human or climactic event — except the 9/11 terrorist attacks — brings its own wave of jokes that tests the listeners' emotional literacy or hidden values. A person's favorite joke is the key to that person's character. Most speakers begin their talk with an appropriate to-the-topic joke to build rapport with their audience. "Those comedians who succeed do so because they have unconsciously brought up to expression, and are able to express it better than others, the unconscious needs, anxieties, and identifications of the audience as well."[41]

Whenever we take ourselves too seriously as adults, we forget how to play without competing. Jesting has an exhibitionist quality that many of us tend to avoid at all costs, especially when the old saying, *Many a true word is said in jest*, is well known. Despite the negative aspects of jests, a positive sense of humor — the ability to laugh at ourselves, our situation, and with others — enhances life, work, and relationships. A fine line exists between not taking ourselves too seriously and not taking ourselves seriously enough. Both begin with a smile.

Public Speaking

"Smile! You're on Candid Camera!" Speaking, listening, reading, and writing require primary communication skills; however, communication involves our deepest feelings about others and ourselves. Public speaking is fearful for most people. Why? Fear that we will not measure up or we will not meet our own or other's expectations! Those fears and insecurities are visible in our bodies and in our voices. Everybody makes assessments of people based on their voices, the content as well as the vocal quality and voice revelations.

There is magic in sound. When we change, our voice changes. Consciousness changes behavior and vice versa; therefore, our voice reveals how we feel about ourselves and how other people react to us. The sound of our voice we hear inside our head is different from that heard by others; you know this from hearing a tape recording of your voice. All of us have suffered from nervousness before a speech or meeting someone we consider important; our voice becomes unsteady; the pitch changes. When the timbre of our voice says one thing and our words say another, the real message is how we feel: annoyed, fearful, irritable, hostile. Vibrations are the life force, and the human voice expresses or blocks these subtle emanations. Through our voices we will be known and know ourselves!

In the process of growing up, we are conditioned not to express ourselves fully. When we give ourselves permission to express our feelings vocally, from a whimper to a shriek, we become less inhibited and become willing to be heard. "Richard Burton said he developed his voice by shouting Shakespeare at sheep in his native Wales."[42] An effective public speaker's voice commands respect, fascination, belief, and interest; it is not flat or a monotone. A monotone voice is a dead-giveaway that the message is controlled; it contains no feelings or input from our true "voice": the emotional right-brain.

Most of us do not use the full range and power of our speaking voices. Girls are taught to be quiet and boys and girls are taught not to show off. Therefore, we modify our voices accordingly. When our body tenses up, breath and voice strength diminish so our voices get pinched, or high or flat, or all three. There are more overtones in a low voice; a high-pitched voice does not have much range or expressiveness. The secret is to breathe deeply and to speak from our chest, rather than from our throat, face, or nose. If we prefer to sound "businesslike" or "professional" and use no inflections in our speech, our presentations will be dull. Stress buildup before a speaking engagement, though fearful, can be a source of heightened energy and performance readiness. When we talk about something we are passionate about, we become animated and fluent, and that is the style we want to emulate in order to get and focus attention on what it is we want to communicate. It is the sound of our voice, more than the words, that attracts people's positive and negative attention.

Self-Defense

Today's reality is we are all targets for those who perceive us as vulnerable, want what we have, or expect to feel more potent at our expense. Our adversaries are willing to poison, maim or kill us for a few dollars, our car, our body, or to control our psyche. If the doors to our homes and cars are locked, it makes it harder for a thief to get in. Similarly, if our attitude transmits confidence and/or the message, "Don't mess with me!" the possibility exists a more willing victim will be chosen instead. If we do not value our own lives, why should someone else? No one can afford to be in public anymore without constant vigilance: our heads and hearts have to be where our feet are at all times in order to be centered, aware of our surroundings, and avoid or fend off prospective attackers: physically and psychologically.

Self-defense and karate courses teach us simulated attack situations and the physical skills to gain time when and if we, men and women, are assaulted. Real life surprise attack situations may put us into the panic mode: our brain downshifts into the Four Fs: fight, flight, freeze, or feign. At that time it is more difficult to gain access to any cognitively learned coping skills, but skills practiced through physically defending self are more available. If we have positive self-esteem and are prepared, our positive attitude will allow us to avoid the Four Fs and gain access to our prepared mental and physical powers. Telling children not to talk to strangers is not enough, as experienced while walking around the neighborhood of an Atlanta suburb. A little boy on his three-wheel bicycle was riding around his driveway. Florence said, "Hi!" He said, "I can't talk to strangers." The second time around, he said, "Hi!" "You're not supposed to talk to strangers," replied Florence. "You're not a stranger. I saw you before," he said.

A woman was walking to her nearby parked car from the New York Public Library (Fifth Avenue and 42nd Street) with her arms full of books. She felt she was being followed. As she reached her car, she turned around quickly and said, "Will you hold these for me, please?" He did. She unlocked her car, thanked him, took the books, and got in. He said, "Lady, I had something else in mind." She thanked him again and drove off. Another woman, a nurse, had to travel the subway late at night from her job at a Brooklyn Hospital. When she left her post, she started talking out loud to herself with gestures and continued to do so all the way home. She was never bothered. Were the foregoing people lucky? Yes and no. Karate, self-defense courses, and physically working-out are confidence-builders that enhance self-esteem so we do not dehumanize ourselves in dangerous situations. Self-esteem enhances creativity, thinking on one's feet, and communication, so we do not become hysterical or verbally abusive or lose access to both sides of our brain's survival and coping strategies. When we lose our humanness, we may be treated as less than human: pseudospeciation occurs.

Women and men, who have been sexually abused in childhood or have unresolved life issues that diminish their perceived right to respect, approval, and love, are more at risk for assaults or abuse. Those ambivalent and sometimes negative feelings and attitudes about themselves are like magnets; they attract negativity. The message transmitted is "It's OK to mess with me!" We have to watch what we think, and we cannot afford to let our minds wander so our lack of awareness or alertness also contributes to our becoming a willing target.

Positive Psychology

There are people in the world who vie to control the minds of other human beings or they covet what others have or are. The field of psychology has been dominated by those who assess what is wrong with human beings instead of what is right or what is unique about them. "Practitioners went about treating the mental illness of patients within a disease framework by repairing damage: damaged habits, damaged drives, damaged childhood, and damaged brains."[43] Positive Psychology's message is "to remind our field that psychology is not just the study of pathology, weakness, and damage; it is also about the study of strength and virtue...work, education, insight, love, growth, and play."[44] The best moments of our lives are when our bodies or minds are stretched to their limits in a voluntary activity. At work, though, is where most of us spend our conscious lives.

Studs Terkel is about ninety years young and is still interviewing people about their lives and writing about them. Repeatedly, he has found that the happy few who liked their work had a common theme: "a meaning to their work well over and beyond the reward of the paycheck."[45] However, people who did not like their jobs reported to Terkel, "Most of us, like the assembly line worker, have jobs that are too small for our spirit. Jobs are not big enough for people."[46] Most jobs are designed so that people are easily replaced, which is better for management. We cannot command more money if we are low value commodities. People who earn high salaries are generally harder to replace; they are a scarce commodity; therefore, they command more money and more respect. In a corporation, money equals respect regardless of what anyone says to the contrary. From a positive psychology perspective, "People who learn to control inner experience will be able to determine the quality of their lives, which is as close as any of us can come to being happy."[47]

Our professional resumés, or curriculum vitae (CV), pay attention to our intellectual professional credentials and achievements, not to our personal and emotional qualities that make us esteemed people, workers, leaders, or managers, and facilitators of others' development. An effective leader has positive self- and other-esteem, a sense of humor, is mature, honest, open to new ideas, flexible, disciplined, courageous, communicative, and has a vision of a better world. "The best leaders inspire people not just to follow the leader, but to follow themselves, to grow in their own abilities, to give direction to their own lives."[48]

The reality is the divided life is not confined to academia for we work within institutions and organizations, from businesses to governmental and social agencies, whose job descriptions and inherent competitive practices are opposed to our hearts and spirit. When hearts, minds, and spirit become subservient to workplace logic, then self- and other-esteem suffer and integrity dies. When we do our personal development work and reclaim our individual identity, we demonstrate the "Fish!" playfulness in any workplace:

> As you enter this place of work please choose to make today a great day. Your colleagues, customers, team members, and you yourself will be thankful. Find ways to play. We can be serious about our work [life] without being serious about ourselves. Stay focused in order to be present when your customers and team members most need you. And should you feel your energy lapsing, try this surefire remedy: Find someone who needs a helping hand, a word of support, or a good ear and make their day.[49]

When we help others, we help ourselves. It is the spiritual thing to do.

Eight

Our spiritual journey is waking up
to the divine sea in which we swim.
—Matthew Fox[1]

Spiritual Development

ESTABLISHED RELIGIONS TEACH US their truth is *the* truth. Dogma captures people's hearts, minds, and souls so they embody unquestioning faith, blind belief, ignorance, and bondage. The suicide-terrorists are an example of an extreme religious ideology that led to their becoming "true believers." Mohamed Atta, the terrorist who steered a plane into a World Trade Center tower, left a Last Will and Testament, dated April 11, 1996, in which he stated, "I don't want anyone to weep and cry...because this is an ignorant thing to do." He also decreed that no women should attend his funeral or visit his grave. He got his wish! His and others' distorted religious beliefs are the antithesis of the traits of humanness and spirituality: health, hope, happiness, harmony, and humor. The boundaries of civilized behavior were breached.[2]

This is a crucial and pivotal time for humanity and spirituality. The term *spirituality* comes to us from the Latin verb for the act of breathing, *spirare*. Spirit, then, is the life, breath, and spirit within us — our invisible but vital essence of mind. What we do with our life, with our choices, and with our freedom, make all the difference in whether or not we are a spiritual being. "Spirituality fosters engagement with the world, not escape from it. It is this-worldly, not otherworldly."[3] In the East, the belief in people's karma is a reason for not helping others who need it. In the West, many wealthy people believe that in a democracy there must be something wrong with someone who needs a helping hand or "I pay my taxes; let Social Services take care of them." Spirituality requires that we move from self-centeredness to a grace-centered response. Through our thoughts, words, and deeds we evade and betray our humanness or we help others and, in the helping process, we demonstrate our love and grace, from which compassion ensues for others and ourselves. Self-understanding and self-esteem help develop our small self. The pathway to the Somebody we were born to be is to develop our larger Self, which includes Other-esteem, then we are connected to the whole of creation. As Albert Einstein said:

> A human being is part of a whole, called by us the 'Universe,'
> a part limited in time and space. He experiences himself,
> his thoughts and feelings, as something separated from the rest
> — a kind of optical delusion of his consciousness. This delusion
> is a kind of prison for us, restricting us to our personal desires
> and to affection for a few persons nearest us. Our task must
> be to free ourselves from this prison by widening our circles
> of compassion to embrace all living creatures and the
> whole of nature in its beauty.[4]

An ecological approach to spirituality, versus an egological one, begins with healing ourselves for, as Chief Seattle of the Squamish Indians said, "all things are connected...'whatever befalls the earth befalls the sons of the earth.'"[5] The word *human* comes from the Latin *humus*, meaning *earth*. A spiritual theologian, Meister Eckhart of Hochheim, Germany (1260-1329), called creation a gift of "grace" in his "Sermon Five: How All Creatures Share An Equality of Being." In discussing the threefold aspect of love in the Lord's commandment given to John (13:34...*love one another as I have loved you*), Meister Eckhart said, "we have to advance from something good (natural love) to something better (graced love) and from something better to something even more perfect (divine love)."[6] We make a spiritual connection as we develop our whole selves so we can bloom, share ourselves, and communicate goodness. We make spiritual connections when we reach out to another in friendship; when we make a stranger a friend; when we love our neighbor as, not instead of, ourselves; when we love and commit to another; and when we understand the impermanence of all beings and things. By having the courage to transform ourselves, we transform our world. In the process, truth, meaning, and happiness ensue.

The Pursuit of Happiness

The U.S. Constitution affirms "the pursuit of happiness." Thomas Jefferson did not use the term *happiness* in the utilitarian sense of pleasure; he meant it in the sense of "living a good life for a human being," from the Greek word *eudaimonia.*[7] Happiness comes when we do not seek it or expect to find it in forbidden or illicit pleasures. Happiness ensues with positive self-esteem, which requires internal and external efforts: we look inside ourselves and heal the rift within our head, heart, and spirit.

There is a Sufi story about the creation of human beings from an Eastern perspective that differs from our Western one, about Adam and Eve, which centers on forbidding them to eat the fruit of the tree of knowledge. The Eastern story is about two gods, one male and the other female. They knew that if they created human beings with happiness as a "given," that humans would not be motivated to grow, learn from experience, and find meaning and happiness in the process. The gods pondered where to hide happiness. In the Earth? No, they decided; they knew that future human beings would develop technology to mine the Earth and plumb the depths of the ocean, so they would find happiness too easily. In the sky? No, they decided, they knew that human beings were going to develop airplanes, space shuttles, and visit planets and would find happiness very quickly. "I know," said the female goddess, "Let's hide it inside human beings. They'll never think to look for it there!" So they did.

Short Cuts to Spirituality

Our quest for love, respect, happiness, and esteem may maximize our sense of responsibility to other human beings and to the other creatures and things with whom we share the Earth. Since there is no smaller person in the world than one who is self-absorbed, anyone who focuses attention upon spiritual development as an end without attention to the whole self and the whole universe is taking a short cut. Some religions have more appeal than others do because they are outlets for expressing emotions or confessing sins in order to be "saved." Several evangelical spiritual stars have fallen from grace due to their materialism or their libido. The fallen media-stars appealed to their followers for forgiveness for doing the same things they preached against, along with appealing to people's fear that they may not go to heaven if they do not seek personal salvation through repentance and by sending money so *the word* may reach other sinners. Too many underdeveloped human beings take short cuts to power under the guise of spirituality. They wear the robes of false prophets and masks of piousness that bespeak bigotry. The eating of forbidden fruit in the Garden of Eden led to the Christian fall and redemption doctrine and to a preoccupation with personal salvation without cosmic connection making.

The issue is to be emotionally literate and at peace with ourselves, not through personal salvation or repentance, but through transformation. To be an instrument of peace and love in the world, we must be at peace with ourselves and have love in our hearts.

Spiritual Bankruptcy

Spiritual bankruptcy began when man detached himself from nature, both human nature and the Earth, and began weeding out "inferior" stock. "The idea that certain individuals or segments of society were predestined by hereditary inferiority to be degenerates of one sort or another had as its converse the idea of hereditary superiority."[8] That doctrine was the basis of the social eugenics movement which led to Hitler's Nazi Germany and the Holocaust. The end of communism in Eastern Europe and Russia was not won by political intervention but by the resistance to manipulation; however, the end of communism also unleashed dormant ethnic hatreds and evil spirits as well. The strife in Europe, Ireland, Eastern Europe, the Middle East, Africa, Russia, China, Canada, and the United States points to the non-spiritual belief that religious, hereditary, and cultural superiority exist. That belief is being preserved and perpetuated despite lip service to the sacredness of life.

Spiritual bankruptcy is socially evident when people's attempt to escape their problems endangers their own and others' welfare by excessive use of alcohol, drugs, verbal and physical abuse, lawlessness, or reckless behavior. Many people seek public recognition for good works or work for peace instead of completing the unfinished issues in their own lives; their intentions may be suspect or toxic unless they resolve their own issues in the process. Spiritual bankruptcy is evident in past and present decades when business values based on greed, money, and power have distanced the haves from the have-nots. Business relationships that are based on trust are nurturing and rewarding; those based on mistrust may be materially rewarding, but they set the stage for the self-fulfilling prophecy: betrayal.

Our cultures and our religions were meant to unite us; instead we are divided by diverse cultures and religions. People in all cultures and of all religious sects are "not exclusively saints or sinners; few adhere to an absolute moral code. Most respond to circumstances, and their integrity and trustworthiness can depend as much on how they are treated as on their basic character."[9] Spirituality is conspicuously absent when we act as if we are the center of the universe, which is a form of spiritual narcissism and negative esteem.

Sin

The failure to trust, which begins with not trusting self, is a sin. Trust is not only a psychological issue; it is a faith issue. Self-negation is a sin: "This sin consists of the refusal to love oneself well, the refusal to celebrate both one's dignity and one's responsibility. When people sin in this way, they become suckers for hero-worship, for projecting onto others their own dignity as images of God."[10] An ego quest for perfection is unreal and harms the individual and society. America and Americans have experienced terrorists who projected their hatred onto us. The alternative to hatred is trust. Trust "softens the body, dilates the arteries, widens the eyes, allows us to open up and welcome the surroundings."[11] We can help transform terrorists' evil into love for humanity and all creation if we can transform ourselves first.

The doctrine of original sin is a weapon to control human beings. The doctrine is not found in any of the writings of the *Old Testament*: no human being enters the world as a sinner.[12] Elie Wiesel agreed, "The concept of original sin is alien to Jewish tradition."[13] The conviction that man's birthright is sin has led to the acceptance of slavery, serfdom, and religious atrocities; it was the rationale by Spanish conquistadors for slaughtering "soulless" Native Americans; and has engendered a colossal disrespect of people from other cultures, animals, and nature. The original sin doctrine has served the purpose of organized religion, empire builders, patriarchy, and political and economic systems. The doctrine is used to justify cruelty and perpetuate misery under the guise of suffering as the wage of sin.

We all suffer, not from original sin, but from the ultimate heresy: the lack of love for others and ourselves, that is, the lack of spirituality. Professor Mitsuo Aoki of Hawaii proposed: sin makes us feel unworthy and gets in the way of our wholeness.[14] He perceived spirituality to be that aspect of ourselves that forever connects us to the whole, that part of us that is open to the energies that surround us all the time. Sin, in its deepest depths, is in the common practice of making oneself the center of the universe, believing everything is ownable and "mine," which is the greatest separation we can create between our universal spirit and ourselves. When we make ourselves the center of the universe, we bend others to our will or exercise power over them. Also, sin is disowning various parts of ourselves and making one part the dominant one. When we diminish ourselves —"I'm no good!" or "I can't do that...should, ought, have to, if, when I..."— we sin.[15] "Original blessing is far more ancient and more biblical a doctrine and ought to be the starting point for spirituality."[16]

Sin is defined as "the refusal of humans to become who we are."[17] Excommunicated Roman Catholic priest, Matthew Fox honors the wisdom of our ancestors when life was lived closer to the Earth long before the Newtonian era when only humans and the food they ate were considered flesh. Today, though, we know that all beings, stars and galaxies are interconnected, including everything animate and inanimate. Sins of the flesh are beyond sexual offenses and encompass those that "destroy children and adults, forests and other creatures...To deny someone decent work or wages, drinking water or health care, shelter or safety...It is in our flesh that we bear the curses of spiritual sins."[18] It is the soul that sins, not the body.

Spiritual Intelligence

When body, mind, and spirit are integrated into a whole, when work life and family life are integrated, when our acts express our interdependence with all life, then life works better for us. We first get sick in the spirit or in the mind and then the body, the messenger, tells us directly through pain and illness to get our act together.[19] Our imperfections often unite us and allow us to assist and be assisted by others. "For it is shared weakness and need that draws from a group its gifts and powers of healing."[20] When we learn to trust, we learn that beauty and imperfection are married. Each flower may be beautiful but close inspection reveals that each is imperfect. The same is true with each human body and mind.

Spirituality represents the most advanced state of being human, and it has nothing to do with perfection. "A spiritual person tries less to be godly than to be deeply human."[21] People who try to be godly often end up being bigots; whereas, to strive to be human and humane returns us to our *wholeness*: a word that shares the same root as *holy*. Spirituality is freeing, not inhibiting. Philosophically, all human beings possess varying degrees of spiritual intelligence. Spiritual intelligence [SQ] is defined as "the intelligence with which we address and solve problems of meaning and value, the intelligence with which we can place our actions and our lives in a wider, richer meaning-giving context. It is the intelligence with which we can assess that one course of action or one life path is more meaningful than another."[22] "Conventional religion is an externally imposed set of rules and beliefs. It is top-down, inherited from priests and prophets and holy books, or absorbed through family and tradition...SQ...is an *internal,* innate ability of the human brain and psyche, drawing its deepest resources from the heart of the universe itself...Spiritual intelligence is the soul's intelligence. It is the intelligence with which we heal ourselves and with which we make ourselves whole."[23]

Spiritual and emotional intelligence have been neglected in the schools across America so we live divided lives. Physically, a "God Spot"[24] is said to be located in human brains' temporal lobes, that is, there is an ultimate intelligence based on a third neural system in the brain which some people call spiritual intelligence. Human beings' brains oscillate at 40-Hertz per second, binding perceptual and cognitive events into an integrated whole. In U.S.

homes, electricity operates at 60-Hz, which current is characteristic of most electrical appliances. Sixty percent of the matter in human bodies are hydrogen atoms, all of which were part of the Big Bang, and the remaining forty percent of the chemical elements in human bodies were forged in the stars: we are recycled stardust.

Science has wrought a radically new picture of how the world began, and we have a better picture of where we came from; therefore, "we are mysteriously connected to the universe, we are mirrored in it, just as the entire evolution of the universe is mirrored in us."[25] Spirituality is one domain where human beings may seek common bonds that bind humanity to produce a radically new picture of human beings, the Earth, its diverse species, and our future together. Our spirituality dimension may be developed earlier in life than currently proposed by age and stage theorists and other social scientists.

Energy Healing

Energy is a more neutral word than spiritual; therefore, some people find it easier to say, "'Your energy is depleted' than 'Your spirit is toxic.'"[26] Caroline Myss, a medical intuitive, not a healer she says, helps people detect the traumas or other life events that are in their energy fields, which are depleting them. Once they attend to their "energy leaks," they are able to regain the power of their spirit to heal themselves.

From India, we learned that a system of energy centers, known as chakras, radiate outside and around each human body, but the energy source begins inside the body as distinct energy clusters in specific locations. *Chakras* is a Sanskrit name, meaning *spinning plates of energy.* There are at least seven chakras; they are considered the seat and source of physical, mental, emotional, and spiritual energy. The *Star Wars* movies familiarized us with the concept of focusing energy to heal and to win over evil: *May the force be with you!* Healers have found that the chakras involve all aspects of being human: survival instincts, sex drive, self-esteem, emotions, intellect, will, and spirituality. Energy healers believe that, in the process of contacting, experiencing, and releasing feelings, emotions, thoughts, and stress or bodily tension, our life force can change the course of our lives.

For those of us who are interested in utilizing the healing perspectives of East and West to achieve wholeness within oneself, we may begin with the seven chakras which are associated with particular areas of the human body. Matthew Fox[27] examines the chakras from a spirituality perspective and equates them with sin (the refusal to become who we are). Caroline Myss[28] equates the seven chakras with the seven Christian sacraments or religious symbolic, archetypal rituals from her medical intuitive perspective. The chakras ascend from 1 (base of spine), 2 (genitals and lower intestines), 3 (solar plexus and navel), 4 (heart), 5 (throat), 6 (pineal gland, third eye), and 7 (above the crown of the head).

> Chakra 1. Live with the wonders of cosmology (a relation to the whole), and live grounded to the earth's ecology (Fox).
> Baptism: Look upon your life and family as the environment in which you were meant to grow up (Myss).

> Chakra 2. Live with passion — better lustful than listless (Fox).
> Communion: Symbolic of the sharing of love and brotherhood with one another (Myss).

> Chakra 3: Live with moral courage and stand up to injustice (Fox).
> Confirmation: Take full responsibility for one's actions and live with a code of honor (Myss).

> Chakra 4: Live with compassion and resist fear (Fox).
> Marriage: Make a loving commitment, first to oneself, on behalf of another person (Myss).

> Chakra 5: Live with telling the truth (Fox).
> Confession: Recognize that the Spirit cannot carry its burdens and mistakes alone (Myss).

> Chakra 6: Live with giving birth and developing all of your creative powers of intellect and imagination (Fox).
> Ordination: Personal and spiritual development achieved through bringing energy to others (Myss).

Chakra 7: Love for the building of community and resist competitive,
envious relationships with others (Fox).
Extreme Unction: A symbolic perspective signifying our
desire to release the excess baggage we carry with us (Myss).

The energy of the seven chakras, according to Fox, may be captured by
one virtue: generosity. "Generosity is about giving from one's abundance, from
the depth of one's heart, from one's very soul. Generosity is about giving
without a guaranteed return."[29] Ordinary Americans are generous, which was
demonstrated by the outpouring of gifts and blood to New York City after the
September 11, 2001 terrorist attacks.

Archetypes are Carl Jung's creation; he believed that archetypes live in the
collective unconscious where all human beings' souls are interconnected
through the energy of universally inherited patterns of thought, ideas, and
images — or models. Those archetypes are portrayed in stories, myths, and
legends by their historical roles in life, which are passed down through the
ages. Examples of archetypes are: the Mother, the Trickster, the King, the
Servant, the Teacher, the Child, the Victim, the Judge, the Rescuer, the
Healer, the Pioneer, the Samaritan, the Seeker, the Wounded Child, the
Student, the Warrior, the Terrorist, the Artist, the Messiah, the Martyr, the
Saboteur. The chakras and archetypes are ways of finding our inner compass
in a society that does not honor emotional and spiritual knowings. Myss
devised an eighth chakra for those who seek their higher potential, to view life
as a spiritual journey to complement the physical one. She perceives twelve
archetypes to be "symbolic 'residents'" of an eighth chakra or Archetypal
dimension. Archetypal energies unconsciously influence us as individuals,
today, and help us understand our day-to-day life.

"The 'child,' 'wounded healer,' 'warrior,' 'wild woman,' and 'hero,' for
example, are but a handful of the many archetypes that have been introduced
into our therapeutic arena as working 'voices' to assist people in understanding
the Symbolic choreography behind their very real physical problems."[30] Carl
Jung's work with archetypes has been expanded upon in the past thirty-five
years by psychologists who believe: "Symbolic perceptions allow us to see that
the real meaning of a crisis lies in showing us what we need to learn about
ourselves."[31] From that perspective, blaming others for our problems needs to
be changed to being grateful to them for presenting us with and helping teach

211

us what we need to learn. China forced The Dalai Lama into exile. Consequently, His Highness says he is grateful to them for he has learned to be compassionate, and, simultaneously, he continues to seek Tibet's liberation. Myss writes, "The two attitudes — gratefulness and the struggle against injustice — are not mutually exclusive."[32]

Human consciousness is undergoing a transformation, and Myss's eighth chakra transcends the physical body and "contains a profile of the archetypal influences that are very much part of a person's spiritual development and everyday life experiences."[33] New-age beliefs that illness can be cured by the power of the mind alone or that the aging process can be reversed have yet to be proved. "The mind alone, without the aid of the human spirit and emotions, is limited in its influence on the body."[34] The body, though, has the ability to heal or to slay the mind, emotions, and spirit.

Medical acupuncture operates on the principle that mind and body are one interconnected entity which uses the emotions as the vehicle for communication. Penetrating emotions via the physical body can help people change their responses to stress, enabling them to heal the physical body-mind entity. Dr. Martha Grout is a physician who (1) uses her Western diagnostic skills and modalities to determine patients' medical illnesses, whether it is a functional illness requiring surgery or a life threatening condition, such as pneumonia, sepsis, diabetic ketoacidosis or cancer; (2) uses her French energetics or traditional Chinese medicine skills (acupuncture) to diagnose any energetic imbalance; and (3) treats the whole person: body, emotions, mind, and spirit. If the disease or problem exists on the emotional level primarily, then treatment is directed to those acupuncture points in the body. If the problem lies in a patient's mindset ("I am not worthy," "I do not deserve the good things in life," or other self-esteem issues), then acupuncture treatment is directed to the cerebral circulation pathways. Dr. Grout states, "Medical acupuncture is extremely useful...in treatment of the physical body, but also...because of its ability to penetrate the layers of defense and coping mechanisms our patients exhibit. Once the defenses are penetrated, patients have the opportunity of choosing to deal differently with their issues."[35a]

Traditional Chinese Medicine acknowledges the whole person: the body, mind, emotions, and spirit. Qi, or energy, powers the body's five major organs: liver, heart, spleen, lung, kidney, each of which has a ruling emotion

— anger, happiness, worry, sadness, and fear respectively. TCM practitioners look for and treat imbalances that create disharmony between the organs; disharmony manifests itself as the external symptoms of disease, excess weight, psychological, or spiritual problems. Stress, for example, compromises the liver's ability to function. Nan Lu, OMD, asserts that when we experience emotions that remain "stuck" or undigested, "Qi cannot move freely through your organs and their meridians and they will become clogged."[35b] His holistic approach to systemic balance requires "eating for healing," which includes eliminating foods that place a burden on the body's digestive system — such as meats and cheeses — and eating fruits, vegetables, pastas, rice, and walnuts so the digestive system can process food, emotions, and stress. In addition, he recommends practicing ten Wu Ming Qigong (energy work) movements each day to help the body, mind, emotions, and spirit connect and function in harmony.

"Regardless of whether an illness is a spiritual crisis or has developed from negativity, human nature is designed to seek a means of healing…people often do not heal because, either consciously or unconsciously, they have more faith in deeply potent belief patterns that interfere with healing than they do in their ability to heal."[36] Wounds that lead to negative esteem may be savored and perpetuated by leading a life of low expectations and irresponsibility. Although such a stance is self-defeating, it is a power play to evoke guilt or sympathy in supportive others. By dwelling on their wounds, they make the wounds deeper, and they are not invested in healing. Similarly, some people who have been criticized or humiliated in their childhood prefer not to make the effort to build positive esteem; they choose life courses that avoid further criticism or humiliation. "Wounds are like diversionary canals that drain water and spirit out of the river of our life. The more wounds we have, the more effort we have to put into calling our energy back, stopping up the energy drains…attending to our healing process…healing requires that our life-force be redirected back into our own life."[37] The choice is between dependency, controlling, being controlled, or empowerment.

Not all illness is due to negativity; sometimes the root cause includes diet, toxic environments, exposure to contaminated water, parasites, germs, bacteria, viruses, or inherited genetics. Finding the positives in the negatives and focusing upon the positives lead to healing and esteem. A journal can be a support group for us all.

Grace

Evolutionary scientists and evangelical and fundamentalist Christians in America are at odds: evolution versus creationism. The Arab religious extremists perceive the West's scientific achievements and multicultures to be threats to their beliefs, way of life, and very existence. Therefore, humanity is in need of a planetary theme that celebrates diversity, all life and the Earth. The search for a global cosmology, an interface between science and diverse religions, is underway but not within today's reach. Grace encompasses what we need to work toward a global cosmology: compassion, equality of being, justice, sharing, goodness, creativity, beauty, nature, love as a relationship among equals, and spirituality.

Meister Eckhart confessed that he found the world "amazing." His theological background and studies of the Bible led him to conclude that *graced love* is a "union between Creator and creature that takes place with those beings who have the fullest potential for consciousness...This kind of love goes beyond 'self-centeredness' and receives enlightenment from a divinely given love." Further, he preached that God is truly in all creatures on an equal basis and that "love is a twofold energy of both receiving and giving...let those who bring about great wonders in big, black books take an animal — perhaps a dog — to help them." From Meister Eckhart we also learn that "the ultimate act of grace and beauty is compassion."[38]

When Bill Moyers presented a program on the hymn, "Amazing Grace," for the first time, many people learned that it was written by John Newton, a former slave-ship British captain, who became an opponent of the slave trade and a minister.[39] Evidently, Captain Newton was transformed by compassion as a result of his slave trade experiences and probably kindled by John Wesley's (founded Methodism in 1761) and his brother John's hymns, for he wrote:

> Amazing grace! How sweet the sound that saved a wretch like me!
> I once was lost, but now am found; was blind, but now I see.
> 'Twas grace that taught my heart to fear and grace my fears relieved;

214

How precious did that grace appear, the hour I first believed.
Through many dangers, toils, and snares, I have already come;
'Tis grace hath brought me safe thus far, and grace will lead me home.

Such words as "wretch," "blind," and "taught my heart to fear" are not common in self-esteem books and seminars; however, "Amazing Grace" has touched more human hearts and has done more for self-esteem that most books and therapeutic interventions. Singing that hymn touches the soul and connects us in a way that is beyond rational understanding of our lives here on Earth.

One therapeutic intervention had a similar effect on a man who used sickness as a crutch whenever he faced difficult situations. When his sickness and attendant lateness became a problem in his professional life, he sought help. His therapist asked him to recall when he first found out that sickness worked for him. After a while, he remembered that, when he was very young, his mother used to have her friends in for lunch and a game of Bridge, and he resented her attention to and fun with them. He was in his room, with his nanny, when he heard the laughter downstairs. He felt sick to his stomach; his nanny called his mother, and she left her friends and spent the rest of the afternoon with him. From then on, he was sickly. The therapist asked him to go back to that day when he heard the laughter downstairs at his mother's Bridge party and, instead of giving in to being sick, to visualize himself running into the hall, leaning over the railing, and calling out to his mother, "Mother, I'm so glad you're having a good time!" He did. In effect, from grace, he gave his mother the gift of permission to have a good time. Amazingly, he felt more in control of how he felt and behaved from then on. Similarly, when Dostoevsky recreated Marey's loving face that Easter Sunday morning in the Siberian prison, he was filled with grace, for he saw his fellow prisoners and situation in a different light. Grace is like sunlight; it illuminates the darkness within human hearts and souls and allows them to blossom and grow.

When a fettered human spirit is unlocked, the mind, heart, and body are free to think, feel, and act differently. When we say a simple "thank you," we could make someone's day or at least a moment. When we say "Grace" at the breakfast, lunch, or dinner table, we are acknowledging the gifts and blessings we have and the people around us. Rituals are necessary to keep us mindful of our connection to the past and to the future. When a fettered human spirit is locked in, the mind, heart, and body are not free to be graceful; it remains self-centered or narcissistic as a negative way to access the "I am Somebody!" within since birth. Grace, though, is not a passive state; it is always found in the process of becoming a whole person with awareness of the divine sea in which we swim. Schools that teach and practice grace would release fettered spirits.

A Vision of Schools With Spirit

The separation of church and state is mandated by the U.S. Constitution's First Amendment. Its intent was to grant all citizens the freedom to express their religious beliefs by protecting them from one religious denomination over all. It was not intended to erase religion or spirituality from Americans' lives. Since World War II, the breakdown of the American family, our culture's emphasis upon materialism, and atheists' and Civil Liberties' objections to prayer and teaching morals and values in public schools' curricula have led to a general breakdown of character and to anarchy in the schools.

Some educators believe that our current dilemmas — violence in the schools, obsession with material things, meaning found outside not inside people — are spiritual dilemmas. Further, generations of young people will not benefit from the wisdom and connectedness needed to be a fully developed human being. Linda Lantieri's position on nurturing children's and teachers' spiritual lives is not aligned with any religion but with universal spiritual values: "compassion, honesty, fairness, responsibility, and respect."[40] Those universal values she attributed to a survey of 271 global thinkers:

> Many young people today are cut off from an understanding of their lives as having a 'higher purpose'— or any purpose at all. The kind of spiritual development we are advocating is not about allowing schools to display the Ten Commandments in their classrooms. We are talking about the kinds of approaches that encourage a commitment to matters of the heart and spirit that are among the positive building blocks of healthy development.[41]

With human beings' spiritual dimension (as well as emotions) excluded from school life, a standards-driven curriculum overrules multiple ways of children's seeing, being, and viewing the world while alienating them from their inner selves and each other. They bring guns to school, kill classmates, use drugs, and violently react to perceived "dissing," from disrespect to disease. "Circles of Courage" was developed by Nancy Carlsson-Paige. The Circles represent a medicine wheel used by tribal peoples to portray four developmental needs of children: "belonging, mastery, independence, and generosity."[42] The four directions, elements, races, and winds have many interpretations and human have many dimensions:

> Four forms of life: human, animal, plant, mineral
> Four elements: earth, air, water, and fire
> Four races: red, black, yellow, and white
> Four winds, Four seasons, Four directions...
> [Individuals] Spiritual, emotional, physical, and mental. [43]

"Every institution and social form we have is devoted to solving problems or to providing pleasure: the school, the family, the church, medicine, entertainment, our jobs...Our society has no place where the ultimate questions are honored as questions."[44] Rachel Kessler developed "'The Passage Program' — a set of principles and practices for working with adolescents to integrate heart, spirit, and community with a strong academic component — [The Passage Program] is a response to what matters deeply to teenagers, their usually unspoken questions and concerns are at its core."[45]

The Schools With Spirit Movement requires teachers with an open heart: "An open heart is what allows a teacher to be trustworthy and to help build trust among his or her students."[46] Kessler believes, "A teacher's love is at the heart of effective discipline. Love does not tolerate behavior that is abusive to anyone. But love does accept and forgive the child from whom this behavior springs."[47] With a focus on spirituality in the public schools, "Self-awareness takes on a new depth of inner exploration; managing emotions becomes self-discipline; empathy becomes a basis for altruism, caring, and compassion. And all of these basic skills for life can now be seen as building blocks of character."[48] Character-educators provide a framework that respects the separation of church and state. It may be possible to teach whole human beings when schools play a crucial role in reuniting people with themselves and others.

The American Character

Americans are individualistic, not collectivist-oriented. We are people first and subjects second, with a history of lawlessness. Our laws may be misdirected at times but often serve as checks on the possible abuses by governmental, industrial, academic, and parental power since, at heart, we are idealists. Researchers are finding that today's older Americans have undergone maturing-out processes and perceive middle age as a time of intense deepening of relationships and of caring, which concurs with Erik Erikson's eighth developmental stage: "Ego integrity."[49] "The American character, whatever its shortcomings, abounds in courage, creative energy and resourcefulness, and is bottomed upon the profound conviction that nothing in the world is beyond the power to accomplish."[50]

The American character was tested on September 11, 2001 and found to be as robust as ever. However, many are in the process of soul searching. The American government was also tested on 9/11 and found to have missed many opportunities: the dots were not connected between disparate intelligence reports about Osama bin Laden and Al Qaeda. Phoenix FBI agent Kenneth Williams' memo to his superiors about Muslim students learning to steer planes at flight schools was filed away. Vital data were ignored; no investigations followed, and buried data were inaccessible to other field offices. Governmental "failures" are due to bureaucrats' ego problems, interagency conflicts, and party-line promotions beyond demonstrated abilities.

American society has been tested since 9/11. A failure of trust occurred at corporate and government levels. Americans can no longer blindly trust its political leaders' and government agencies' competence. "Thinking outside the box" and stewardship are lacking in government's bureaucratic culture. Americans can no longer trust corporations are who they say they are on its financial statements; hence, trust in the stock markets has eroded. "No one has changed a great nation without appealing to its soul."[51] Soul murder occurred on many levels. The hatred, threats, and attacks we are experiencing from the

Middle East, since 9/11, have been exacerbated by our wars and the shocking actions of our domestic terrorists. Healing requires a cultural renewal.

The first task for Americans is healing the terrorist within!

The second task is to make the U.S. a better global citizen by making Corporate America more accountable and responsible by reinstalling trust and respect; by Americans' demanding a safer, cleaner, and greener America with products that reduce energy consumption and global warming; and by committing our resources to ensure human development by ending global poverty. Then the U.S. may be perceived by the world as a good global citizen.

The third task is to transform hatred, evil, and fear — misdirected love and abused safety — in souls, nations, institutions and organizations, and religious sects into compassionate ones. After 9/11, America's youth demonstrated their interest in doing good works, and no projects have been forthcoming. The first question "How can we live together peacefully on this planet?" requires creative solutions. "A change of meaning is necessary to change the world politically, economically, and socially. But that change must begin with the individual."[52] And there are many individuals, youths especially, who are not steeped in bureaucracy or corporacy and are not lacking in imagination. Their energy and resources must be tapped to find answers to that question and to strengthen America at home and abroad. In a democracy, money talks; it also impedes the phoenix from taking flight.

It is a sad irony that in our democracy the priorities are the global franchising of money-making ventures, such as McDonalds, Pizza Hut, Taco Bell, and Kentucky Fried Chicken, and supporting oil interests, while totally ignoring the creative people who have done their personal, professional, and cultural soul searching and have questions for us all: *"Why are institutions, everywhere, whether political, commercial, [educational], or social, increasingly unable to manage their affairs? Why are individuals, everywhere, increasingly in conflict with and alienated from the institutions of which they are part? Why are society and the biosphere increasingly in disarray?"*[53]

Institutional and organizational successes or failures are primarily due to its people and the cultures they endorse. Matters of the heart, mind, and spirit affect people's ability to lead and to work. "Primal"[54] leaders have self-awareness, self-esteem, empathy, and a vision of a better future. They have solid ideas and innovative ways to humanize institutions and organizations to make them work for Americans and to engender respect from abroad. As the richest and most powerful nation of the world, we need to balance business matters with people's concerns. We need other nations to collaborate with us against global terrorism. In addition, we need the experienced wisdom of our younger and older citizens to guide us.

The Graying of America

Life begins with an unfolding in youth as we respond to or ignore our world of possibilities. However, in later years we nourish ourselves through infolding when we focus upon insight from life experiences. Creative aging allows us to maximize our intake of the breath of life — prana, ch'i, flow, grace, life force or energy — that animates each of us and connects us to the universe within and outside ourselves. Our life tasks are to let go of the negative aspects of our histories, our habits of thought that make us feel old, our wish to set back the clock; the foregoing consumes enormous amounts of energy. Forgiveness is one way to release the drain of the past; however, it is not the only way to free up energy.

Some of us dread the loss of our youth, our looks, or the athletic abilities we used to have so we hold onto our thirties by wearing dated or youthful clothes, make-up, or hair styles that do not fit the times, our figure, or our individuality. Men also purchase sports cars, acquire trophy wives, or prefer the company of younger women to feel young. Toxic behaviors and toxic substances take a toll on our life force, impair our immune system, or make us prone to accidents.[55] Acceptance of others and ourselves is one of the conditions which must be present for esteem to occur. When we are open to personal transformation, our innate character or spirit emerges and releases who and what we are meant to be. Change is a part of life. We transform the food we eat to fuel our minds and bodies. We are transformed as the world changes: *The old order changeth, yielding place to new.*

The graying of America has led to the fear of aging and of looking old in our youth-oriented society, so many Americans exercise to be fit. Exercising the mind is equally important; yet, change is often perceived as having to reject the old self for a new self. Adding new ideas, the gift of imagination, and being original at least once a day keep boredom at bay and provide the incentive to sort through the old self's mental closet to see what does and does not fit us today. We do not have to wait for a crisis, such as an illness or 9/11, before we undertake change. Healing programs that encompass the physical, mental, emotional, and spiritual are the bases for internal and external makeovers to uncover our original selves. When we view life as a gift, we may review the many factors that make our lives work, not work, connect or disconnect us from our energy and the life force. Spiritual growth comes from sharing with others. With a gift perspective, we form a group or a think tank to devise projects to work for the betterment of all life on our planet; then we become part of the solution.

Nature Revisited

Biblical stories, such as in Genesis, granted dominion to man over the Earth and its plants and creatures. Such a literal approach to creation is the antithesis of Native American peoples' approach to creation whereby one creature sustains another so we are all interdependent. It used to be considered pagan and a threat to the "civilized" world to have empathy and compassion for the Earth's creatures and nature. This is still the cultural norm for economic, political, and religious reasons. With public awareness of the planet's changed condition and the need for changes in government policies and people's attitudes and actions, there is an openness to saving endangered species, regulating the burning of fossil fuels, limiting the production of hazardous chemicals, limiting pesticides and fertilizers, and to generating environmentally sustainable technologies: solar and wind power and natural or organic processes.

There is also awareness and acknowledgment that man's dominance over the Earth and the animal kingdom has led to redundant and unnecessary experimentation, exploitation, suffering, and extinction of some species. Most people have not lost their capacity to empathize with other human beings or with animals and to enjoy nature. Through communion with animals and nature, a sense of our basic human nature is revived or awakened. Some educators, such as Dr. Sam Ross of the Green Chimneys School in Brewster, New York, utilizes animals to redevelop children who have been physically, psychologically, emotionally, or sexually abused. The president emeritus of

The Delta Society (Dr. Leo K. Bustad[56]) asserted that our survival as a species is contingent upon fostering compassion for living things and that our nurturing contact with animals and nature ensures individual and communal health. Strong bonds exist between animals and humans. A former Human Development student, Carol, told us about her husband's dog. Her husband died of cancer. The day after his death, she noticed that his Dalmatian had grown increasingly anxious and continuously ran to the front door. Finally, she decided to take the dog to the funeral home. Seeing her husband, the dog wagged his tail and ran to the casket. He jumped up, sniffed the body, and "knew" his master was dead, for he turned around and immediately wanted to go home. The dog did not run to the door any more.

Jeanne rescued a dog from the streets of Philadelphia, near her apartment, when she was attending college. She saw him lying next to a telephone booth; he was so dirty that she could not tell what kind of dog he was, and one of his eyes was glazed over. She coaxed him into the elevator. At home, she gave him water, food, and at least three baths. He was beautiful, looked like a wolf with some collie, and about a year old. She named him "Amadeus" after Mozart. He became very attached to her; then she was told no dogs were allowed in her building so she brought him home to New York. When she left, he had fears of abandonment; he kept one of her shoes in his mouth and constantly ran from her bedroom door to the front door. Left alone, he chewed doors so Florence took him to her appointment with Dr. Verter, a chiropractor in New Jersey. The receptionist kept him at her desk. After the session, the doctor patted Amadeus on the head and realized that his neck was out of alignment. He said he had not treated dogs but, as a favor, Amadeus could share Florence's next session. On the floor, Florence stroked Amadeus' head while the doctor manipulated his body. When the doctor finished, Amadeus whipped around, faced the doctor, and held up his paw to shake. He lived for fourteen more years with one good eye; the other eye did not need a glass replacement as recommended by our veterinarian. He was Jeanne's constant companion until he died in her arms last year. Her painting of him is hanging in her living room. Amadeus lovingly touched our lives.

When we accept that the universe and "Life includes, in its essence, hardships of many kinds,"[57] we do not make avoidance of our own pain and suffering central to our lives. Within the universe and within human beings, there are "Violence, destruction, and disruption, on the one hand; creativity, synthesis, integration on the other."[58] That does not mean we condone the cruelties and injustice practiced on Earth today; it means that tension exists, hatred exists, and people respond humanely or inhumanely, depending upon their level of self-development. "Case studies reveal that people who voluntarily help others — no matter how demanding the work they take on — are happier and healthier than the rest of us."[59] Most of us are familiar with the biblical story of the Good Samaritan. We call his actions "altruism" — a word coined by Auguste Comte (1798-1857), a French mathematician and philosopher. Today, altruism is tinged with a reward — "What's in it for me?" — since we may get publicity for our company or ourselves, it looks good on our resumé, or we get a tax credit. Strictly defined, though, altruism means voluntarily helping others without an expectation of external rewards, even if it may entail a risk or costs. An internal reward, that is, feeling good about helping another, is the motive and reward.

A sacred dimension to our existence emerges when we exercise our creativity-synthesis-integration side to develop positive esteem, not to "live happily ever-after" but to activate the diverse dimensions of our being, to respond to those who need help, to work for the well-being and empowerment of others, and for the betterment of the Earth and its community. Human beings have minds so we will have thoughts and emotions, just as the ocean has waves. Waves go back to the ocean; thoughts and emotions remain in the mind. When we observe our negative thoughts and emotions from an unbiased attitude, the nature of our thoughts and emotions can change. When our attitude toward ourselves and others changes, our meaning changes, and so does our world. It is through our relational Self that we perceive the larger picture, the cosmos. When global problems can be addressed from a spiritual base, then the ideal world that has been in our hearts will also be in our thoughts, feelings, and actions.

Chaos exists, but there is order even in chaos; so order, harmony, and compassion exist in the universe and within human beings. Our common task is to become a single tribe by understanding our common origins. Our human story is not separate from the cosmic story, the plant story, or the animal story. Our destinies are intertwined. The human soul shrivels as the natural world shrinks in resources and capacity to regenerate itself. We nourish each other,

223

and when that intimate dynamic relationship is destroyed, we collude in extinguishing species of plants and animals and in degrading our environment. When we value the collection of objects more than the communion of life, we deny our natural tendencies and exploit the natural world.

When Grandfather (Pop) Edmund Frampton, Anglican lay preacher, ship captain, and shipbuilder, visited us in Brooklyn, NY, after World War II, the Cathedral of St. John the Divine in New York City was first on his list. That Episcopalian, yet ecumenical, community is the epitome of creative spirituality at work with its celebration of Earth, art, animals, and people. The Cathedral's building program may never be finished, especially since the fire on December 18, 2001, with ensuing soot and water damage. We human beings will never be finished either; however, many of us abort our natural impulse to grow, learn, and respond to the creative impulse and spirituality within us all.

The Healing Path

All humanity's spiritual teachers have the same message: "the purpose of life on earth is to achieve union with our fundamental, enlightened nature."[60] The Tower of Babel failed to be completed in Biblical times when the people's language was "confounded" by a displeased God, so they no longer communicated. In the 21st century, "Babel" is the struggle to hold onto literal translations of sacred texts, from the Bible to the Koran, when the roles of women, banking, and punishment have changed. Strict adherence to scriptures written in ancient times (7th century or so) causes much of the conflict between people, nations, and diverse religions, so international and interreligious relationships fail to be built.

An enlightened or spiritual vision is necessary for our survival when terrorism and disintegration are imminent. Raw egos' success and power celebrate greed, which is destroying the sacredness of life and our planet. The path to self- and other-esteem is strewn with spiritual charlatans who want us to believe that they are saints. We need a master mirror: a journal can be a mirror that reflects back to us all our confusion with clarity. When the doors of perception are open, all the old concepts of self and the world dissolve and an entirely *new* way of seeing and being opens up to us. As Blake said, *If the doors of perception were cleansed, Everything would appear...as it is, infinite.*[61]

224

The United Nations has a forum to work with global conflicts. Episcopalian Bishop William Edwin Swing[62] believes that the world's religions need a forum to resolve religious conflicts. He founded United Religious Initiative in response to a "calling" in 1993 to honor all spiritual expressions on Earth. URI is an organization, not a religion, and the global organization was officially born in 2000. URI's mission is to focus on building bridges across diverse spiritual boundaries. With 9/11 and the ensuing wars, there is a need for such a forum. Like viruses, Internet rumors and global satellite TV fuel more hate, reinforce stereotypes, and infect people's minds, which make it harder to work with global conflicts through human relations.

Since 9/11, three of the world's religions are in crisis: "Roman Catholics learned that some of the princes of their church protected priests who sexually abused children. Muslims have seen their scholars condemned and their scriptures deconstructed for signs that Islam encourages terrorism. Jews in Europe have suffered a wave of anti-Semitic attacks as world opinion hardened toward Israel."[63] Such a confluence of crises occurred during a violent period in the world, from 800 to 200 BC, according to Karen Armstrong, and the result was spiritual thinkers and leaders forged religious development. She said, "We could use this suffering to create wonderful new religious systems, as the Buddha did, or we could retreat into the spiritual barbarism of hatred."[64] Religion could be a healing not a divisive force.

In transitional times, we need faith, hope, love, and a journal to sustain us. A life review is rewriting, possibly writing for the first time, the story of our lives through anecdotes, past and present. Since the purpose of life is to live it, "without stories there is no pattern, no understanding, no art, and no character — merely habits, events passing before the eyes of an aimless observer, a life unreviewed, a life lost in the living of it."[65] A paradigm shift from physiology (the selfish gene theory: the perpetuation of one's genes or of self) to psychology ("What is important for my character?"[66]) redirects our lives toward life reviews, insight, wisdom, compassion, companionship, the arts, and service: an epiphany. Ultimately, there needs to be a paradigm shift that includes spirituality to understand the true meaning of life. The Dalai Lama says, "if we wish to die well, we must learn how to live well: Hoping for a peaceful death, we must cultivate peace in our mind, and in our way of life."[67]

The Life, Breath, and Spirit Within!

"My house is your house, and my arm is your arm," said an elderly native of Anegada, British Virgin Islands, as he welcomed us into his humble cottage. He shared his homemade plum wine with us as his stories and our stories blended into one. Thousands of miles north, another island — Newfoundland — is dear to our hearts. Newfoundlanders' acts of kindness and generosity are not random; it is part of their Newfie philosophy, similar to our experience in Anegada. Newfoundlanders had an opportunity "to walk their talk," to demonstrate their spirituality to strangers and to the world on 9/11/2001. After the terrorist attacks on New York City and Washington, DC, the U.S. closed its air space, so all flights enroute to the U.S. were forced to return or land in other countries, particularly Canada. *The Day The World Came to Town*: 9/11 in Gander, Newfoundland,[68] is a true story of the compassion of people who responded from their hearts, minds, spirit, and resources to the nearly seven thousand passengers with children and animals who descended from thirty-eight jetliners and smaller planes upon their tiny town, with a population of ten thousand or so. At a time when the boundaries of civilized behavior were being breached by some human beings, other human beings were making visible the often invisible but vital essence of being human.

In the next chapter, there is an opportunity to gain self-knowledge through a self-administered, self-scoring, self-evaluation instrument. SEA consists of 100 statements about the domains of esteem. Your responses may show that you have (a) considerable self-awareness and self-understanding, (b) resolved many negative experiences from childhood, or (c) learned from your experiences and do not wish to pass them on to others. Your responses to the statements may reflect your growth, not the facts of your life. Only you know the difference! The SEA statements and scores focus attention on what has yet to be learned and where to start building or enhancing positive self- and other-esteem. SEA is not a test; you may use it as a coach to heal the terrorist within and outside self and to attain a higher level of human development. When we have a higher perspective from which to understand and accept ourselves, we are more empowered to exercise our free will, to manage our own dark side, the terrorist within, and to confront the terrorists outside ourselves. When we become whole, we contribute to healing the universe.

Nine

No wind is favorable for the sailor who doesn't know
in which direction he is going. —Anon.

SELF-ESTEEM ASSESSMENT (SEA)
©1993 by Florence Pittman Matusky and Jeanne Elodie Matusky

SEA consists of 100 statements covering diverse aspects of the self-esteeming process. SEA is designed to access the extent to which a statement has meaning for you, in the here-and-now, from a value of 5: TRUE to a value of 1: FALSE. SEA is not a psychometric test. Our current situation, attitudes, behavior, and responses reveal our esteem status; however, SEA is a quick way to focus your attention on the sources, processes, and consequences of positive to negative self-esteem in life and at work that may be out of your awareness. SEA is an assessment: the quantitative results are a guide to what you have yet to learn and how to maintain or enhance self-esteem in the spirit of self-discovery. Statement numbers with responses that afflict your comfort level may be recorded on page 203 for later journaling.

In the blank spaced provided before each statement, write a number, from 5 to 1, depending upon the extent to which you think or feel the statement applies to you in the here-and-now, using the following scale:

> 5 = TRUE to a VERY GREAT EXTENT
> 4 = TRUE to a GREAT EXTENT
> 3 = TRUE to a MODERATE EXTENT
> 2 = TRUE to a SMALL EXTENT
> 1 = FALSE or TRUE to a VERY SMALL EXTENT

_____1. When I was a child, at least one caring person gave me a view of myself as a lovable and capable human being.

_____2. At school, I experienced one or more teachers who valued me or inspired me to learn.

_____3. I am responsible for the results of my thoughts, feelings, actions, and life choices.

_____4. My work (career or studies) gives me a genuine sense of fulfillment.

_____5. I am curious about others' ideas, beliefs, and experiences for I am interested in expanding my worldviews.

_____6. I feel physically attractive.

_____7. I like my name.

_____8. I share power with others; I do not seek to control them.

_____9. I am comfortable learning new skills, working, or relating without extreme self-consciousness or shyness.

____10. I attribute my successes to my abilities, beliefs, and efforts, not to luck or my IQ.

____11. My relationship with my mother (or mother figure) gave me a positive foundation for building other relationships.

____12. When I was a child, I was proud of my family and felt I belonged to a special group.

____13. I have the inner strength to say "No" when I want to, without feeling I have to go along to be accepted or liked.

____14. I turn potentially dull, everyday tasks into enjoyable activities.

____15. I let people know I love, admire, appreciate, or respect them in a manner they understand.

____16. I perceive my emotions and feelings as valid data to be integrated with my intellectual, moral and ethical data before taking action.

____17. I like how tall I am.

___18. I accept others' values, beliefs, lifestyles, and special interests as valid for them, even if they do not agree with mine.

___19. The challenge and enjoyment of an activity motivate me more than any pressure to perform or any expectation of a reward.

___20. I have a purpose in life that is larger than myself or my own self-interest.

___21. My sexual self was and continues to be treated with respect by others and myself.

___22. I have learned to think for myself, to be open to new ideas or information, and to discriminate between facts and fears, needs and wants.

___23. I follow through on all my appointments, commitments, and promises.

___24. I have a sense of control over my life and work.

___25. I grant myself and others the freedom to make mistakes and to learn from experience.

___26. I am physically healthy: free of any chronic illnesses or any recurring problems.

___27. I am in charge of and control my intake of alcohol, drugs, food, and cigarettes.

___28. I learn from my life experiences, choosing to recall and focus upon the positives.

___29. I resolve conflicts or problems where they arise, instead of creating new ones or magnifying old ones elsewhere.

___30. When I receive praise, I thank the giver for sharing his or her perceptions.

___31. When I was growing up, my parents (or caregivers) showed me they cared for me and for our relationship.

___32. When I was an infant, my father (or father figure) participated in rearing and caring for me.

___33. I look for people's positive intentions for their actions instead of judging them.

___34. I pull my own weight in social and business situations. I am neither a big spender nor a freeloader.

___35. I trust that the problems I encounter or the hard times I experience are opportunities to learn or to improve myself.

___36. I have a positive sense of self that allows me to listen objectively and dispassionately to others' criticisms or insults.

___37. Despite social restraints or others' expectations, demands, or lack of direction, I develop career goals and follow my own definition of success.

___38. I focus more on improving my credibility and knowledge and on gaining experience than on promoting my public image.

___39. I am comfortable expressing my opinions and speaking in front of a class or group.

___40. I value my uniqueness, and I exercise my creativity.

___41. My parents (or caregivers) set clearly defined rules and limits for me as a child, and they practiced what they preached.

___42. I function more effectively when I listen to and respond from my body, mind, emotions, and spirit.

___43. I seek primary sources of data instead of relying upon hearsay or rumors.

___44. I believe in lifelong learning, and I actively pursue it.

___45. I accept my own and others' imperfections.

___46. My physical self was treated with respect by all during my childhood.

___47. I am competent and capable and feel comfortable demonstrating my talents, skills, and ideas.

___48. I represent myself accurately on self-assessments; I have no need to lie or embellish.

___49. My sense of self is based upon more than my role, job, title, status, possessions, relationships, or other outside-self things.

___50. I perceive differences among people and nations as opportunities to learn more about others and myself.

___51. My relationship with my father (or father figure) gave me a positive foundation for building other relationships.

___52. My religious, spiritual, or philosophical learnings and experiences reinforce my belief that all human beings are worthy.

___53. I am honest and fair with everyone.

___54. I use humor to dissolve tension, defuse conflict, minimize resistance, and just for fun.

___55. When I give from my heart, I also receive.

___56. Sometimes I like to be alone.

___57. Only I can embarrass myself, not the behavior or looks of my family, friends, associates, or acquaintances.

___58. My commitment to myself is balanced by a commitment to the common good of the human family and the Earth's family.

___59. I choose to experience and express the full range of emotions, from joy to anger (without repressing or projecting them onto others), in ways that are not harmful to others and myself.

___60. I help people to help themselves instead of doing for them what they can learn to do.

___61. My parents, caregivers, teachers, or mentors instilled in me the idea I could become whatever I choose to do and be.

___62. I make friends easily and have long-term relationships.

___63. I help, not hinder, others with their personal and professional development.

___64. Even when the odds appear to be against me or when faced with personal losses, I still have positive future expectations.

___65. I appreciate and acknowledge others' ideas and achievements.

___66. I eat a healthy, balanced diet and exercise; I am in good physical condition.

___67. When my opinions, beliefs, or actions are challenged, I do not become defensive; nor do I have an overwhelming need to defend myself.

___68. I expend more energy on improving myself and my condition rather than on blaming my parents or others for what I did not get when I was growing up.

___69. In a sensitive and assertive way, I deflect others' attempts to control or undermine me.

___70. I would mentor (or coach) someone unlike me or someone who is more competent or ambitious than I am.

___71. I have fond memories of my childhood and of those with whom I shared it.

___72. When I "step into others' shoes" to understand them, I keep my own perspective as well.

___73. I am nice, fair, reasonable, and hardworking; yet, I do not let people lacking those qualities take advantage of me.

___74. I am able to go to movies, theatres, or restaurants by myself and to travel alone to unfamiliar places.

___75. My definition of success includes helping others to succeed.

___76. The best resource I bring to any situation is myself.

___77. I have friends who are of different racial, cultural, religious, and ethnic origin than I am.

___78. There is nothing in my personal and professional lives that I need to hide from anyone.

___79. I ask for what I want from others: I do not expect them to guess or to intuit what I want or to interpret passive messages.

___80. I enjoy working with my hands (gardening, cooking, cleaning, painting, odd jobbing, hobbies) and/or walking, running, jogging, dancing, etc.

___81. I was spoken to with respect when I was growing up, and any criticism I received was constructive.

___82. When I interact with people of different races and cultures, I am aware that our verbal/nonverbal communication differences may affect our perception of any intended meanings.

___83. I encourage people to do their best; I do not put people down or set them up to lose.

___84. If things do not work out as planned, I may not like it; I consider it a temporary setback, and I still feel worthy and capable.

___85. I view the world from a trust-oriented, not a fear-oriented perspective.

___86. I am content with my weight for my height and frame.

___87. The world is a better place because I am here.

___88. I treat myself, men, women, children, animals, and the Earth with equal respect.

___89. I can let go of things and people and move on for my own good or for theirs.

___90. I accept and genuinely love myself "as is."

___91. When I was a child, my family accepted and respected me for who I was, for not only what and who I would become.

___92. I believe and practice that winning or success is achieved through honest and moral means.

___93. I respect others' rights, successes, and property without feeling envy, competitive, malice, or resentment.

___94. I have supportive, give-and-take relationships in my life.

___95. I can admire something without needing to own it; I can love someone without being possessive.

___96. I know that belittling, blaming, or contributing to others' powerlessness reveals more about me than about another.

___97. Before responding, I look for the positive in others' actions.

___99. I market myself and receive rewards commensurate with my skills, expertise, efforts, education, or experience.

__ 100. I believe and practice that all of Earth's human beings, living things, and creatures are interconnected.

Self-Esteem Assessment Data for Journaling

SEA statements that require my extra attention are:

1. Statement #_____

2. Statement #_____

3. Statement #_____

4. Statement #_____

5. Statement #_____

6. Statement #_____

7. Statement #_____

8. Statement #_____

9. Statement #_____

10. Statement #_____

The Self-Esteem Assessment (SEA) Table for scoring the assessment may be found on the next page.

HD	CD	MD	PD	SD
1.____	2.____	3.____	4.____	5.____
6.____	7.____	8.____	9.____	10.____
11.____	12.____	13.____	14.____	15.____
16.____	17.____	18.____	19.____	20.____
21.____	22.____	23.____	24.____	25.____
26.____	27.____	28.____	29.____	30.____
31.____	32.____	33.____	34.____	35.____
36.____	37.____	38.____	39.____	40.____
41.____	42.____	43.____	44.____	45.____
46.____	47.____	48.____	49.____	50.____
51.____	52.____	53.____	54.____	55.____
56.____	57.____	58.____	59.____	60.____
61.____	62.____	63.____	64.____	65.____
66.____	67.____	68.____	69.____	70.____
71.____	72.____	73.____	74.____	75.____
76.____	77.____	78.____	79.____	80.____
81.____	82.____	83.____	84.____	85.____
86.____	87.____	88.____	89.____	90.____
91.____	92.____	93.____	94.____	95.____
96.____	97.____	98.____	99.____	100.____
T: ____ %	T:____ %	T:____ %	T:____ %	T:____%

(Total SEA scores for each of the domains)

BREAKDOWN: FIVE HUMAN DEVELOPMENT PROCESSES

Psych- ological.	Physical Processes	Interper- sonal	Intraper- sonal	Emotional Literacy
1.____	6.____	11.____	16.____	57.____
21.____	26.____	31.____	36.____	59.____
41.____	46.____	51.____	56.____	68.____
61.____	66.____	71.____	76.____	74.____
81.____	86.____	91.____	96.____	90.____
**_____	____	____	____	_____**
***_____	____	____	____	_____***

SCORING: CONVERSION TABLE

** Total 5 6 7 8   9 10 11 12 13 14 15 16 17 18 19 20 21 22 23 24 25
*** Adj.T 0 5 10 15 20 25 30 35 40 45 50 55 60 65 70 75 80 85 90 95 100

237

SELF-ESTEEM ASSESSMENT SCORING

The SEA Scores are determined by inserting the numerical score assigned to each of the SEA statements (1-100) under the columns for HD, CD, MD, PD, and SD. The scoring is easy. Transfer the numerical scores for SEA statements 1 through 5 to the first line of the five columns headed HD, CD, MD, PD, and SD. Transfer the scores for SEA statements 6 through 10 to the second line of the five columns, until completed.

Total the numerical responses for HD and place it at the bottom of the HD column under Totals: Human Development. Continue to add the next four columns and transfer the totals to each domain. The score for each column represents the score, based upon 100 percent, for each of the Self-Esteem domains. To ascertain your Overall SEA Score, add the totals for HD, CD, MD, and SD under SEA OVERALL SCORE, in the spaces provided, to get each score, then divide by 5 to get your SEA Overall Score.

Human Development is divided into five processes: (1) Psychological, (2) Physical, (3) Interpersonal, (4) Intrapersonal, and (5) Human Brain: Emotional Literacy. Under "BREAKDOWN," there are five columns with SEA statement numbers and blank spaces for numerical scores. For the first four processes, refer to HD only to complete the blanks with the scores from 1–96. For (5), the Emotional Literacy process, complete the blanks with the scores sprinkled throughout CD, MD, PD, and SD. Then total each of the five columns and list them in the spaces with **Scores to the extreme right. To convert these **Scores, refer to the CONVERSION TABLE at the bottom of the page and find the adjusted score *** for each of the five ** scores. The adjusted score for those in each column is based upon 100 percent.

Scoring ranges and an interpretation of them for learning purposes are discussed below.

Suggested Range of SEA Scores

90 - 100	IDEAL Self-Esteem	Positive Self-Esteem
80 - 89	HEALTHY Self-Esteem	Positive Self-Esteem
70 - 79	MODERATE Self-Esteem	Positive Self-Esteem
60 - 69	LOW Self-Esteem	Negative Self-Esteem
0 - 59	VERY LOW Self-Esteem	Negative Self-Esteem

Positive: Ideal and Healthy Self-Esteem

Ideal Self-Esteem (90-100) is not necessarily better than Healthy Self-Esteem (80-89). An Ideal score may be interpreted as our having experienced excellent self-esteem development, and we are functioning at optimum. It may also be due to idealizing or not wishing to examine our parenting and our transition into the world beyond family. Either of these positions may lead to complacency or to passivity; if so, it is time to address our delusions and perfectionism so we may become what we are capable of becoming.

Positive (Healthy) self-esteem is attainable by most of us, but it is not always practiced. It represents a reflective, objective yet positive perception of past and present experiences. If there seems to be a discrepancy between low SEA scores and our positive self-esteem, a felt sense of self-esteem is more reliable than an assessment covering only 100 pertinent statements that are more indicative of a trend than a fact. If, however, there is a discrepancy between high SEA scores and negative self-esteem, a felt sense of self-esteem may call for an attitude adjustment. All of us have capabilities we are not channeling into action; or we may have specific thoughts, feelings, and unconscious motivations that are not empowering us to learn from past mistakes and disappointments or to take risks. Artists, for example, may be talented and creative but must produce art to make the talent and creativity visible.

If we are high achievers or performers and our self-esteem is not positive, it is possible that (a) it is time to upgrade our opinion of ourselves, which may be stuck at an earlier or adolescent level; or (b) we may be more extrinsically (external rewards; external pressures) motivated than intrinsically (internal rewards; internal pressure) motivated. Some of us overestimate our skills; others underestimate theirs, but most of us estimate our skills accurately, if we are not self-centered or narcissistic, which is negative self-esteem.

There are differences between what people do and what they say they do in life, at work, and on tests and assessments. If the self-assessment data is understood and utilized for its intended purpose, then the human tendency to inflate or deflate scores may not be operative. Some people practice self-deception, especially under conditions perceived to be a threat to egos, image, or survival. However, at a deep level of knowing, people know the difference.

They know when they are fooling themselves and others. It is important to access our deep knowings, if only for ourselves.

Positive: Moderate Self-Esteem

Moderate self-esteem (70-79): On most assessments, a score between 70 and 79 is considered a good enough score. Because of self-esteem's role as buffer between the ego and its environment, we emphasize the necessity of improving the sense of self as master and creator of our lives. Just as a woman cannot be just a little bit pregnant, we cannot settle for just a little bit of self-esteem.

Unsocialized, underdeveloped, or unprotected human egos with moderate scores are less liable than those with negative self-esteem to resort to raw, uncivilized, undersocialized emotional expressions in interpersonal and environmental situations. Real or imagined physical, verbal, and nonverbal attacks evoke the innate fight, flight, freeze, or feign syndromes and self-destructive or antisocial behavior.

Negative: Low and Very Low Self-Esteem

Those who are under- or oversocialized, undernourished, or underprotected, or have unexamined human egos, usually experience low or negative (60-69) and very low or negative (0-59) self-esteem. There are many people whose negative self-esteem leads to underutilizing their talents and abilities; they may be underemployed despite their earned academic credentials and work experience. And then there are those with unacknowledged negative self-esteem, the narcissists who feed on others; they hold high positions, climb the social ladder, and are often toxic to those whose lives they touch. Negative self-esteem requires a "Yes" to self-development.

We may not be able to change the facts of our past, but we can seek new facts, reinterpret old facts and view experience from a more positive, objective, less negative emotional schema. "Except in a limited biological sense, in fact, we are shaped less by our environment and our past experiences than by the image we create of the past,"[1] present and future. We may adopt new behaviors, including behaving "as if." There is a difference between the false front of a negative self-esteem person, which is a defense mechanism to protect

240

or enhance an insecure ego, and behaving "as if" we already have positive esteem. Behaving "as if" is a conscious position since we are practicing, not just playacting. If, however, the practicing eventually leads to becoming what we project, then the "as if" stance is positive. Otherwise, the stance is negative. The evidence comes from many sources that self-enhancing beliefs impact on motivation, persistence, and performance.

Self-esteem is based upon perception. Our perception of our self-esteem influences what we do and how we think, feel, and act. If we think we have positive self-esteem and act as if we do have it, then we do. However, if we think we have positive self-esteem and act as if we do not have it, then there is a lack of congruence, that is, we think one way and behave in another way; a mixed message is sent. Astute receivers of mixed messages tend to unconsciously perceive and believe the nonverbal communication.

Other SEA Scores: The Five Domains

The Human Development (HD) SEA scores appear to be the lowest for most people who have completed the sample assessment in the U.S., Canada, and Russia. Our human development experiences and our perceptions of them prepare us well or poorly for entry into the world beyond our immediate family. Class discussions and dialogues with individuals informed us that parenting and teaching in Russia and the U.S. have much in common.

The Biblical commandment, "Honor Thy Father and Thy Mother," does not encourage us to examine our upbringing.[2] Unfortunately, we do not have a commandment for parents, teachers, and society to "Honor Thy Children."

Cultural Development

The Cultural Development (CD) SEA scores appear to be the next lowest for most people completing the sample self-assessment. We learn early to stereotype, distinguishing between friend (the familiar) and foe or stranger (the unknown). Opposites may initially be attracted to each other, but the "we" versus "they" attitudes emerge, and the "they" become the scapegoats for the faults and deficits of the dominant "we."

The human mind leaps to make sense out of its world; hence, people have a tendency to label, categorize, and perceive people as the embodiments of their conceptual constructs, perceptual biases, and cultural imperialism. Our brains have a built-in schema to seek out and reinforce our biases and to ignore those that do not fit our mindset.

Moral and Ethical Development

From the prior samplings of the SEA Assessment, Human Development had the lowest score, Cultural Development had the next lowest score, and Moral and Ethical Development had the highest scores of all the Self-Esteem domains. We appear to learn our moral lessons well and usually operate within the safety of our own moral and ethical system with people who are like-minded or of the same culture.

New research from Princeton University indicates that the emotions are key to tough moral judgments and decisions. Images of what parts of the brain are operative, when presented with moral issues, show major activity in the emotion-related brain area. Evidently, the emotional brain is located in the frontal lobes as well as in the right hemisphere. Human beings are symmetrical; therefore, the right side of the brain governs the left side of the body and vice-versa. However, right-handed people's emotional brain is usually in the right hemisphere; whereas, in left-handed-people the emotional brain may be in the left or in the right hemisphere. Social and political issues that divide us are not resolved through logical, analytical reasoning of the left-brain. The brain's cognitive side, the left, may balance emotional, moral, and ethical compulsive responses when there is a little time in between the stimulus and the response.

Personal and Professional Development

The Personal and Professional Development scores from the SEA samples have been the third lowest scores for participants. The traits we are expected to learn on our own are emotional literacy, self-discipline, self-reliance, religious tolerance, mutual respect, free inquiry, honesty, democratic humanism, and spirituality. Few of these are part of education systems' curricula. Those who concentrate on intellectual development only may achieve status, money, and power due to their professional competence or importance in the system; however, their Achilles heel will be their emotions. They may use their power to dehumanize or womanize or use drugs and alcohol to assuage felt ego deficits. Those who do not concentrate on their intellectual development may also get stuck at the emotional, adolescent level and adopt macho behaviors, cultural stereotypes, and perceptual prejudices to overcome their fear of differences.

Our personal and professional development in the 21st century is also hindered by traditional male-female stereotyping, poor attitudes about work, disvaluing the arts, media's emphasis upon violence, society's obsession with short-term versus long-term planning, materialism, consumerism, image versus substance, competition, and its obsolete family, educational, and bureaucratic systems that do not work for the majority, leading to violence, substance abuse, and poverty. The huge gap between the haves and the have-nots is undermining our democracy and freedom.

It is our responsibility to develop our talents to capacity and to seek our niche where our mind is not imprisoned so we may fulfill ourselves and participate in the activity of the world.

Spiritual Development

The Spiritual Development scores from the SEA samples have been the next highest to Moral and Ethical Development, except for the youngest participants. The SEA scores in the SEA samples taken in Russia (Novosibirsk, Siberia, and St. Petersburg) were the highest in Spirituality of the five domains. "Why is Russia called 'Mother Russia'?" The origin of the word *Russia* is Scandinavian, from the Vikings who pronounced Russia — Russ-she-ah — which is a feminine word encompassing *nature and spirit*, in the nurturing sense.

Concern for and reaching out to others become issues for older and wiser adults who are no longer preoccupied with their personal selves. However, more young people are becoming conscious of and responding to our social and environmental problems. The terrorists' attacks have galvanized them to action as they respond with dollars, letters, flowers, and discussions at home, in school, and in church.

Other SEA Scores: Human Development's Five Processes

1. Psychological Processes

As dependent infants cry for food, touching, and changing, they feel secure and loved if their basic needs are met. With their basic needs met, the stage is set for trusting others and loving themselves. If we did not get what we needed to affirm ourselves, earlier, we seek affirmation elsewhere, job, money, material things, but we can learn to reparent ourselves so our positive self-esteem is vested inside ourselves, not outside.

2. Physical Processes

Looking like a disliked or feared aunt, uncle, or cousin is not conducive to accepting or liking one's physical self. Schools' physical education departments have contributed to our early views of our physical selves: the usual team selection process ultimately stigmatizes those who are chosen last. The Jocks are revered; the Nerds are despised, and all labeled students are diminished by Bullies and by the belittling of adults, parents, teachers, and other peers.

Not looking like the fashion models or stars, not knowing that most magazines airbrush their subjects, and having siblings and peers who are more attractive than we are could lead to negative views of our face or bodies. At 5' 7" and 135 lbs. in high school, Felix wished to be 6' 2" and 175 lbs. Now he jokes that he got half his wish. While we cannot grow inches taller, we can grow inches wider. Some women use extra pounds to avoid their sexual selves; others add extra pounds that take extra physical space to compensate for not asserting their psychological space or power. Our physical and psychological selves are intertwined to heal each other.

3-4. Interpersonal and Intrapersonal Processes

Interpersonal processes means how we get along with others. Intrapersonal processes mean how we get along with ourselves. It makes sense that how we view ourselves is intertwined with how we get along with ourselves and with others. Children are told, "If you want to make friends, be friendly." Some of us are outer-directed and seek others' applause or approval. Others of us are inner-directed and do not seek applause, but if we get it, it's a shared gift. In our interactions, a "Yes" to either of the following questions is a litmus test for esteem status: Are you interested in people? Are you interested in people becoming interested in you? Therein lies the difference. Ultimately, the relationship we have with ourselves is the best one we will ever have and will impact the rest of our life and the lives we touch.

5. The Human Brain: Emotional Literacy

The statements for Emotional Literacy include all of the HD statements; however, the statements and scores are culled from the four other developmental processes (cultural, moral and ethical, personal and professional, and spiritual development), which are indicative of how we emotionally play the hand we are dealt. Brain research indicates that our emotions have the power to supersede, override, or undermine our "good intentions." Early emotional memories may reach consciousness; others may be out-of-awareness and initiate actions that are independent of thought. Early precognitive or preverbal emotions may be at work in many areas of our mental life and actively run our lives. With self-awareness, we learn to integrate our emotional and cognitive responses.

Unresolved fears, hurts (inside self), or felt threats (outside self) to the ego, body, security, or family may trigger or provoke emotional reactions to programmed, new, or unexpected life situations and involve an instinctive response from one of our preferred Four Fs: fight, flight, freeze, or feign. We engage in old responses to new but similar experiences when we bypass the rational mind, but the mind provides a self-serving rationale for doing what we do due to its need for control. Emotions and feelings are an integral part of rational thought and reasoning. Too much emotion or affect impairs reasoning. The lack of emotion or feeling in reasoning leads to cold, cruel, or inhumane behaviors.

Environments that are too anxiety-provoking or too boring do not promote healthy growth and learning. The love or acceptance response is not as "natural" as the Four F responses. However, the love or acceptance response is a conscious way to acknowledge, learn from, and regain control of our feelings, thoughts, and physical reactions. When our emotions are secure, we utilize our mental, sensory, visceral, emotional, intuitive, and spiritual assets to maximize brain-mind information processing in order to love, learn, work, and relate healthfully. Our emotional assets are inside ourselves, but our behaviors make the state of our emotions visible to all.

What's Next?

Most of us have been looking outside ourselves for life's answers. Our answers are within. We must begin with ourselves, but we do not end there. "We are here for such a brief period of time. We come and go like flickers of a flame. Sometimes we get so serious about what it all means. The important thing is to play the hand you've been dealt."[3] Above all, to enjoy the game, enjoy the process!

The U.S. Constitution affirmed that the pursuit of happiness was humankind's natural right. Wise men have long taught that we cannot find happiness by seeking it. We can only find happiness by being involved in life. Positive esteem is the key to unlocking the human spirit to create a humane world where respect for all life reflects the respect and esteem we have for ourselves.

Awakening

Transformation processes take time and effort, just like life itself. Consciously doing our own selfwork may awaken our unconscious and divulge answers to our questions, needs, and wounds in healing ways.

To explore our mind's island with an awakened eye and a feeling heart, create your own journal for *Healing The Terrorist Within!* and recreate your life as you reconnect with the world.

246

Ten

*Writing helps keep our
psychological compass oriented.*
– J.W. Pennebaker[1]

JOURNALING —
The Right- and Left-Brain Way

JOURNAL KEEPERS ARE PART OF A LONG CULTURAL-HISTORICAL TRADITION, from England's Samuel Pepys (1600s) and his diaries to King Louis XVI's sole diary entry, "Nothing!" on July 14, 1789, the day the French Revolution began. The King's entry informs us he was, by choice or default, out of touch with himself, his people, and his country. Many people, such as Louis XVI, who write every day may not grapple with fundamental issues. While his diary reflected his elite position and passive attitude, double-entry journaling is not an ivory tower exercise.

Why Journal? Self-esteem explored through a journal, with a right- and left-brain focus, is an opportunity to examine who we are, what we have going for us, what we are up against, how to get others (and ourselves) out of our way, how to manage our thoughts and feelings and the responses we give and get, and when to make interventions to get more of what we want for ourselves and others. University researchers found that people "Writing about their deepest thoughts and feelings about traumas resulted in improved moods, more positive outlook, and greater physical health."[2]

Journaling is a form of confession. "Within any given society, whoever controls the confession market has the power to shape the society's belief systems."[3] As journalers, we are in control and have the power to reshape our own lives. Confession is used in most cultures, in therapy, religion, politics, self-help groups, twelve-step programs, and brainwashing, for example. People are more inclined to disclose intimate secrets in darkened places, from a Roman Catholic confessional, a candlelit church, or on a barstool to a moonlit

247

tryst or remote campfire. Public confession occurs in unique settings, on airplanes, buses, and trains and in the TV studios of Jay Leno, David Letterman, or Oprah Winfrey. Self-disclosures tend to occur when people are in an altered state of consciousness, emotional or biological; when relaxed, excited, anxious, exhausted, or fearful; or when under the influence of alcohol or drugs, deprived of sleep or food. In such emotional-oriented, persuasive settings, the emotional brain dominates the thinking or rational brain, so people ignore any intuitive feelings or common sense. Also disarming is an accepting audience that encourages us to talk. Interestingly, people's stories change to fit the implicit and explicit values of particular audiences and of ourselves. There are no techniques that can erase our memories and values; however, we can learn to manage them and to endorse new values. When we journal, we disclose our secrets, emotions, thoughts, ideas, and experiences on paper. Reflecting on and/or reading the objective (left) side of our journal (representing the left side of the brain) to another is a way to learn from our writings. During journaling, "it can be beneficial to reflect on the underlying values you are working from: 'What are your basic beliefs about right and wrong, about life and death, about sex, love, and hate, and about the nature of friendship and God, and about yourself?' Once you know those basic values that are influencing your thought processes, you can be more informed in evaluating your perceptions, emotions, and life experiences."[4]

Journaling is not to be used as a substitute for or as an avoidance of action. Keeping a journal is a means of recording and organizing our jumbled thoughts and feelings and reflecting upon them to find meaning or to make sense out of events and our lives. It is easy to be caught up in telling our stories of being wounded over and over without breaking out of the circles of "Poor Me," terrorism, psychic pain, or dysfunction. We cannot heal what we do not acknowledge or understand. A journal is a safe place to explore our pain. Journal entries or anecdotes provide clues as to who we are and why we behave the way we do, and they suggest questions, new ideas, and areas to explore. None of us is perfect. By writing for ourselves, we will recognize and honor what we already know, which may have been out of our conscious awareness. In addition, we will see the dual aspect of our lives, the meanings in both, and how to integrate them.

With minimum journaling, each of us will rediscover our lost uniqueness — what's right about us instead of what's wrong with us — and uncover our unfolding myths. The personal myths that run our lives may be compared to an iceberg which is 10 percent above and 90 percent below the surface — a metaphor for our unconscious. Our journal writings may be snatched from oblivion, selected with care, or chosen at random. Once committed to paper, our anecdotes become the genesis of our self-knowledge and provide the impetus to act on our insights and knowings. In real life, what we do and what we feel like doing are not always coordinated. Journaling helps us relive an incident at a distance to reflect upon what was missing or missed and discover what we don't know. What we don't know does hurt us but may help us momentarily. With self-knowledge we are free to make interventions, let go of obsolete patterns, habits, or ways of relating, and live the life we want to live. We do not have to write every day; just keep all the anecdotes together in one place for rereading later.

Before we choose self or another to be the subject of our journal, remember the big picture. If I were to stand before you with a dollar bill held between the fingers of both hands and to ask, "What do you see?" What would you say? Would you describe the dollar bill? Would you talk about its value or uses? Would you report seeing the fingers holding the bill? The whole person? The background? That is the whole picture. In our culture we are taught to pay attention to the details. The human brain sees the big picture, but we are taught not to think or see outside the box. The big picture is necessary to understand human behavior. When we become an observer of our own and other's behavior, instead of a critic, we may hypothesize about the possible reasons for the behavior to understand what is happening to us or to them.

To comprehend the complexity of each unique human being, again picture in your mind's eye a set of Russian dolls to represent the many facets of human growth and development. The largest doll represents a human being in the here-and-now; the smallest doll represents the infant each of us once was. In between the smallest and the largest dolls, there may be a series of five or more dolls; each represents the diverse layers of human experience we encounter in our developmental processes. Through journaling, we examine the development each of us undergoes, from human, cultural, and individual development to moral, ethical, spiritual, and professional development. Each layer of experience thwarts or promotes our potential to be humanly and humanely developed individuals.

In addition to the diverse influences that affect who we are today — which each of us brings to every interaction, situation, and context — there is also an information overlay of known and unknown data that we act upon, consciously and unconsciously. With the help of a concept called the Johari Window,[5] we may actually learn how known and unknown factors, blind spots, and façades enter into and control human communication processes. Blindspots become visible through journaling. The Johari Window has four panes:

1. Communication Arena
   Data known by Self and Others
	2. Blindspot: Data known
	   by Others

2. Image or Façade:
   Data Known by Self
	4. Unknown Data by All:
	   Data Unknown by Self and Others

Windowpane #1 is the communication area where data are known by self and others, such as the obvious physical data and attributes, features, hairstyles, clothing choices as well as data from what we say and do when we reveal our likes and dislikes and when we disclose what we do and do not want. If we are willing to be seen and heard and actively seek life experiences and feedback from others, then we reduce the size of our blindspot or Windowpane #2.

Windowpane #2 is our unknown area: we are unaware of others' reactions to or impressions of us, from our tone voice, body language, body odors to others' first and lasting impressions of us. The content of Windowpane #2 usually remains unknown unless we ask for others' specific feedback or they give it to us anyway, which may change from person to person since different people have different impressions. Even then, many people are reluctant to divulge negative feedback; most negative feedback stemming from emotional outbursts is not reliable for it discloses more about the giver than the receiver.

Windowpane #3 contains information that we choose not to reveal about ourselves to another (and, perhaps, even to our journal). Our fear may be that people may not like us if we told them who we really are — assuming we know. We may have things in our past that we wish to hide or think that others would misunderstand or think less of us if they knew. For example, a friend will not reveal her age; she knows she may be stereotyped, and she also knows there are ages beyond the chronological, such as mental age, physical age, emotional age, and spiritual age. In response to, "How old are you?" Rene responds, "Age is a number and mine is unlisted." Aunt Peg never revealed her age to anyone. At her funeral, some friends asked her daughter Dallas, "How old was your mother?" Dallas responded, "Didn't she ever tell you?" "No!" they said. Dallas kept her mother's secret. The obituary in the local newspaper was headed, "Patience Blanche Dalton, nee Frampton, 69" and on the next line: "Portugal Cove Road…" etc. Aunt Peg would have liked that!

Beyond age and obvious data best kept to oneself, if we keep a low profile by revealing little and seeking little in return, that is, we choose not to make waves or to raise issues that may affect us, then the "Lottery" approach to life is operational: If you don't play, you can't win! When we are relatively open, rather than closed, then what we hide may not affect a relationship. However, if we are reserved, closed, or secretive, then our façade may make others suspicious of us or lead them to mistrust us, becoming cautious and wary around us. Note that there is a difference between data that reveal data about the world, business, sports, the weather, and that of inner world data.

Windowpane #4 is our unknown or limbo self, which neither others nor we are aware of. The unknown self could be our underdeveloped or underutilized skills, potentials, and attributes. It could be unexamined beliefs, values, and attitudes we have inherited from our culture or family, which are out of our awareness and of those like us. We may have unconscious scripts, tapes, schemas running in our heads that undermine positive behavior or have suppressed life experiences embedded in our unconscious which contribute to self-destructiveness or affect our functioning at optimum levels.

251

Some of us have different sized windowpanes for each of the four Johari Windows. It is useful to utilize the Johari Window as a visual guide to assess our progress in journaling toward self- and other-esteem.

Before we begin double-entry journaling, look around you and select an object that interests you. The task is to compose a paragraph or jot down a few sentences about the chosen object. Describe the object without naming it.[6] You may describe how it looks, its purpose, potential, value, or whatever the object generates in or says to you. The purpose in not naming the object is not to mislead but to challenge you to see an object without its label. It is not essential to pay attention to grammar, sentence structure, spelling, or handwriting. You may prefer to make a list, write a poem, or a riddle about the chosen object.

When you complete the first task, you may complete the rest of the exercise by yourself, or ask a friend or family member to do the same thing you did without revealing to each other the names of the objects chosen to write about. You may exchange papers and deduce what the object is from the written description. When you think you know, turn the paper over and write down the name of the object. Then, from your own experience, write how it would feel to be that object.

In a Human Development class, all the students chose objects and wrote about them without naming them. The papers were exchanged. One student chose to describe a picture on the wall. The student who read it thought it was a description of a rug on the floor. As a rug, she felt put down and trod upon. We project onto others, events, animals, and inanimate objects how we feel about ourselves now. Our perceptions — how we see an event, others, and ourselves — are keys to how we think, feel, and respond.

The purpose of the exercise was to see an object clearly without dismissing it by using its label. The more attention we pay to things and people, without making assumptions about who they are and what they are doing to us, the more we can appreciate their uniqueness as well as our own. The exercise also demonstrates how we project our interpretations of our experience onto the world around us. Often we cannot get past our thoughts, feelings, and expectations to clearly see the things and the people around us, or the events in our lives. As psychologist Carl Jung and journaler Anais Nin have observed, we do not perceive things and others as they are, but rather as we are.

Double-Entry Journaling: Left- and Right-Brain Approach

The left side of the notebook or journal is used to record objective-descriptive details of what actually happened during an event or interaction (left-brain activity). The right side of the journal is used to record what happened inside you, the journaler — subjective-reflective feelings about the same event — such as unexpressed feelings and words at the time and afterwards, upon reflection, as well as what you wish had been said or had happened (right-brain activity). The double-entry approach utilizes both the left and right sides of a notebook for recording a single event. Each entry or anecdote is broken down into its descriptive (objective) and reflective (subjective) observations.

Note that we are following the attributes for the left and right sides of the human brain. The left hemisphere is concerned with language and is logical, analytical, linear, rational, sequential, detail-oriented, and unemotional. The left brain is task- and bottom-line-oriented. The right hemisphere is concerned with the emotions and feelings, spatial matters, recognition of faces, visual patterns, the big picture, reflection, intuition, music, moral and ethical decisions, and body or nonverbal language. The right brain is people-oriented. The division between the two brains is an incomplete one; its main connection is a bridge called the corpus callosum with millions of nerve fibers carrying information both ways. The brain operates as an intricate system, as a committee, as a whole, but each half has different assignments.

We cannot see or hear clearly or behave congruently when one brain dominates the other. When we arbitrarily separate their different data in a journal, we learn to value the function of each and to give each brain equal weight so that they are more likely to act in concert than to oppose one another to our detriment. It is our nonverbal communication that indicates our two brains are not in agreement. The disagreement may be invisible to us but visible to observant others, even on an unconscious level, and influences their behavior toward us. Recording what we think, say, and do, and recording how we feel and what we wish we had said, are opportunities to become chairperson of our brain's committee and to become more in charge of our communication processes.

Journaling is not expensive and, for the general populace, may be more accessible and as effective as psychotherapy, in some instances. Journaling is not new, and there are many ways of keeping a journal, from the self-reflective writings of Anais Nin to depth psychologist Ira Progoff and his Intensive Journal.

Our double-entry journal method is different, and it works. A similar journaling method also worked and had been taught in a learner-centered Human Development master's program at a New Jersey university for about twenty years. One of the founders of the program, Dr. Alice Z. Castner, had obtained her doctorate at the University of Maryland's Institute for Child Study under Director Daniel A. Prescott. In the Human Development program, the students were primarily teachers, social service workers, policemen, priests and nuns, business people, and parents. Each was required to take 12 credits in the Direct Study of Human Beings, or Practicum I-IV. Some of those students were selected to take an extra 12 credits in leadership by leading study groups with faculty consultants. The master's students learned to see, hear, and write so well in the two year course, through studying another human being for one year and oneself for another year, that they improved the quality of their personal and professional lives. Two graduates of the program became Teacher of the Year in New Jersey in successive years.

Administrators who are more power- than learner- or student-centered find ways to destroy a program that is perceived by them to be out of their control. The demise of the Human Development masters' program, in the 1980s, may also be attributed to the NJ State Department of Education's policy of Thorough and Efficient Education (T&E). Only a master's degree in one's field (not in Human Development, for example) warranted teachers' reimbursement or salary increases. Primarily, the program's demise was due to some faculty who used the program as a haven, rather than for ongoing growth and development. The demise was also due to administrators who loaded expenses against the program to make it appear unprofitable. Today, to appear profitable is preferable. Business examples are the profitable-on-paper giants: Enron's creative number-crunchers who hid losses and WorldCom's tricksters who hid expenses. Figures do not lie, but liars figure. Keeping a journal is the best way to figure out the positive and negative aspects of any situation, how to work with the challenge of integrating our inner and outer lives, and how to avoid becoming an accomplice to white collar crime.

Direct or Indirect Study of Human Beings

The focus of the journal may be yourself, your child, spouse, friend, foe, your job, a problem, or your dreams. In the beginning, it is more comfortable to journal about another than oneself. Keep your journal away from prying eyes. If you do study another, give the person a pseudonym. It is your choice whether or not to tell your subject what you are doing. Videotaping a class makes a difference in behavior for the first few minutes; then the students revert to their usual behavior. Most subjects do the same when informed of journaling plans. Many people may think it is an invasion of privacy for us to record their interactions with us in a journal. However, we keep files on people in our heads, and we do not separate what is their stuff from what is our stuff. Journaling is a fair process. The double-entry journal is a way to understand the other person as he or she is without being tainted by our biases, judgments, expectations, or needs. Often, through journaling, the relationship with our subject (whether self or another) deepens. When we pay positive attention to people, they may respond in kind. In rare cases, negative people continue to be negative. We retain control in the relationship, if we do not collude in their negativism or desire to control us.

The journal method is fair and positive because it is whole-brain and whole-person based. If you find you have recorded three or more anecdotes that are negative, then look for three or more positive anecdotes. Balance the negatives with the positives, since none of us is either all negative or all positive. If we cry all the time, we have a problem. If we laugh all the time, we have a problem. Balance is the key to health and to journaling for positive results.

The journal method is whole brain-based because each anecdote is divided into the objective (left side) and subjective (right side). It is self-esteem oriented. As anecdotes are randomly collected and recorded, they may be identified according to the five domains of self-esteem: Human, Cultural, Moral and Ethical, Personal and Professional, and Spiritual Development. Note that all these developmental processes are layers added to the tiny human infant, consciously and unconsciously, from conception to death. The task of journaling is to pierce the layers to understand, not to criticize. Criticism is like a spark; it can cause an explosion in the powder keg of pride. "You can

255

make more friends in two months by becoming interested in other people than you can in two years by trying to get other people interested in you."[7]

The Beginning

The study of self or another requires writing, in an ordinary notebook or journal. Before recording actual anecdotes, on the left page of the journal, write a description of self or the person to be studied, the behavior you would like to understand, and what you would like to learn or improve through the journaling process. List any negative thoughts and behaviors that you are aware of that get in the way of positive self-esteem. List any positive attributes that contribute to positive esteem or action. On the right page of the journal, write your subjective thinking, feeling (positive and negative) about how the person is like and not like you or how the public self differs from the private or idealized self. Include any stereotypes, beliefs, or expectations that you have about yourself or are aware of about the person you chose to study.

Set the stage of each narrative, or anecdote, concerning a particular incident, event, or person, by recording the date, time, setting, and who was present. Since we behave differently in different contexts, describing the setting and who is present are important. The writing may be short and does not have to be recorded immediately; although it may be more accurate when less time has elapsed. Some journalers write a week's worth of anecdotes in one sitting; others write two or three times a week.

If you are keeping a journal on yourself, and have no problems on the job or in relationships, choose particular statements from the Self-Esteem Assessment and use them as a basis for your writing anecdotes to enhance self- and other-esteem. The writing will jog your memory and the anecdotes will be a way to reprocess and resolve any residual issues. Life has lessons, and we are our own best teachers.

A master's student, who worked in a pharmaceutical company, found the courage to confront her "character flaw" during the last of a four-semester journaling class. Her husband, a pilot, had told her one evening that he was leaving her. Her impulse was to get his gun from the bedroom and kill herself. He took the gun from her and left with it. Too confused and without a quick way to kill herself, she decided to do it the next day. At work, she had access to poisons. After work, at home with pills in hand, she was about to take them when she realized, as a biologist, that her decomposing body would not be found for days, so she decided to clean out the refrigerator first, take the pills, and then get in it. She was so exhausted after cleaning the refrigerator, she decided to kill herself the next day after work and went to bed. She arrived home with the full intention of killing herself, when a question flashed through her mind, "Why should I kill myself over that SOB?" So she didn't!

However, a nagging thought had lingered. She had fully intended to commit suicide, which was against her religious upbringing, so her character must be flawed. In class, through reading aloud the left side of her journal's anecdote, she realized, from feedback, what terrific coping and timing skills she had exercised as her perception of her problem changed from negative to positive, even though her belief system plagued her. Through delaying the suicide act, as in counting to ten or higher, to distance us from acting on intense emotions, she was able to override negative emotions and intentions and balance them with more positive, rational, and life enhancing ones. Through journaling, we can turn negatives into positives.

The Objective or Left Side of the Journal

On the left side of the journal, where we record what actually happened (left-brain activity), the task is to select and collect data on observed human behavior, that is, to pay attention to the events, tensions, or incidents, which may seem trivial or important but are somehow relevant. Describe what actually happened to recapture the experience for later processing. Description is more than a transcription of reality. It is not a tape recording. It is a re-creation of your perception of a particular piece of reality. Therefore, the entry on the left side of the journal is an attempt to recreate an event, incident, or describe yourself or another person's interpersonal or intrapersonal communication in such a way that the entry speaks for itself on the written page. That is, the description can stand-alone and be understood by an objective reader as if present as a fly on the wall. It does not need the journal keeper to explain, furnish more data, or answer questions in order for another reader to see the whole picture and the details.

An anecdote is well-written when the journal keeper and any potential listener or reader are able to see and hear or recreate for themselves what actually happened in the incident instead of having to deal with hearsay, lost, secondhand, or filtered data whose flavor or essence is missing from the writing. After writing a few anecdotes, you will become aware of your interpretations, assumptions, or perceptual biases that are interfering with an attempt to be objective.

In the context of Direct Study of Human Beings in the Human Development master's program, the students brought their journals with them each session and had the option to read or not read aloud to the class an objective (left-side) anecdote only. As when anecdotes were read, each received comments about the subject's behavior in the form of hypotheses. Students also learned, from questions about an anecdote, how to write the anecdotes so their listeners did not have to ask questions to flesh-out the scene.

The Subjective or Right Side of the Journal

On the right side of the journal — representing the right brain: where you record how you felt about what happened and what you wish had happened — it is the behind-the-scene, unobservable data ruled by our conscious and unconscious belief and value systems — as well as our schemas that influence what happened (as described on the left side of the journal) — that are important. We separate the objective from the subjective data because each tells its own story without interference from the other. Subjective experience includes lived data, inner dialogues from Self 1 (left-brain) and Self 2 (right-brain), adjectives, labels, stereotypes, biases, judgments, hidden agendas, emotions, feelings, and intuitions that were not acknowledged, articulated, or discernible in the interaction. Subjective data include observations such as our own and another's nonverbal or body language, from voice intonation and breathing to facial and body movements. Important to the anecdote are any observed and/or felt incongruence between what is said verbally and what is expressed nonverbally.

Reflective writing — a commentary on the data written on the left — is also a source of subjective data that reveal cognitive meanings in emotional reactions. The right side is also used to acknowledge and record unexpressed needs, feelings, attitudes, reactions, expectations, interpretations of the event or the other person, as well as what you would like to have said or happen, not said or not happen, during the interaction. It is also a place to become aware of what was missing for you in the interaction and whether or not you felt inhibited, victimized, or valued.

Through journaling, we become aware of recurring life themes or patterns. Sometimes we do not need a journal to record what is happening under our noses; however, a journal entry illuminates a potential problem. Eileen and John have seven children. One of the children was particularly sloppy when he ate his meals. Andrew, at three, was the identified slob of the family. Eileen is a keen observer. One day she watched Andrew deliberately throw his food on the floor while saying "I'm a 'weal shwob'!" each time he dropped a potato chip. She put him on the floor and helped him to pick up the chips, saying, "You're a neat boy!" She alerted the family and put a stop to their calling him a slob; she insisted that the whole family make comments only when he was neat. Shortly thereafter, Andrew became the neatest sibling. Sometimes caring adults recognize, as Eileen did, that "slobs are made, not born."

Working and Journaling in Negative Environments

Journaling is a way to record complex interactions that wound, hinder, or rob us of our right to esteem and respect. When we live out others' self-fulfilling prophecies, we disown our real selves, and it takes effort to maintain a construct. Until we uncover and examine any negative labels we live by, we will not be in touch with or become the fully functioning human being we were meant to be. Journaling is helpful when a person is having a problem at work and/or with a supervisor. It is essential to keep a log of our work accomplishments and troublesome encounters that affect us emotionally and intellectually or impair our relationships, careers, and nation.

Bureaucracies are notorious for fix-the-blame-not-the-problem cultures where CYA (cover your ass) is operative. Top bureaucrats in field offices do not make waves. Nor do they encourage others to do so. They micromanage, are indecisive, and ignore employees' suggestions and vital reports. An example of "not my job" occurred long before 9/11 when vital data about possible terrorist activities were ignored at the FBI and not shared with other government agencies. A Washington (DC) FBI spokesperson declined to comment on the stonewalling within the agency that closes the lines of communication. He is quoted as saying, "They [former agents] write the letters after they leave because they don't have the (courage) to write them while they're still agents."⁸ That FBI official still doesn't "get it." If former agents have to wait until after they leave the agency to give feedback, what does that say about the culture at the FBI? It says the FBI does not encourage honest reporting or value its agents' intelligence. It says nothing about former agents' courage for they know from experience what happens when an individual makes waves: they are transferred, fired, demoted, or ruined. It said too much about some of people who made it to the top in government agencies: they were petty power-oriented and more concerned about their jobs than defending America and Americans. Changing the FBI's priorities after the fact of 9/11 will not change entrenched habits and attitudes without intensive retraining and keeping a journal to record the handling and processing of all the data, not just what the top wants to hear. What happened at the FBI is a lesson for all of us who work in "controlled environments" as a precedent for future action that benefits all, not just the self.

Since 9/11, we relearned what we have known all along: our institutions, organizations, and government agencies are not working for America or Americans. Citizens, investors, and workers are the victims of too many greedy executives whose motto is "Nothing succeeds like excess!" Elites at Enron, consulting-auditing firms, and other large corporations succeeded in enriching themselves at the expense of employees, investors, banks, and our government. Our political parties let us down. The FBI-CIA also let us down. The old-boy network is out of control. Corporate America's scandals are providing bad role models for the rest of the world and are becoming more of a focal point for Americans' perception of America than the 9/11 transnational terrorist attacks.

Two women emerged as new versions of whistle-blowers. Sherron Watkins at Enron had the temerity to write a memo to the then-president Kenneth Lay warning him of improper accounting and management practices before its downfall. Lay's "response" to her was to sell more company stock. It was her testimony before the U.S. Congress that is leading to criminal indictments and to possible changes in corporate accounting and practices. Coleen Rowley was also an FBI whistle-blower. In her 13-page letter to the new FBI chief, Robert S. Mueller, she had the courage to dispute the FBI's hard line that no terrorist intelligence before 9/11 had been mishandled. Both women were insiders, in positions of power, and both did not play by the rules when they experienced government incompetence and corporate wrongdoing.[9] Whistle-blowers are usually punished for challenging the status quo; both women realized they had to "go public" with their data. The FBI is undergoing a shake-up and reforms are being urged in corporations. Both men and women on the inside know when their personal values are being violated by work values. We are not in charge of our career if we let things happen or, later, we wonder what happened. We are in charge of our career when we make things happen for the greater good. Keeping a journal keeps us mindful.

American businesses have been in a downturn since the presidential election in 2000, after which the Internet dot-com sector bubble burst and many are dot-gone. The market had declined and was on a rebound when 9/11 occurred. The ensuing corporate excesses led to the lack of investor and consumer confidence in the U.S. marketplace. In fact, Henry M. Paulson, Jr., Chairman and CEO of Goldman Sachs said, on June 5, 2002 at the National Press Club, "I cannot think of a time when business over all has been held in less repute."[10] He acknowledged the "black eye" given to the business community by some CEOs and insiders for selling company shares before they declined in value. Chief executives are under pressure, he said, to report higher profits every quarter. It appears that in repayment of financial favors, our politicians have allowed Corporate America to influence the watering down of our accounting and business practices. Thus, the accounting principles set by the Financial Accounting Standards Board made the system "ripe for manipulation." Hence, the accounting institutions, organizations, and government agencies are ripe for an overall change, beginning at the top. Today, we have an opportunity to right wrongs: to get our nation refocused on a more equitable distribution of power, wealth, and opportunity that is compatible with human spirits and planet Earth in the 21st century. When we keep a record of our lives, we will find clues as to what needs attention before it is too late. Hindsight improves foresight!

Most of us think that at work we will receive loyalty and admiration by exhibiting our confidence and competency. Instead, we may engender fear or threat, not admiration, as we reveal who we are under the pressures of work. We do not have to overcome others' fears, but we do have to know what their fears are. To stand up to another's fear, we have to confront our own. Our refusal to speak or to act confirms, in a supervisor's eyes, our vulnerability. When we live in the shadow of our fears, our professional mask makes it possible to preserve our jobs but not our realness. Exhausted from sustaining our fears, an insecure, threatened, or power-hungry supervisor will sense our weakness and increase the pressure. "The boss doesn't like me" or "It's impossible to work in a negative environment" are judgments based upon personal emotional reactions that do not include a systemic understanding of what we are up against. We will encounter workplace negatives, repeatedly, until we learn the lessons to be learned. However, learning our lessons does not mean that those who do not will not continue to foist theirs onto us. Our tasks are to confront our fears, our intimate terrorist, and those of our adversary, the workforce terrorist. How?

The fog of work clears when we pay attention to the world of work around us by keeping a journal. First, we learn from journaling what is our part of the problem, how we collude in the problem, and what part is the supervisor's problem. "Many times in our work lives we walk through the office door with our shoulders hunched to our necks, feeling powerless and bullied by those who hold power over us. Our refusal to stand up to those who harass us on a daily basis is a lack of faith in our own voice."[11] Silence is agreement with the intimate terrorist's voice that diminishes us in our own eyes and increases our vulnerability. "We feel certain that we will lose our job, our position, our career, and no one will ever look at us again."[12] When we inventory our fears, we learn we do not have to overcome them, but we do have to know what we are afraid of. When we inventory the talents, gifts, or experience we have to give to our job, we may become aware of the gifts we fear receiving, such as feedback about our work ethic, competence, or human relations. And we become more accountable workers.

Risk Mitigation[13]

Keeping a journal of our work environment, especially a negative one, is a way to lessen risks, such as litigation, damaging one's reputation or career, being blackmailed, blamed, or being told to do something by a supervisor that may be against company policy or illegal. To be a legal instrument, the journal cannot be a loose-leaf book or a computer file. A composition book is the best. Use a black ink pen, not a pencil. Follow the guidelines for keeping a journal: date, time, setting, people present, or situation. Such a journal is similar to but more detailed than the daily records kept by many professionals. Pay attention, though, to balancing the number of your positive and negative entries.

Keeping a record of what we are told to do by a supervisor, such as to shred documents, create false data, destroy computer files — or cover up on-the-job environmental, work or product hazards — allows us to become aware of the risks we take and to mitigate such risks when and if we are blamed by a supervisor, fired, sued, or have to testify. It is unfortunate that in the business and academic worlds there are some people in power positions who demonstrate no morals, ethics, integrity, or conscience. They rise and excel in an organization because performance at any cost makes money. They demand, "Get the sales up! Do whatever you have to do to do it!" When or if problems become visible, they fall hard, have memory lapses, and refuse to testify. People with integrity and a conscience are considered a liability because they put people and product concerns above profit. Thus, in such negative work environments, we have to be prepared to lessen or manage any unexpected blows to our personal and professional self. Supervisors, too, may journal workers' performance, behavior, attitudes, and consequences of unhealthy habits.

The Journal as Confidant

Consider your relationship with a journal similar to that of a new friend or a trusted confidant. New friends allow us to perceive ourselves differently; trusted confidants allow us to feel comfortable to reveal ourselves and be accepted *as is* so we can learn and grow. When we record the facts of an interaction with another and our feelings as well as what was said or not said, we may focus on what triggers the person's negativity and what kind of person is emerging from the pages. From that data, we may find a way to change our response, to clarify versus collude in his response, or to refuse to take his negativity as personally imprisoning us by focusing on what it is like to walk in his shoes, what it would take to make him look good, or why he has an agenda to make us look bad. We can learn to cope with workforce terrorists. First, though, we learn to love and accept self unconditionally.

"With dignity comes honesty and an unwillingness to sell yourself short...There are certain things we should not do, certain people we should not work for, lines we should not cross, conversations to which we should not descend, money we should not earn."[14] A survey of chief executives of a manager's potential for advancement indicated that integrity was number one, followed by an ability to get along with others, followed by industriousness. Inner character strengths matter for business success and advancement. People's *personae*, esteem, and people skills are 75 percent of most jobs.

Journaling is a way to examine our good and bad experiences. Journaling diminishes inhibitions; it increases self- and other-awareness and self-responsibility when we turn every negative thought ("You botched that job again!") into an appropriate affirmation ("You did the best job you could under the circumstances!"). Then the next step is the learning experience, which is, "What is the message waiting to be acknowledged or the lesson yet to be learned?" By following the foregoing format, we learn the lessons embedded in negative experiences so that they will not have to be repeated elsewhere. "If you are still being hurt by an event that happened to you at age twelve [25, 35, 60, or older], it is the thought that is hurting you now."[15] We are in charge of our thoughts, so questions to journal are: "What can I do today to change what I would otherwise think of myself tomorrow?" "What's in it for me to collude in my inner terrorist's blackmail?" We can make peace with our bad experiences, such as journaling about forgiving someone for their transgressions or forgiving ourselves for our mistakes. We can make room for gratitude by journaling our blessings. Albert Einstein wrote: "There are two ways to live your life. One is as though nothing is a miracle. The other is as though everything is a miracle." It is our choice. Emphasizing our good experiences increases the likelihood of having more of them. Journaling is a way of uncovering and healing the terrorist within.

The first step is to work on self-esteem by focusing on an internal locus of control. If we continue to base our esteem for self on what we accomplish, accumulate, or get from the world in the form of money, prestige, power, or negative feedback, then the more vulnerable we are to external influences. When we do not love, believe in or accept ourselves *as is*, we look for others to do it for us. Self-doubt creeps in when we get any negative feedback. Self-doubt is similar to an open wound that others, with negative esteem (bullies), like to pick on to deflect attention or negativism away from themselves or to make themselves feel or look good. As Eleanor Roosevelt said, *No one can make you feel inferior without your consent.* However, it takes a positive self- and other-esteem person to keep that in mind when being abused or wanting to abuse others. Learning to count to ten (or higher!) is one way to bring reason to emotions in a volatile situation. Journaling is a way to reflect upon and make sense out of a challenging situation and to reinforce one's resolve to be alert to the signs of discontent so we may avoid colluding in the problem; then we can be part of the solution.

Example: One Journal Entry

Below is a real life incident Jeanne experienced; it is written in the left- and right-brain way for you to reflect on what you might have done in a similar situation or to use as a guide for your own anecdotal writing:

Left-Brain (objective facts)	**Right-Brain** (subjective emotions)
What happened in class:	What happened inside me, the teacher:
Time: After lunch. Date: 4/02	*Looking forward to getting started on a*
Setting: Inner city school	*new project with this class:*
Art Class, Grade 9	*A Global Art Project (Student Art*
	Exchange) with a small African nation
While I was talking with a student, two boys began insulting each other and, in seconds, were face-to-face	
	That's a familiar stance: chest-to-chest, that means a fight!
I hurried over and pulled them apart; got in-between them, and faced the angriest one (bigger than I am!) And said, "Sit down!"	*I'm not going to let students hurt each other! Ineffectual commands, probably fed his anger!*
"Get out of my face before I 'sneak' (hit) you!" he said.	
"Sit down!"	
The other student headed for the hall. I turned away from the angry student and told the other, "Go down to the office!"	
	I figured, "He started it!"

Instead, he hurled another insult in the direction of the still-angry student

I hear the class getting excited.

Now I'm disgusted with everyone, including myself! They want a fight. Fun for them!

The angry student started swinging; I grabbed him by the shirt collar and held him back Another student grabbed the other one. I was losing my grip when a big kid in class stepped up from behind and restrained him. One kid wouldn't let up and the other took all the insults to heart.

A male teacher appeared in the hall and forcibly held the other student, face down on the floor.

Two days' detention for both!

The lesson on "Peace" was absurdly ineffectual. I was still in shock, almost in tears.

Class was over and the next class was arriving. I sat at one of the 8th grader's desks, as one of them, and discussed what had happened and asked what would they have done.

Bewildered by the fast and furious encounter, I felt comforted by the 8th graders' perspective.
They are a sensible bunch: not easily angered or moved to fight.

Later I visited the Detention Room and spoke with the two detainees from a distance. I wanted them to know I am interested in their welfare.

As is customary, teachers supply work assignments for detainees.
My assignment: write an apology to me and list five possible alternative behaviors they each could have chosen instead of what had happened.

A nagging question, "What could I have done to be more effective?"

266

At the end of the day, I visited my Mentor and the Principal to discuss the classroom incident and told them why the two had been given Detention and I suggested that Anger Management be part of the detention.

Both students did the assignment and did it well. The angriest student expressed himself freely in a whole page; he apologized to me and to the entire staff.

Days later, I was walking my feisty cocker spaniel on a leash and noticed her aggressive side when on leash, a "Let me at him!" attitude that is missing when she's off the leash. I thought of the fight in school and wondered if my presence and agenda could have encouraged them to be more aggressive. Not wanting to hurt each other left little room for my alternatives. Now I have five.

What I want to happen:

I can't give these kids self-esteem. I create an environment in class where they can respect and get along with each other, and I feel frustrated when they don't. I am determined to keep trying anyway.

Conclusion from the Journal's Anecdote:

The troublemakers are good kids, and they have talent. They are not ready or able to learn due to emotional illiteracy. If they don't get help now, they will be disrespectful of themselves and others for the rest of their lives and will be vulnerable to insults and put-downs. And they won't be able to learn the academic skills necessary to graduate from high school or to get a job that will enable them to become good citizens. Interestingly, during Back-to-School night only three parents came. So, it is up to the schools and teachers to make a difference in some of these kids' lives. Until schools' Missions include educating bodies, minds, emotions, and spirits, we will be part of the problem.

Reprocessing the Data

After you have collected a sizeable number of anecdotes over the period of a month or so, take an hour or more to reread what you have recorded. Note what may be missing: whether you have balanced the positives with the negatives and whether you have included anecdotes about your own or another's Human (physical, psychological, emotional, interpersonal and intrapersonal processes), Cultural, Moral and Ethical, Personal and Professional, and Spiritual Development processes. It is not in the writing or recording that most insight comes but in the rereading, hypothesizing, and looking for patterns and themes.

When we see on paper how we repeat self-defeating patterns and evoke the same games and mistakes, it takes courage to admit we create our own reality and to take responsibility for a future that is not a repeat of the past. Learning the language of esteem, diminishing the power of others' negative voices, licking our wounds, accepting our imperfections, loving ourselves, and reaching out to, loving and helping others are ways of discovering and healing the terrorist within and outside self.

When we see on paper or through our retrospectroscope that we are, or have been, in a situation that is beyond our control, it takes the virtue of acceptance — from discipline, endurance, and perseverance to self-respect, self-esteem, and dignity — to accept "what is" and move on. Blaming self or others is not a virtue; it is a vice. Those who feel responsible for conditions over which they have no control are children who blame themselves for their parents' divorce, women and men who blame themselves for choosing partners who betray them, people with illnesses who consider them personal failings, and men and women who lose their jobs due to downsizing or who experience all sorts of misfortunes.

When we believe we bring bad outcomes into our lives, we feel culpable and think, "*If only* I had done so and so, *then* such and such would never have happened." Then we are in the victim stance. And in the victim stance we feel powerless to change and become self-destructive too. Such a mode is a killer of self-esteem, self-respect, and self-worth. Some things are beyond our individual control, from earthquakes and terrorism to many other life events. To overcome such felt personal inadequacy, many people turn to psychotherapy in the hope that self-knowledge will put an end to the psychic pain and poor quality of life. There seems to be no end to personal failures since many of us rarely get all we aspire to have. We face defeat, frustration, and rejection — stress — in our daily lives, and in our culture where individualism — the self — is a priority, and we get little comfort from society when personal losses occur. Without nurturance, helplessness becomes hopelessness. However, preoccupation with self and self's problems advertises our need to be rescued by someone who needs to be needed or our willingness to drown at sea rather than swim to shore; such situations present us with an opportunity to defeat the terrorist within and without. By behaving "as if" we are OK, we may learn our problem's lesson, change our body stance, and our attitude.

Our Attitude Determines Our Altitude

Happily, a negative explanatory mode for bad outcomes and personal losses can be changed to a positive one. When we help others, we help ourselves: self-healing occurs. The dilemmas of our lives are deeply spiritual ones, and it is the spiritual domain of our lives that connects us to others, nature, and our wholeness. With self-awareness, we know who we are: our strengths and weaknesses. When we learn from mistakes (mis-takes), our own and those of others: we have the ability to be flexible with a higher tolerance for ambiguity; we embody compassion or the reluctance to cause unnecessary harm; we practice random kindness by "making someone's day;" and we learn to monitor our attitude to break the tyranny of pessimism. When we are at peace within ourselves, esteem ourselves and are open to esteeming others, we are able to be tolerant of those who are intolerant of us. The lack of esteem breeds intolerance and perpetuates it. Thus, our attitude determines our altitude, our ability to rise above intolerance with tolerance. Reach out to others and help them grow as you maintain your esteem by writing, breathing deeply, and walking. When you cannot take one more step, take one more.

Positive self- and other-esteem is the way through our self-imposed silence, fears, impatience, boredom, and other debilitating inner and outer obstacles to enjoying our life, work, and play. When our body, mind, emotions, and spirit are dynamically balanced, our life, work, and play are dynamically balanced, and we move on and leave the intimate terrorist behind. Then we are fluent in the unique language of self. When who we are is not negotiable, we find meaning in our lives and treat all with respect and dignity. The Johari Window becomes a window of opportunity to explore our inner world, to make ourselves visible in the world, and to show ourselves to the world as we really are.

Only in America, though, do the optimistic poor, the near-rich, and the wannabe-rich vote for tax cuts for the ultra-rich. Why? Many of us believe that *tomorrow* we could be rich and that we will benefit. There's always luck — the lottery, the slot machines — or that our dreams will come true, mostly without effort. Such self-deceptive attitudes affect not only our altitude (a lower economic class and standard of living yet socially connected by TV to the upper class: the rich and famous) but also our latitude (*freedom from narrow restrictions; permitted freedom of action, options*). When laws that favor the rich also include limiting ordinary Americans' right to know political and economic facts, the right to their own bodies (women's choices), and to choose how they live, we will have colluded in betraying ourselves and our freedom, for our courts would then be saddled with those who have the power to impose their ideology, their agendas, and their worldview on American citizens. Self- and other-esteem is about educating ourselves from the inside out and from the outside in. Remember, Thomas Jefferson warned Americans, a long time ago, that nobody's liberty is secure if Americans neglected their civic responsibilities. The same warning applies today. We live in a culture of abundance; we admire our rich icons whether in the media, sports, or politics; however, our cultural elites have been betraying us and our country. Our need to believe that we are part of the action has gotten in the way of reality and of our demanding that our leaders be accountable to us. A journal's paper trail begins the reclamation process.

Esteem development is an all encompassing and a proactive process, and it requires activism, patience, perseverance, learning, and behavorial results. Our positive life task is to develop esteem and practice it by perceiving problems as opportunities and by maintaining and sharing the original blessings of this world with all creation. Rekindling positive esteem can be a task as difficult as rubbing two sticks together to start a fire, or it can be as easy as taking a pen in hand and drawing ourselves out through the journaling process to become the person we are meant to be.

270

A Creative Quest

A new class has emerged in the U.S., which is beyond gender and economic lower, middle, and upper classes; it is the Creative Class,[16] which spans the economic gamut of low to upper. Individuals of the Creative Class have a vision of a more tolerant, diverse, better, and prosperous future for all, and they use their creativity in all aspects of their lives — especially their work, which drives most human lives — to improve the quality of their lives, to lessen the growing economic and social divide between the haves and have-nots, and to satisfy their lifestyle preferences. Periods of crisis, such as today, are times for personal and social change. All of us may become part of the Creative Class when we are challenged, beyond the dollar, to use our human capacities to develop ourselves to be part of the sea of change.

The future is in us now, so the quality of our lives depends upon the amount of risk we can handle today to live our dream tomorrow. *What you can visualize, you can actualize!* There is no risk involved in envisioning who you would like to be in two or five years from today. To create a future that is different or better than the one we are living today, we have to have a dream and a plan or chart, so sit down in a comfortable chair, take off your shoes, put your feet on the floor, close your eyes, think purple, and relax! Breathe in through your nose on Re- and exhale through your mouth on lax. Re–lax. Re–lax. In your mind's eye, visualize responses to questions about your life today: Do you love yourself? With whom do you live? Where do you live? What is your work? Do you feel there is something missing in your life? Are you living all you can or want to be and do? *Pause.* Let's move on from today to create a vision of your tomorrows. Breathe in deeply on Re– and breathe out thoroughly on lax. Re–lax. Re–lax. It's two years from now, and you are creating the you that you want to be. Where are you? Where are you living? Describe your home. With whom do you live? Who are you? What do you look like? What are you wearing? What are your interests? Where do you work? Describe your work? How do you make yourself happy? What do you do to be healthy? Who are your friends? Where do you vacation? How are you contributing to your community? To world peace? To the sustainability of the Earth? Now answer a question that only you can ask yourself.

Open your eyes and take the time, now, to write in your journal what you just experienced, so you will have a written record of your vision to read and re-read. Add more data, for the more details you write down, the more specific you are, the more real the vision becomes. Finally, what are you willing to give up to get what you want?

Without a vision, we muddle through life. Knowing and asking for what we want for ourselves, and putting it out to the universe, become clearer when we find a reason to create what we want that is more compelling than our excuse not to begin to achieve it. Our positive intentions are our compass. Life isn't about finding ourselves: it's about creating ourselves.

The Butterfly Effect[17]

When we exercise our spiritual freedom to participate in, pay attention to, and make a difference in what happens in the world — instead of just worrying about our individual yesterdays, todays, tomorrows, and the hereafter — then we will know we do have an effect on the whole. So do butterflies! The notion that a butterfly stirring the air today in China can create storm systems next month in America, is only half-jokingly known as The Butterfly Effect.

When we work our way out of the cocoon of our own making, we will not think, feel, see, hear, do, or be the same old way any more. "Man's mind stretched to a new idea never goes back to its original dimensions," said Oliver Wendell Holmes, Jr. Yet, "we have in this country, dominated by corporate wealth and military power and two antiquated political parties. . .characterized as 'a permanent adversarial culture' challenging the present, demanding a new future."[18] We are free to follow our inner voice, our magnetic compass, to the opportunities and relationships we desire, to practice our critical powers of discrimination, and to live life as a spiritual journey. Or, according to Stephen Covey, "We are not human beings on a spiritual journey. We are spiritual beings on a human journey."

Together we can meet the challenges of international and domestic terrorism. Together we can create a more creative, personal, institutional, and organizational world. Together we can ignite a 21st century Global Renaissance based upon human beings' self- and other-esteem whose empowering actions will have more meaning than any words used to define esteem.

Afterword

To write a book about self-esteem is both an arrogant and a humbling thing to do: an oxymoronic undertaking. Arrogant because it presumes that we know, like praise, something that you don't know. Humbling because we realize how much we don't know, how much there is to know about people and esteem, and how more research and many more books are out there that we did not read yet or that are not yet written.

We began with life experience and questions, so we designed the Self-Esteem Assessment first. SEA was honed in workshops in the U.S., Canada, and Russia and copyrighted in 1993. Then we built a book around SEA by researching diverse aspects of esteem until it was time, after 9/11, to synthesize our learnings from many sources and to share our story of esteem.

The writing of this book helped us to make sense out of and direct our own personal and professional lives. We discovered that without positive other-esteem there is no self-esteem, only negative-esteem or narcissism. It is our hope that you will find at least one thing in the book that helps you to grasp the complexity and possibilities of esteem. It is also our hope that you will recognize terrorism for what it really is: fear and lack of positive respect or esteem. We trust that each of us will learn the lessons we need to learn from the transnational and domestic terrorists and will empower ourselves to be change agents. It is not true that nothing can be done about terrorists or that change cannot occur in inhumane institutional and organizational entities created or misused for nefarious purposes. As Uncle Two Crows said, "Throughout your life, there will be people who will try to buy you and tell you what to do and what you should be like. Will you be willing to sell yourself or, like Smokey, are you not for sale? That is your measure of self-worth." It is true that change will not happen unless we make it happen in a way that honors each human being's uniqueness. A popular poster's message honors each of us:

Walk ahead of me, and I may not follow.
Walk behind me, and I may not lead.
Just walk beside me, and be my friend.

If you have questions, comments, criticism, are a long lost-to-us student or friend, or if you just want to share something with us, we welcome your e-mail:

drflorencem@cs.com
Florence and Jeanne Elodie

Notes/References

Chapter I: Human Beings' Polarities and Possibilities (pages 1-35)

1. Wilson, E. O. (2002). *The Future of Life.* NY: Alfred A. Knopf.
   See: Wilson, E. O. (2002, February). "The Bottleneck."
   Scientific American. Vol. 286. No. 2. pp. 82-91.
2. Sulloway, F. J. (1996*). Born to Rebel*: Birth Order, Family Dynamics,
   and Creative Lives. NY: Pantheon Books. p. xv.
3. May, R. (1981). *Freedom and Destiny.* NY: W.W. Norton & Co. p. 202.
4. Friedman, T. L. (2002, 17 April). "George W. Sadat." *The New York
   Times*, Op-Ed Page A25.
5. Bennett-Goleman, T. (2001). *Emotional Alchemy*: How the Mind Can
   Heal the Heart. NY: Harmony Books.
6. Branden, N. (1994). *The Six Pillars of Self-Esteem*. NY: Bantam.
7. Rank, O. (1941/1958). *Beyond Psychology.* NY: Dover Books. p. 290.
8. Latner, J. (1992). Anton Chekhov is quoted in "The Theory of Gestalt
   Therapy." In *Gestalt Therapy: Perspectives and Applications.* E. Nevins,
   Ed. Cleveland, OH: The Gestalt Inst. of Cleveland Press. p. 30
9. Popcorn, F. w. Hanft, A. (2001). *Dictionary of the FUTURE*: The words,
   terms and trends that define the way we'll live, work and talk. NY:
   Hyperion. During a Fall, 2001 NYC radio interview, Ms. Popcorn
   mentioned the term "intimate terrorist."
10. Marrs, J. (2000). *rule by secrecy*: the hidden history that connects the
    Trilateral Commission, the Freemasons, and the Great Pyramids.
    NY:HarperCollins.
11. Phillips, K. (2002). *Wealth and Democracy*: A Political History of the
    American Rich. NY: Broadway Books. p. xi.
12. Maslow, A. (1968). *Toward a Psychology of Being.* 2nd Ed. NY:
    D. Van Nostrand Co. p. 196.
13. Greven, P. (1991). *Spare the Child*: The Religious Roots of Punishment
    and the Psychological Impact of Physical Abuse. NY:
    Alfred A. Knopf. p. 123.
14. Dorsey, J. M. (1971). *The Psychology of Emotion*: Self-Discipline by
    Conscious Emotional Continence. Detroit, MI: Wayne State
    University Press. p. xxxvii.

15. Swihart, E. W. Jr & Cotter, P. (1996). *The Manipulative Child*: How to Regain Control and Raise Resilient, Resourceful, and Independent Kids. NY: Macmillan, A Simon & Schuster Macmillan Co. pp. 17-18.
16. Branden, N. (1994), pp. 90, 21-22.
17. Hutschnecker, A. A. (1974). *The Drive for Power*. NY: M. Evans. p. 211.
18. Bellah, R. N., Madsen, R., Sullivan, M., Swidler, A. & Tipton, S. M. (1985). *Habits of the Heart*: Individualism and Commitment in American Life. NY: Harper & Row.
19. Gross, R. E., Ed. (2000). *Thunderbird on Global Business Strategy*. NY: John Wiley & Sons, Inc., p. 158.
20. Prescott, D. (1938). The American Council on Education appointed a Special Committee to investigate emotions and the educative process. Chairman Prescott's Committee Report (1938) included a transmittal letter containing the quotation, p. vii. In *Emotion in Man and Animal*: Its nature and dynamic bases. P. T. Young (1973). Melbourne, FL: R. E. Krieger. p.193.
21. Szent-Györgi, A. (1970). *The Crazy Ape*. NY: The Universal Library, Grosset & Dunlap. p. 13.
22. Ibid., p. 77.
23. Meeker, J. W. (1988). *Minding the Earth*: Thinly Disguised Essays on Human Ecology. Alameda, CA: The Latham Foundation, Pub. p. 11.
24. Friedman, T. L. (2002, January 2). "Let's Roll." *The New York Times*. p. A25.
25. Greven, P. (1991). *Spare the Child*: The Religious Roots of Punishment and the Psychological Impact of Physical Abuse. NY: Alfred A. Knopf. p. 221.
26. Carson, R. (1962). *Silent Spring*. Boston, MA: Houghton Mifflin Co., The Riverside Press, Cambridge, MA.
27. Bloom, A. (1987). *The Closing of the American Mind*: How Higher Education Has Failed Democracy and Impoverished the Souls of Today's Students. NY Simon & Schuster.
28. Garrett, L. (2001). *Betrayal of Trust*: The Collapse of Global Public Health. NY: Hyperion. p. 585.
29. Pennebaker, J. W. (1990). *Opening Up*: The Healing Power of Confiding in Others. NY: Avon. p. 174
30. Fox, M. (1999). *Sins of The Spirit, Blessings of The Flesh*: Lessons for Transforming Evil in Soul and Society. NY: Three Rivers Press. p. 148

31. May, R. (1981*). Freedom and Destiny.* NY: W. W. Norton. p. 16

32. Conner, R. L. (1989, 29 December). "Individual Rights Are Just Part of the Cocktail." *The Wall Street Journal.* p. 6. Quoted Harvard Law Professor M.Glendon. p. 6.

33. Mecca, A. M., Chair, California Task Force to Promote Self-esteem and Personal and Social Responsibility. (1990. January). *Toward A State of Esteem* (The Final Report). Sacramento, CA: CA State Department of Education, Office of State Printing. p. 37

34. May, R. (1981), p. 1.

35. Landgraf, K. M. (2002, 23 April). "Literacy is the Key to Unlocking Potential." Kurt M. Landgraf, President & CEO of Educational Testing Service, Princeton, NJ. *The New York Times*, p. A6.

36. Waldman, A. (2002, 24 April). "How in a Little English Town Jihad Found Young Converts." *The New York Times*, p. A12.

37. Wilson, E. O. (1998). *Consilience*: The Unity of Knowledge. NY: Alfred Knopf.

38. Jourard, S. (1968). *Disclosing Man to Himself.* NY: D. Van Nostrand Co.

39. Kessler, R. (2001). "Soul of Students, Soul of Teachers: Welcoming The Inner Life to School." In *Schools With Spirit.* L. Lantieri, Ed. Boston, MA: Beacon Press. p. 108.

40. Miller, A. (1981). *Prisoners of Childhood*: The Drama of the Gifted Child and the Search for the True Self. NY: Basic Books, Inc. pp. 81-82.

41. Emoto, M. (1999/2002)*Messages From Water* (Volumes I & II), Japan: HADO Kyoikusha Co, Ltd. http://www.hado.net

Chapter II: Human Beings' Esteem: A Work in Progress (pages 36-64)

1. Beck, A. T. (1989). *Love is Never Enough.* NY: Perennial Library, Harper & Row. p. 2

2. Zunin, L.& Zunin, N. (1973). *Contact*: The First Four Minutes. NY: Ballantine Books. p. 209

3. Long, D. E. (1990). *Anatomy of Terrorism.* NY: MacMillan Coll.

4. Fallows, J. (2002, April). "Behavior Modification." *The Atlantic. Vol.* 289, No. 4. pp. 28-29.

5. Mecca, A. M., Chair (1990, January). *Toward A State of Esteem*. Sacramento, CA: CA State Department of Education, Office of State Printing, p. 1.

6a. Ibid., p.1.

6b. Ibid, p. 1.

7. Ibid., p. 144.

8. Rosenberg, M. (1965). *Morris Rosenberg's Self-Esteem Scale*. Princeton, NJ: Princeton University Press.

9. Emler, N. (2002, 3 February). In "The Trouble with Self-Esteem" by Lauren Slater. *The New York Times*. pp. 44-47.

10. Baumeister, R.F. (2001, April). "Violent pride." *Scientific American*. *Vol.* 284. No. 4. pp. 96-101. Internet http://first search.oclc.org/ WebZ/FSP — *WilsonSelectPlus*. pp. 1-8.

11. Ibid., pp. 4-5.

12. Ibid., p. 6.

13. Ibid.

14. Hutschnecker, A. A. (1974). *The Drive for Power*. NY: M. Evans & Co., Inc. p. 85

15. Baumeister, R. F. (2000, April), p. 7.

16. Adler, J. with Wingert, P., Wright, L., Houston, P., Manly, H. & Cohen, A. D. (1992, 17 February). "The Curse of Self-Esteem: What's Wrong With the Feel-Good Movement." "Hey, I'm Terrific!." *Newsweek*. pp. 46-51.

17. Slater, L. (2002, 3 February). "The Problem with Self-Esteem *The New York Times Magazine*. pp. 44-47.

18. Sanford, L. T. & Donovan, M. E. (1984). *Women & Self-Esteem*: Understanding and Improving the Way We Think and Feel About Ourselves. NY: Penguin Books. p. 9.

19. Baumeister, R. F.(2001, April), p. 1.

20. Hutschnecker, A. A. (1974), p. 100.

21. Epstein. S. (1980). "The Self-Concept: A Review and the Proposal of an Integrated Theory of Personality." In *Personality*: Basic Aspects and Current Research. Ervin Staub, Ed. Englewood Cliffs, NJ: Prentice-Hall. p. 84.

22. Hutschnecker, A. A. (1974), p. 183.

23. Baumeister, R. F. (2001, April), p. 8..

Healing The Terrorist Within!

24. Coué, Emile: French pharmacist who urged his patients to accompany their medication with the affirmative thought: "Every day..." In Seligman, M. E. P. (1993). *What You Can Change And What You Can't*: The Complete Guide to Successful Self-Improvement. NY: Fawcett Columbine. p. 27.

25. Browning, R. (1951). "Pippa Passes." *Selected Poetry of Robert Browning*. Ed. K. L. Knickerbocker, NY: Random House, Inc.

26. Minsky, M. (1986). *The Society of Mind*. NY: Simon & Schster. p. 50.

27. Satir, V. (1990). "The Meaning of Family." In *Toward A State of Esteem*. A. M. Mecca, CA Task Force to Promote Self-Esteem & Personal and Social Responsibility. Sacramento, CA: CA State Department of Education, Office of State Printing. p. 46

28. Branden, N. (1994). *The Six Pillars of Self-Esteem*. NY: Bantam.

29. Caplow, T., Hicks, L. & Wattenberg, B. J. (2001). *The First Measured Century*: An Illustrated Guide to Trends in America, 1900-2000. Washington, DC: AEI Press, Publisher for American Enterprise Inst.

30. Prescott, D. A. (1957). *The Child in the Educative Process*. NY: McGraw-Hill Book Co. p. 357.

31. Ibid., p. 358.
32. Ibid., p. 357.
33. Ibid., p. 358.

34. Ginott, H. (1965). *Between Parent and Child*. NY: Avon Books. p. 233

35. Natiello, P. (2001). *The Person-Centred Approach*: A passionate presence. Ross-on-Wye, England (UK): PCCS Books. p. 8.

36. Coopersmith, S. (1969, 6 February). "Implications of Studies on Self-Esteem for Educational Research and Practice." Paper presented in Los Angeles, CA, at the American Education Research Association Convention. p. 1.

37. Rogers, C. (1977). *Carl Rogers on Personal Power*. NY: Delacorte Press. p. 8.

38. May, R. (1972). *Power and Innocence*: A search for the source of violence. NY: Delta.

39. Gracey, D.R. & DeRemee, R.A. (1981). "The University of Vienna Medical School." *Mayo Clinic Proceedings*. Vol. 56:834-838.

40. Harlow, H. (1958). "The nature of love." *American Psychologist*. Vol. 13. pp. 637-685.

279

41. Welch, M. G. (1988). *Holding Time*: How to eliminate conflict, temper tantrums, and sibling rivalry and raise happy, loving, successful children. NY: Simon & Schuster.

42. Krystal, H. (1988*). Integration & Self-Healing*: Affect, Trauma, Alexithymia. Hillsdale, NJ: The Analytic Press, Lawrence Erlbaum Assoc., Inc. p. 147.

43. Welch, M. G. (1988), p. 215.

44. Fromm, E. (1973). *The Anatomy of Human Destructiveness*. NY: An Owl Book, Henry Holt & Co. p. 223.

45. Ibid.

46. Ibid., p. 228.

47. Ibid.

48. Baumeister, R. F. (2001, April), p. 2.

49. Holt, J. (1989). *Learning All The Time*. NY: Addison-Wesley.

50. Ibid., pp. 240-141.

51. Kindlon, D. (2001, 12 September). "'Indulged kids actually short-changed,' author says." *The Arizona Republic*. Article by S. Newman, Social Psychologist. p. E4.

52. Caputo, P. (2001, 4 October). "Twenty Years of Training for War." *The New York Times*. p. A27.

53. Prescott, D. A. (1957). *The Child in the Educative Process*. NY: McGraw-Hill Book Co. p. 405.

54. Fox, M. (1988). *The Coming of the Cosmic Christ*. San Francisco, CA: Harper & Row. p. 23.

55. Lederer, W. J. & Burdick, E. (1965). *The Ugly American*. NY: Norton

56. Hall, E. T. (1976/1981). *Beyond Culture*. Garden City, NY: Anchor Press/Doubleday. p. 57.

57. Ibid., p. 240.

Chapter III: The Language of Diplomacy, Terrorism, and Esteem (pages 65-87)

1. Hock, D. (1999). *Birth of the Chaordic Age*. San Francisco, CA: Berrett-Koehler Publishers, Inc. p. 158.

2. Hutschnecker, A. A. (1974). *The Drive for Power*. NY: M. Evans. p. 242.

3. Sheehy, G. (1981). *Pathfinders*: Overcoming the Crises of Adult Life and Finding Your Own Path to Well-being. NY: Bantam Books. p. 524.

4. Hutschnecker, A. A. (1974), p. xi.

5. Machiavelli, N. (1952/1903/1935). *The Prince.* NY: Mentor Book. p. 98.

6. Rioch, M. J. (1975). "All we like sheep (Isaiah 53:6): Followers and Leaders." In A. D. Colman & W. H. Bexton (Eds.). *Group Relations Reader*: An A. K. Rice Series. San Rafael, CA: Associates Printing & Publishing. pp. 161, 165.

7. Albrecht, K. (1983). *Organization Development.* Englewood Cliffs, NJ: Prentice-Hall, Inc. p. 113.

8. Evans, P. (1996). *The Verbally Abusive Relationship*: How to recognize it and how to respond. Holbrook, MA: Adams Media Corp.

9. Thunder Strikes & Orsi, J. (1999). *Song of the Deer*: The Great Sun Dance Journey of the Soul. Malibu, CA: Jaguar Books, Inc. p. 40.

10. Lewis, B. (2001). *What Went Wrong?* Western Impact and Middle Eastern Response. NY: Oxford University Press.

11. Machiavelli, N. (1952), p. 95.

12. May, R. (1984). *American Politics and Humanistic Psychology*: Rollo May, Carl Rogers, and Other Humanistic Psychologists. T. Greening, Ed. NY: Saybrook Publishing Co. p. 8.

13. Goldin, H. J. (1990, 28 August). "Hussein's Support Deeper Than We Think." *The New York Times.* p. A21.

14. Coopersmith, S. (1967). *The Antecedents of Self-Esteem.* San Francisco, CA: W. H. Freeman & Co. p. 196.

15. Rogers, C. (1977). *Carl Rogers on Personal Power.* NY: Delacorte Press. p. 12

16. Natiello, P. (2001). *The Person Centered Approach*: A passionate presence. Ross-on-Wye, England (UK): PCCS Books. p. 59.

17. Thunder Strikes & Orsi, J. (1999), p. 23.

18. Schumacher, E. G. (1977). *A Guide for the Perplexed.* NY: Harper & Row. p. 30.

19. Powell, J., SJ (1969). *why am I afraid to tell you who I am?* Chicago, IL: Peacock Books.

20. Rogers, C. (1980). *A Way of Being.* Boston, MA: Houghton Mifflin. p. 2.

21. Tolle, E. (1999*). The Power of Now*: A Guide to Spiritual Enlightenment. Novato, CA: New World Library. p. 29

22. Selye, H. (1993). "History of the Stress Concept." In *Handbook of Stress*: Theoretical and Clinical Aspects, 2nd ed. L. Goldberger & S. Breznitz, Eds. NY: The Free Press, a Div. of Macmillan, Inc. pp. 7-17.

23. Ibid., p. 17.

24. Pinker, S. (1997). *How the Mind Works.* NY: W.W. Norton. p. 24.

Healing The Terrorist Within!

25. Ibid., p. 50. [Quotation from Sommers, C.H. (1994). *Who stole feminism?* NY: Simon & Schuster.]

26. Lundin, S. C., Paul, H. & Christenson, J. (2000). *Fish!* A Remarkable Way to Boost Morale and Improve Results, Catch the Energy & Release the Potential. NY: Hyperion. pp. 38-39.

27. Drucker, P. F. (1985). *Innovation and Entrepreneurship*: Practice and Principles. NY: Harper & Row. pp. 248-249.

28. Csikszentmihalyi, M. (1990). *Flow*: The Psychology of Optimal Experience. NY: Harper & Row. p. 59.

29. Deming, W. E. (1991, 26 October). "Managing for the 21st Century." American Interests, Program No. 1105. Moderator, Morton Kondracke. Produced by Neal B. Freeman, TV Channel 13, NYC. Transcript (c) 1991. The Blackwell Corp. News Transcripts, Inc., 1333 H Street, N.W., Ste. 500, Washington, DC 20005.

30. Gibran, K. (1966). *The Prophet*. NY: Knopf.

31. Reynolds, D. K. (1980). *The Quiet Therapies*: Japanese Pathways to Personal Growth. Honolulu, HA: University of Hawaii Press. p. xvi.

32. Suzuki, D. T. (1980). *Zen and Japanese Culture*. NY: Random House. p. 104.

33. Hammerschlag, C. (1988). *The Dancing Healers*: A Doctor's Journey of Healing with Native Americans. San Francisco, CA: Harper & Row. p. 15.

34. Zeig, J. (1980). *A teaching seminar with Milton H. Erickson, MD*. NY: Brunner/Mazel.

35. Hammerschlag, C. (1988), p. ii.

Chapter IV: Human Development (pages 88-124)

1. Pittman, F. (1993). *Man Enough*: Fathers, Sons, and the Search for Masculinity. NY: G. P. Putnam's Sons. p. 125.

2. Ibid., p. 121.

3. Ibid., p. 132.

4. Ibid., p. 231.

5. Wallerstein, J. S., Lewis, J. & Blakeslee, S. (2000). *The Unexpected Legacy of Divorce*: A 25-Year Landmark Study. NY: Hyperion.

6. Josefowitz, N. (1980). *Paths to Power*: A woman's guide from first job to top executive. Reading, MA: Addison-Wesley.

7. Chira, S. (1988). *A Mother's Place*: Taking the debate about working mothers beyond guilt and blame. NY: HarperCollins. p. 77.

8. Pittman, F. (1993), p. 126.

9. Ibid., p. 133.

10. Ibid.

11. Kindlon, D. & Thompson, M. (1999). *Raising Cain*: Protecting the Emotional Life of Boys. NY: Ballantine Books. p.15.

12. Caplow, T., Hicks, L. & Wattenberg. B. J. (2001). *The First Measured Century*: An Illustrated Guide to Trends in America, 1900-2000. Washington, DC: AEI Press, Publisher for American Enterprise Institute. p. 220.

13. Ibid., p. 226.

14. Ibid.

15. Ibid., p. 220.

16. Lewis, T., (2001, 12 November). "Having a Two-Way Learning Experience." Interview: Dr. T. Berry Brazelton at his Baby College in Harlem. *The New York Times*, Spec. Section F: GIVING. p. F30.

17. LeDoux, J. (1996). *The Emotional Brain*: The Mysterious Underpinnings of Emotional Life. NY: Simon & Schuster.
Goleman, D. (1995). *Emotional Intelligence*. Why It Can Matter More than I.Q. NY: Bantam.

18. Young, P. T. (1973). *Emotion in Man and Animal*: Its nature and dynamic bases. Melbourne, FL: R. E. Krieger. p. 193. Quoted Chairman Prescott's transmittal letter with his Committee's Report (1938, p. vii) to the American Council on Education.

19. Goleman, D. (1995).

20. Csikszentmihalyi, M. (1990). *Flow*: The Psychology of Optimal Experience. NY: Harper & Row. p. 223.

21a. Sarno, J. (1982) *Mind Over Back Pain*: A Radically New Approach to the Diagnosis and Treatment of Back Pain. NY: Berkley Books.

21b. Fried, E. (1970). *Active/Passive*: The Crucial Psychological Dimension. NY: Harper Colophon Books, Harper & Row.

22. Zastrow, C & Kirst-Ashman, K. K. (1997). *Understanding Human Behavior and The Social Environment*. Chicago, IL: Nelson-Hall Publishers. p. 56.

23. Ibid., p. 57.

24. Ibid.

25. Sears, B. (2002). *The Omega Rx ZONE*: The Miracle of the New High-Dose Fish Oil. NY: ReganBooks, HarperCollins, p. 41.

26. D'Adamo, P. with Whitney, C. (2001). *Live Right For/4 Your Type*: The Individualized Prescription for Maximizing Health, Metabolism, and Vitality In Every Stage of Your Life. NY: G. Putnam's Sons. p. 74.

27. Ibid., p. 97.

28a. Ibid., p. 98.

28b. Agatston, A. (2003). *The South Beach Diet:* The Delicious, Doctor-Designed, Foolproof Plan for Fast and Healthy Weight Loss. PA: Rodale. p. 76.

28c. Weill, A. (2000) *Eating Well for Optimum Health:* The Essential Guide to Food, Diet, and Nutrition. NY: Alfred A. Knopf, p. 89.

29. Selye, H. (1993). "History of the Stress Concept." In *Handbook of Stress*: Theoretical and Clinical Aspects, 2nd ed. Eds. L. Goldberger & S. Breznitz. NY: Free Press, a Division of Macmillan, Inc. pp.7-17.

30. Hall, N. (2000, 26 March). "Stress and Disease: A seminar for health professionals." Mesa, AZ. Printed Handout. p. 6.

31. Goleman, D. (1995), p. 60

32. Bennett-Goleman, T. (2001). *Emotional Alchemy*: How the Mind Can Heal the Heart. NY: Harmony Books. p. 109.

33. Ibid., p. 171.

34. Ibid., p. 173.

35. Sanday, P. N. (1997). *A Woman Scorned.* CA: Univ. of CA Press. pp. 25-26, 199, 309.

36a. Mondoa, E. I. & Kitei, M. (2001) *Sugars That Heal:* The New Healing Science of Glyconutrients. NY: Ballantine

36b. Mahler, M. S., Pine, F., & Bergman, A. (1975). *The Psychological Birth of the Human Infant*: Symbiosis and Individuation. NY: Basic Books.

37. Siegal, B. (1986). *Love, Medicine & Miracles.* NY: Harper & Row. p. 4.

38a. Peal, N. V. (1982). *The Power of Positive Thinking.* NY: Ballantine Books

38b. Lundin, S. C., Paul, H. & Christensen, J. (2000). *Fish!* A Remarkable Way to Boost Morale and Improve Results, Catch the Energy & Release the Potential. NY: Hyperion. p. 38.

39. Ibid., p. 68.

40. Gardner, H. (1993). *Multiple Intelligences*: The Theory in Practice. NY: Basic Books. p. 9.

41. Hall, E. T. (1984). *The Dance of Life*: The Other Dimension of Time. Garden City, NY: Anchor Press/Doubleday. p. 4

42. Loewenstein, W. (1980, 16-19 October). Lecture: "Cancer Dialogue" Symposium. Grand Hyatt Hotel, New York, New York.

43. Rogers, C. (1977). *Carl Rogers on Personal Power.* NY: Delacorte Press. p. 49.

44. Albrecht, K. (1983). *Organizational Development.* Englewood Cliffs, NJ: Prentice-Hall, Inc.

45. Hall, E. T. (1969). *The Hidden Dimension*: An anthropologist reveals how we communicate by our manners and behavior. Garden City, NY: Anchor Press/Doubleday. p. 30.

46. Hall, E. T. (1984), p. 4.

47. Pearce, J.C. (1981). *The Bond of Power.* NY: E. P. Dutton. p. 110.

48. Gardner, H. (1993), p. 9.

49. Dostoevsky, F. (1985, 23 October). "Dostoevsky in Siberia." Based upon Joseph Frank's five-volume study [*Dostoevsky*: The Years of Ordeal, 1850-1859. NJ: Princeton U. Press, 1983]. *Manas. Vol.* XXXVIII, No. 3. p. 3-4.

50. Ibid., p. 4

51. Ibid., p. 8

52. Bly, R. (1990). *Iron John*: A Book About Men, NY: Addison-Wesley Publishing Co. p. 42.

53. Gallwey, T. (1976). *Inner Tennis.* NY: Random House.

54. Loehr, J. E. & McLaughlin, P. J. with Quillen, E. (1986). *Mentally Tough*: The Principles of Winning at Sports Applied to Winning in Business. NY: M. Evans & Co.

55. Krystal, H. (1988). *Integration & Self-Healing*: Affect, Trauma, Alexithymia. Hillsdale, NJ: The Analytic Press, Lawrence Erlbaum Assoc. Inc. p. 68.

56. Plimpton, G. (1990). *The X-Factor*: A quest for excellence. Memphis, TN: Whittle Direct Books c/o FedEx, 2005 Corporate Ave. 38132. pp. 15-17.

57. Csikszentmihalyi, M. (1990).

58. LeDoux, J. (1996). *The Emotional Brain*: The Mysterious Underpinnings of Emotional Life. NY: Simon & Schuster. p. 35

59. Goleman, D., Boyatzis, R. & McKee, A. (2002). *Primal Leadership*. Boston, MA: Harvard Business School Press. p. 6.

60. LeDoux, J. (1996). p. 137

61. Ibid.

62. Bennett-Goleman, T. (2001). p. 141.

63. Ibid., p. 110.

64. Ibid.

65. LeDoux, J. (1996). p. 242.

66. Hart, L.A. (1983). *Human Brain and Human Learning.* NY: Longman. p. ix.

67. Erikson, E.H. (1959/1980). *Identity and The Life Cycle.* NY: W. W. Norton.

68. Bennett-Goleman, T. (2001), pp. 75-85, 87-95.

69. McKowen, C. (1986). *Thinking About Thinking*: A Fifth-Generation Approach to Deliberate Thought. Los Altos, CA: William Kaufmann, Inc.

70. Hart, L.A. (1983), p. 52.

71. Drucker, P. F. (1985). *Innovation and Entrepreneurship*: Practice and Principles. NY: Harper & Row., p. 193.

72. Goleman, D. (1995). p. 88.

73. Drucker, P. F. (1985).

74. Frye, N. (1969). *Fearful Symmetry,* A Study of William Blake. NJ: Princeton University Press, p. 223.

75. Shlain, L. (1998). *The Alphabet Versus The Goddess:* The Conflict Between Word and Image. NY: Penguin/Compass, p. 180.

76. Ibid, p. 186

Chapter V: Cultural Development (pages 125-146)

1. Turnbull, C. M. (1972). *The Mountain People.* NY: Simon & Schuster.

2. Crosette, B. (2001, 4 November). "Living in a World Without Women: It's a Man's, Man's, Man's World." *The New York Times.* Section 4. pp. 1, 5.

3. Premson, R. (2001, 4 November). "Allure Must Be Covered. Individuality Peeks Through." *The New York Times.* Section 4. p. 14.

4. Hall, E. T. (1976/1981). *Beyond Culture.* Garden City, NY: Anchor Press/ Doubleday. p. 42.

5. Ibid., p. 14.

6. Gallwey, T. & Kriegel, N. (1977). *Inner Skiing.* NY: Random House.

7. Fox, M. (1999). *Sins of The Spirit, Blessings of The Flesh*: Lessons for Transforming Evil in Soul and Society. NY: Three Rivers Press. pp. 71-75.

8. Hall, E. T. (1976/1981), p. 12.

9. Goleman, D. (1989, 10 October). "Sensing Silent Cues Emerge As Key Skill." *The New York Times.* pp. C1, 11.

10. Holton, S. W. (1984). *Down Home and Uptown*: The Representation of Black Speech in American Fiction." Cranbury, NJ: Associated Univ. Press. p. 25.

11. Ibid., p. 45.

12. Ibid., p. 30.

13. Calvin, W. H. (1989). *The Cerebral Symphony*: Seashore Reflections on the Structure of Consciousness. NY: Bantam Books. pp. 98-99.

14. Sagan, C. (1977). *The Dragons of Eden*: Speculations on the Evolution of Human Intelligence. NY: Random House. p. 54.

15. Gardner, H. (1983). *Frames of Mind*: The Theory of Multiple Intelligences. NY: Basic Books, Inc.

16. Scollon, R. & S. (1983). *Narrative, Literacy, and Face in Interethnic Communication*. NJ: Ablex Publishing Co. p. 101.

17. Nohlgren, S. (1991, 18 January). "Involved parents called key in class." *St. Petersburg Times* (FL). pp. B1, B6.

18. Goleman, D. (1995). *Emotional Intelligence*: Why It Can Matter More than I.Q. NY: Bantam.

19. Goleman, D. (1988, 10 April). "An Emerging Theory on Blacks' I.Q. Scores." *The New York Times*. p. EDUC 23.

20. Ibid., p. EDUC 24.

21. Breggin, P. R. (1989, 7 November). "The Scapegoating of American Children." *The Wall Street Journal*. p. A30.

22. Lambert, B. (1992, 11 January). "James E. Hair, 76, Naval Officer Whose Unit Broke Color Bar, Dies." *The New York Times*. p. 26L..

23. Goleman, D. (1988, 10 April), p. EDUC 23.

24. Larson, R. W. (2000, January). "'Toward a Psychology of Positive Youth Development." *American Psychologist*. Volume 55. No. 1. Special Edition: Positive Psychology. pp. 170-183.

25. Hall, E. T. (976/1981), p. 107.

26. Berman, M. (1989). *Coming to our Senses*: Body and Spirit in the Hidden History of the West. NY: Bantam Books. p. 22.

27. Drucker, P. F. (1985). *Innovation and Entrepreneurship*: Practices and Principles. NY: Harper & Row. p. 261.

28. Seligman, M.E.P. (1993). *What You Can Change...And What You Can't*: The Complete Guide to Successful Self-Improvement. NY: Fawcett Columbine.

Chapter VI: Moral and Ethical Development (pages 147-168)

1. Sharpe, K. (2000). *Sleuthing the Divine*: The Nexus of Science and Spirit. Minneapolis, MN: Fortress Press. p. 127.

2. Greening, T. (Ed.), (1984). *American Politics and Humanistic Psychology*: Rollo May, Carl Rogers, and Other Humanistic Psychologists. NY: Saybrook Publishing. p. 1.

3. Ibid., p. 2.

4. Krystal, H. (1988). *Integration and Self-Healing*: Affect, Trauma, Alexithymia.Hillsdale, NJ: The Analytic Press, Lawrence Erlbaum Assoc., Inc. p. xii.
5. Machiavelli, N. (1952/1903). *The Prince*. NY: Mentor Book. p. 94
6. Fox, M. (1979). *A Spirituality Named Compassion*. San Francisco, CA: Harper & Row. p. 159.
7. Ibid.
8. Milton, J. (2002). *The Road to Malpsychia*. NY: Encounter.
9. Ray, P. H. & Anderson, S. R. (2000). *The Cultural Creatives*: How 50 Million People are Changing the World. NY: Three Rivers Press.
10. Ibid. p. back cover.
11. Seligman, M. E. P. & Csikszentmihalyi, M. (2000). "Positive Psychology: An Introduction." *American Psychologist* Special Issue on Happiness, Excellence, and Optimal Human Functioning. Journal of the American Psychological Association, Volume 55, Number 1. p. 5.
12. Ibid.
13. Wade, N. (2002, 19 March). "Scientist at Work — Leon R. Kass: Moralist of Science Ponders Its Power." *The New York Times*. pp. D1, 2.
14. Ibid., p. 2.
15. Yankelovich, D. (1981). *New Rules*: Searching for Self-Fulfillment in a World Turned Upside Down. NY: Random House. p. 231.
16. Ibid., p. 226.
17. Ibid., p. 246.
18. Ibid., p. 248.
19. Ibid., p. 149.
20. Friedman, M. (1984). "The Nuclear Threat and The Hidden Human Image." In *American Politics and Humanistic Psychology*. Ed. T. Greening. NY: Saybrook Publishing. p. 40.
21. Ibid.
22 Ibid.
23. Ibid., p. 39.
24. May, R. (1972). *Power and Innocence*: A search for the source of violence. NY: Delta. pp. 113-114.
25. Ekman, P. (1991). *Telling Lies*: Clues to Deceit in the Marketplace, Politics, and Marriage. NY: W. W. Norton
26. Gilligan, C. (1982). *In A Different Voice*: Psychological Theory and Women's Development. Cambridge, MA: Harvard University Press.

27. Kanter, R. M. (1989). *When Giants Learn to Dance*: Mastering the Challenges of Strategy, Management and Careers in the 1990s. NY: Simon & Schuster. p. 77.

28. Bellah, R. N., Madsen, R., Sullivan, M., Swidler, A. & Tipton, S. M. (1985). *Habits of the Heart*: Individualism and Commitment in American Life. NY: Harper & Row. p. 162.

29. Bell, D. (1976). *The Cultural Contradictions of Capitalism*. NY: Basic Books. p. 1.

30. Margolick, D. (1991, 12 August). "Wooed, Wined and Overworked, Wall St. Lawyers Served Pink Slips." *The New York Times*. p. A1.

31. Eisler, R. (1987). *The Chalice & The Blade*. San Francisco, CA: Harper & Row. p. 132.

32. Herbert, B. (1999, 22 April). "Addicted to Violence." *The New York Times*. p. A31.

33. Barron, J. (1990, 20 August). "Anger Over Verdicts in Jogger Case Is Mixed With Calls for Compassion." *The New York Times*. p. B4

34. Goleman, D. (1989, 5 December). "Fear of Death Intensifies Moral Code, Scientists Find." *The New York Times*. p. C1, 11.

35. Fox, M. (1988). *The Coming of the Cosmic Christ*. San Francisco, CA: Harper & Row. p. 23.

36. Hall, E. T. (1976/1981). *The Hidden Dimension*: An anthropologist reveals how we communicate by our manners and behavior. Garden City, NY: Anchor Press/Doubleday.

37. Robbins, A. (1986). *Unlimited Power*: The way to peak personal achievement. NY: Fawcett Columbine, Ballantine Books.

38. Maslow, A. (1968). *Toward A Psychology of Being*. 2nd ed. NY: D. Van Nostrand Co.

Chapter VII: Personal and Professional Development (pages 169-201)

1. Prescott, D. A. (1957). *The Child in the Educative Process*. NY: McGraw-Hill Book Co. p. 4.

2. Lewin, K., Lippitt, R. & White, R. K. (1939). "Patterns of Aggressive Behavior in Experimentally Created Social Climates." *J. Soc. Psycho. Vol.* 10. pp 271-299.

3. Lippitt, R. (1940). "An Experimental Study of the Effects of Democratic and Authoritarian Group Atmospheres." *Univ. of Iowa Stud. Child Welfare, Vol.* 16, No. 3.

4. Larson, R. W. (2000). "Toward a Psychology of Positive Youth Development." *American Psychologist, Volume* 55. Number 1. p. 173.

5. Phillips, K. (2000). *Wealth and Democracy*: How Great Fortunes and Government Created America's Aristocracy. NY: Broadway Books.

6. Bernstein, P. (1985). *Family Ties, Corporate Bonds*. NY: Doubleday. p. 9.

7. Ibid., pp. 127-128.

8. Ibid., p. 153.

9. Overbeek, A. M. C. (1986). "Growth, Development, and Integration in Human and Social Services in The Netherlands: An International Approach." Unpublished Ph.D. dissertation, *The Union Institute & University*, Cincinnati, OH

10. Kolb, D. A. (1984). *Experiential Learning*: Experience as the source of learning and development. Englewood Cliffs, NJ: Prentice-Hall..

11. Drucker, P.F. (1972).*Concept of the Organization*. NY: John Day. p. 26.

12. Chubb, J. E. & Moe, T. (1990). "Reform Can't Be Left to the Education Establishment." *The New York Times*. p. E19.

13. Bronfenbrenner, U. (1979). *The Ecology of Human Development*: Experiments by nature and design. Cambridge, MA: Harvard University Press. p. 231.

14. Ibid., p. 53.

15. Kolb, D. A. & Smith, D. N. (1986). *User's Guide for The Learning Style Inventory*. Boston, MA: McBer & Company.
    Albrecht, K. (1983). *Mindex*: Your Thinking Style Profile. San Diego, CA: Karl Albrecht & Associates, P.O. Box 99097 (92109).

16. Prescott, D. A. (1957). pp. 22-30.

17. IBM Advertisement (1980, 7 May) "Dreamers, Heretics, Gadflies, Mavericks, and Geniuses." *The Wall Street Journal*.

18. Ueland, B. (1987). *If You Want To Write*: A Book about Art, Independence and Spirit. Saint Paul, MN: Graywolf Press. p. 6.

19. Prescott, D. A. (1957), p.23.

20. Galbraith, J. K. (1990). *A Short History of Financial Euphoria*: Financial Genius is Before the Fall. Memphis, TN: Whittle Direct Books by Federal Express.

21. Mellan, O. (1992, March/April). "The Last Taboo." *The Family Therapy Networker*. Vol. 16. No. 2. p .46.

22. Gallagher, N. (1992, March/April). "Feeling the Squeeze." *The Family Therapy Networker*. Vol. 16. No 2. p. 19.

23. Fox, M. (1979). *A Spirituality Named Compassion*. San Francisco, CA: Harper & Row. p. 71.

24. Kearns, D. (1989, 17 December). "Improving the Work Force: Competitiveness Begins at School." *The New York Times*. p. F2.

25. Csikszentmihalyi, M. (1975). *Beyond Boredom and Anxiety*. San Francisco, CA: Jossey-Bass. p. 44.

26. Coonradt, C. A. with Nelson, L. (1984). *The Game of Work*: How to enjoy work as much as play. Salt Lake City, UT: Shadow Mountain Press, P.O. Box 20178. pp. 2-6.

27. Hart, L. A. (1983). *Human Brain and Human Learning*. NYC: Longman. p. 70.

28. Rein, I. J., Kotler, P. & Stoller, M. R. (1987). *High Visibility*: How Executives, Politicians, Entertainers, Athletes, and Other Professionals Create, Market, and Achieve Successful Images. NY: Dodd, Mead.

29. Goleman, D., Boyatzis, R. & McKee, A. (2002). *Primal Leadership*: Realizing the Power of Emotional Intelligence. Boston, MA: Harvard Business School Press.

30. Kelly, M. (2001). *The Divine Right of Capital*: Dethroning the Corporate Aristocracy. San Francisco, CA: Berrett-Koehler.

31. Phillips, K (2000).

32. Oshry, B. (1980). *Middle Power*. Boston, MA: Power & Systems, P.O. Box 388, Prudential Station, Boston, MA 02199.

33. United Technologies Corp., Hartford, CT (1984, 12 April). "Let's Get Rid of Management." *The Wall Street Journal*. Full page ad, p. 32.

34. Hock, D. W. (1999). *Birth of the Charodic Age*. San Francisco, CA: Berrett-Koehler

35. Ibid., p. 6.

36. Goleman, D., Boyatzis, R., & McKee, A. (2002*)*.

37. Ibid., p. 3

38. May, R. (1975). *The Courage to Create*. NY: Bantam Books. p. 4.

39. Nemy, E. (1992, 12 April). "New Yorkers, etc.: You have the nerve to say that I don't have a sense of humor? Ha, ha, ha, ha, ha." Cited Don Nielsen, Arizona State University. *The New York Times*. pp A 1, B7.

40. Heinlein, R. A. (1961/1987). *Stranger in a Strange Land*. NY: An Ace Book, The Berkley Publishing Group.

41. Legman, G. (1975). *No Laughing Matter*: Rationale of the Dirty Joke. NY: Breaking Point, Inc, (P. O. Box 328, Wharton, NJ 07885). p. 40.

42. Lang, D. (1980). *The Secret of Charisma*: What it is…and how to get it. NY: New Choices Press. p. 170. (Anecdote re: Richard Burton)

43. Seligman, M.E.P. & Csikszentmihalyi, M. (2000). "Positive Psychology: An Introduction." *American Psychologist* Special Issue on Happiness, Excellence, and Optimal Human Functioning. Journal of the American Psychological Association, *Volume* 55, Number 1. p. 6.

44. Ibid., p. 7

45. Terkel, S. (1972). *Working*: People Talk About What They Do All Day and How They Feel About What They Do. NY: Avon. p. xiv.

46. Ibid., p. xxix.

47. Csikszentmihalyi, M. (1990). *Flow*: The Psychology of Optimal Experience. NY: Harper & Row. p. 2.

48. Kahn, S. (1982). *Organizing*: A Guide for Grassroots Leaders. NY: McGraw-Hill. p. 21.

49. Lundin, S. C., Paul, H. & Christensen, J. (2000). *Fish!* A Remarkable Way to Boost Morale and Improve Results, Catch the Energy & Release the Potential. NY: Hyperion. p. 107.

Chapter VIII: Spiritual Development (pages 202-226)

1. Fox, M. (1980/2000). *Passion for Creation*: The Earth-Honoring Spirituality of Meister Eckhart. Rochester VT: Inner Traditions. p. 55

2. Friedman, T. L. (2002, 17 April). "George W. Sadat." *The New York Times*, p. A25.

3. Coffin, W. S. (1989, December). "Making the Spiritual Connection." Articles by William Sloane Coffin, President, Sane/Freeze. Campaign For Global Security. *Lear's* (magazine: now defunct). p.75.

4. Einstein, A. (1954). *Ideas and Opinions*. Translated by Sonja Bargmann. NY: Crown Publishers. p. 203.

5. McKowen, C. (1986). *Thinking About Thinking*: A Fifth-Generation Approach to Deliberate Thought. Los Altos, CA: Wm. Kaufmann. p. 24.

6. Fox, M. (1980/2000), p. 91.

7. Gifford, D. (1990). *The Farther Shore*: A Natural History of Perception, 1798-1984. NY: The Atlantic Monthly Press. pp. 138-139.

8. Money, J. & Lamacz, M. (1989). *Vandalized Lovemaps*: Paraphilic Outcome of Seven Cases in Pediatric Sexology. p. 23.

9. Bhide, A. & Stevenson, H. H. (1991, Spring). "The Cost of a Clean Conscience." *Best of Business Quarterly. Vol.* 13. No. 1. pp. 38-42, 44-45. (p. 42).

10. Fox, M. (1983). *Original Blessing.* Santa Fe, NM: Bear & Co. p. 120.

11. Keen, S. (1980). *What To Do When You're Bored And Blue.* NY: Wyden Books. p. 221.

12. Fox, M. (1983). p. 47.

13. Wiesel, E. (1976/1994). *Messengers of God*: Biblical Portraits and Legends. NY: A Touchstone Book, Simon & Schuster. p. 30.

14. Aoki, M. (1980, 10-16 February). "Holistic Healing" presentation at Young President's Organization Annual Meeting, Madrid, Spain.

15. Ibid.

16. Fox, M. (1983). p. 49.

17. Fox, M. (1999). *Sins of The Spirit, Blessings of The Flesh*: Lessons for Transforming Evil in Soul and Society. NY: Three Rivers Press. p. 4.

18. Ibid., p. 13.

19. Aoki, M. (1980).

20. Fox, M. (1983), p. 111.

21. Coffin, W. S. (1989, December), p. 75.

22. Lantieri, L. (Ed.) (2001). *Schools With Spirit*: Nurturing the Inner Lives of Children and Teachers. Boston, MA: Beacon Press. p. 18

23. Zohar, D. & Marshall, L. (2000). *SQ: Spiritual Intelligence*: The Ultimate Intelligence. NY: Bloomsbury Press. p. 91.

24. Ibid., pp. 91, 95

25. Havel, V. (1994, 8 July). "The New Measure of Man." *The New York Times.* Op-Ed p. A27.

26. Myss, C. (1996). *Anatomy of the Spirit*: The Seven Stages of Power and Healing. NY: Three Rivers Press. p. 63.

27. Fox, M. (1999), pp. 165-329.

28. Myss, C. (1997). *Why People Don't Heal and How They Can.* NY: Harmony Books. pp. 221-223.

29. Fox, M. (1999. p. 332.

30. Myss, C. (1999). p. 90.

31. Ibid.

32. Ibid.

33. Ibid., p. 89.

34. Ibid., p. 92.

35[a] Grout. M. (2002, August). "Medical Acupuncture in the Treatment of Chronic Stress-Related Illness." *Acupuncture Today. Vol. 3*, No. 8. pp. 18-19, 32.

35[b] Lu, N. & Schaplowsky, E. (2000). *A Natural Guide to Weight Loss That Lasts.* NY: Quill, An Imprint of HarperCollins. p. 6.

36. Myss, C. (1999). p. 30.

37. Ibid., p. 31.

38. Fox, M. (1980/2000), pp. 94, 95, 96, 97, 99, 415.

39. Steinfels, P. (1990, 29 September). "Beliefs: One hymn above all others stands out in demonstrating their power in religion." *The New York Times.* p. L11.

40. Lantieri, L., Ed. (2001). p. 11.

41. Ibid., p. 15.

42. Carlsson-Paige, N. (2001). "Nurturing Meaningful Connections With Young Children." In *Schools With Spirit.* L. Lantieri (Ed), p. 41.

43. Ibid., p. 43.

44. Needleman, J. (2001). "Wendy, Sim, And Other Philosophers: High School and The Love of Wisdom. In *Schools With Spirit* L. Lantieri (Ed). p. 90.

45. Kessler, R. (2001). "Soul of Students, Soul of Teachers: Welcoming the Inner Life to School." In *Schools With Spirit.* L. Lantieri (Ed). p. 109

46. Ibid., p. 121.

47. Ibid., p. 123.

48. Goleman, D. (2001). "Foreword." In *Schools With Spirit.* L. Lantieri (Ed). p. i.

49. Erikson, E. H. (1959/1980). *Identity and The Life Cycle.* NY: W. W. Norton.

50. Schlesinger, A. M. (1956). "What Then Is The American, This New Man." In *The Pursuit of Learning.* Ed. N.C. Starr. NY: Harcourt, Brace. p. 297.

51. Bellah, R. N., 1975, p. 162.

52. Bohm, D. (1987). *Unfolding Meaning*: A Weekend of Dialogue with David Bohm. London, England: Ark. p. 107.

53. Hock, D. (1999). *Birth of the Chaordic Age.* San Francisco, CA: Berrett-Koehler Publishers, Inc. pp. 2-3.

54. Goleman, D., Boyatzis, R. & McKee, A. (2002). *Primal Leadership*: Realizing the Power of Emotional Intelligence. Boston, MA: Harvard Business School Press.

55. Myss, C. (1997). p. 19.

56. Bustad, L. (1990). *Compassion*: The Last Great Hope. Pullman, OR: Delta Press.

57. Swimme, B. & Berry, T. (1992). *The Universe Story*. San Francisco, CA: HarperSanFrancisco. p. 59

58 Ibid., p. 56.

59. Knaster, M. (1991, November/December). "The Good That Comes From Doing Good." *EastWest:* The Journal of Natural Health & Living. *Vol.* 21. p. 65

60. Rinpoche, Sogyal (1992). *The Tibetan Book of Living and Dying.* San Francisco, CA: HarperSanFrancisco, p. 127

61. Blake, W. (1972). *Blake*: Complete Writings. NY: Oxford University Press. p. 154.

62. Swing, W. E. (1998). *The Coming United Religions*. San Francisco CA/Grand Rapids, MI: United Religions Initiative; CoNexus Press.

63. Goodstein, L. (2002, 2 June). "O Ye of Much Faith! A Triple Dose of Trouble." *The New York Times.* p. WK5.

64. Armstrong, K. (2002, 2 June). In "O Ye of Much Faith! A Triple Dose of Trouble" by L. Goodstein. *The New York Times.* p. WK5.

65. Hillman, J. (1999). *The Force of Character and The Lasting Life.* NY: Random House. p. 91.

66. Ibid., p. 55.

67. The Dalai Lama (1992). "Foreword." In *The Tibetan Book of Living and Dying* by Sogyal Rinpoche. CA: HarperSanFrancisco. p. xix.

68. DeFede, J. (2002) *The Day The World Came To Town:* 9/11 in Gander, Newfoundland. NY: Regan Books/Harper Collins.

Chapter IX: Self-Esteem Assessment [SEA] (pages 227-246)

1. Dubos, R. (1974). *Beast or Angel?* Choices that make us human. NY Charles Scribner's Sons. p. 178.

2. Miller, A. (1984). *Thou Shalt Not Be Aware*: Society's Betrayal of the Child. NY: Farrar, Strauss, Giroux.

3. Hammerschlag, C. A. (1988). *The Dancing Healers*: A Doctor's Journey of Healing with Native Americans. San Francisco, CA: Harper & Row. p. 136.

Chapter X: Journaling: A Right-Left Brain Way (pages 247-272)

1. Pennebaker, J. W. (1990). *Opening Up*: The Healing Power of Confidence in Others. NY: Avon. pp. 205-206.
2. Ibid., p. 50
3. Ibid., p. 193
4. Ibid., p. 192
5. Luft, J. (1969). *Of Human Interaction*. Palo Alto, CA: Mayfield Publishing. Joseph Luft and Harry Ingham's Johari Window Theory was developed by them in the 1960s.
6. Fairfield, R. (1980). Exercise by Dr. Roy Fairfield, Union Institute & University, Cincinnati, OH, during Peer Days at Fairfield Univ., CT.
7. Carnegie, D. (1936). *How to Win Friends and Influence People*. NY: Pocket Books. p. 77.
8. Krikorian, G. & Connell, R. (2002, 25 May). "Phoenix FBI 'stonewalled.'" *The Arizona Republic*. pp. A1, A8.
9. Hill, A. (2002, 6 June). "Insider Women With Outsider Values." *The New York Times*. p. A31.
10. McGeehan, P. (2002, 6 June). "Goldman Chief Urges Reforms In Corporations." *The New York Times*. pp. A1, C5.
11. Whyte, D. (2001). *Crossing the Unknown Sea*: Work as Pilgrimage of Identity. NY: Riverhead Books. p. 52.
12. Ibid.
13. A term coined by Malcolm J. Matusky, BFA, MBA, a marketing and media consultant.
14. Whyte, D. (2001), p. 90.
15. Bly, R. (1990). *Iron John*: A Book about Men. NY: Addison-Wesley Publishing Co. p. 116 (Quoted James Hillman).
16. Florida, R. (2002) *The Rise of the Creative Class:* and how it's transforming work, leisure, community, and everyday life. NY: Basic Books/Perseus Book Group
17. Gleick, J. (1987). *Chaos*: Making a new Science. NY: Penguin Books, Viking-Penguin. p. 8.
18. Zinn, H. (2001) *A People's History of the United States: 1492-Present*. New York Perennial Classics/HarperCollins Publishers.

INDEX

www.ingramcontent.com/pod-product-compliance
Lightning Source LLC
Chambersburg PA
CBHW031146270326
41931CB00006B/160